REFLECTIVE PRACTICE IN CHILD AND YOUTH CARE

REFLECTIVE PRACTICE IN CHILD AND YOUTH CARE

A Manual

Donicka Budd

CANADIAN SCHOLARS

Toronto | Vancouver

Reflective Practice in Child and Youth Care: A Manual
Donicka Budd

First published in 2020 by
Canadian Scholars, an imprint of CSP Books Inc.
425 Adelaide Street West, Suite 200
Toronto, Ontario
M5V 3C1

www.canadianscholars.ca

Library and Archives Canada Cataloguing in Publication

Title: Reflective practice in child and youth care : a manual / Donicka Budd.
Names: Budd, Donicka, 1966- author.
Description: Includes bibliographical references.
Identifiers: Canadiana (print) 20190212950 | Canadiana (ebook) 20190212993 | ISBN 9781773381398 (softcover) | ISBN 9781773381404 (PDF) | ISBN 9781773381411 (EPUB)
Subjects: LCSH: Social work with children—Handbooks, manuals, etc. | LCSH: Social work with youth—Handbooks, manuals, etc. | LCGFT: Handbooks and manuals.
Classification: LCC HV713 .B83 2020 | DDC 362.7—dc23

Cover design by Rafael Chimicatti
Page layout by S4Carlisle Publishing Services

Printed and bound in Ontario, Canada

Canadä

To Mom and Dad
and Indiana

CONTENTS

APPENDICES

PREFACE

The absence of a resource in the Child and Youth Care curricula to foster reflective practice has prompted my interest in writing this book. While the concept of reflective practice is not a novel one, the field lacks a book on the practical aspects of doing reflective practice that encompasses the essential characteristics of a reflective practitioner. I have realized throughout my diverse experiences as a Child and Youth Care Practitioner how little reflective practice is utilized and cultivated across the distinct systems within which Child and Youth Care Practitioners are employed. Issues of power and control and a discernable lack of self-awareness have and continue to dominate the culture of systemic organizations. The implications for engaging reflective practice as a Child and Youth Care Practitioner are significant, not only for students but for professors as well; the method for which to support students in developing the skills fundamental to reflective practice is lacking across many Child and Youth Care programs. It is my hope in creating this book that it will offer learning professionals an experience of the fundamentals of reflective practice that embodies the very attitudes that underlie professional Child and Youth Care practice.

ACKNOWLEDGEMENTS

True to Child and Youth Care fashion, I acknowledge those who have been influential, albeit unknowingly, in my inspiration to write this book. I would like to extend my appreciation to Peter H, for opening my eyes to how much there was still to be known about reflective practice; to the students whom I shared the learning space with; and my colleagues from various work experiences who reminded me, unknowingly, about the significance that reflective practice has to our role as Child and Youth Care Practitioners. I would not be the practitioner I am today without the experiences of learning from the children, youth, and families whom I have had the privilege of meeting during my 18+ years as a Child and Youth Care Practitioner, each of whom has been the greatest influence on my curious nature, learning, and development as a practitioner; nor would I have grown into my practice without the help of the different professional community members who influenced my learning and development as a practitioner. I extend my appreciation to Canadian Scholars for supporting me through this exciting endeavour, and to Montana, whose eye-rolling moments have reminded me of the need to stay grounded and appreciative for the many learning moments parenting has brought.

INTRODUCTION

Reflective practice is a dialogue of thinking and doing through which I become more skillful.

— Schon, 1983

Child and Youth Care is an active and diverse field (White, 2007) that involves supporting the emotional, social, and spiritual development of children, youth, and families (CYCCB, 2018), within the context of their environment (White, 2007). This is no easy task and requires more than the good intentions of wanting to help or provide others with a different set of experiences. Supporting others involves a distinct way of engaging with people, many of whom bring their own ways of thinking about the world. Engaging others is an art that requires a special set of skills, knowledge, and experiences (Anglin, 1999) and that involves a way of knowing and being with others (Bellefeuille & Ricks, 2010; Garfat & Fulcher, 2012; Ricks & Bellefeuille, 2003; White, 2007). The art of Child and Youth Care is cultivated through your ways of knowing and being with others, which aligns with relational practice and your ability to learn from your experiences as a means to improve your practice. Learning from experiences is the essence of reflective practice and is an essential aspect of professional practice[1] (CYCCB, 2018; Johns, 2009; Mann, Gordon, & MacLeod, 2009), which calls for students to think critically about their ways of thinking, their actions, and their opportunities for further learning. Learning from experiences, however, requires an awareness of who you are in relation to others. Experiential learning is the foundation on which reflective practice develops (Coulson & Harvey, 2013).

The process for how to *do* reflective practice that supports students' learning has resulted in the absence of a standardized practice of doing reflective practice (Mann et al., 2009; Moon, 2004). The doing aspect of reflective practice that involves reflective and critical thinking skills, essential for students to develop as professional practitioners (Bellefeuille, McGrath, & Jamieson, 2008; Bellefeuille & Ricks, 2010; Garfat & Newcomen, 1992; Kinsella, 2009; White, 2007), has been absent from the academic curriculum. That absence inspired the development of this book.

One cannot demonstrate reflective practice without engaging in the experiential learning skills that are fundamental to this core aspect of professional practice. Fewster and Beker (2014) highlight the importance of combining academic and experiential learning experiences with field experiences to develop as professional practitioners.

Overlooking these fundamental processes of reflective practice refutes the very professionalism that Child and Youth Care seeks to promote. It is therefore your professional responsibility to yourself, your client, your employer/organization, the community, and the profession to see that reflective practice is cultivated as a universal standard that embodies professional Child and Youth Care practice. Integral to this learning are the day-to-day experiences, both within the classroom and outside of it. It warrants repeating that reflective practice is ongoing and does not end at the completion of a course. The initial concepts and exercises included in this book will prepare you for the experience-based learning that underlies reflective practice. By engaging in the experiential process this book offers, rather than simply reading and memorizing the content, learning professionals will develop the skills and knowledge fundamental to reflective practice.

Reflective practice is not a new concept and has been documented in the literature across Child and Youth Care and other disciplines for decades (Bellefeuille, McGrath, & Jamieson, 2008; Bellefeuille & Ricks, 2010; Garfat & Ricks, 1995; Garfat & Fulcher, 2013; Johns, 2009; Krueger, 2005; Ricks, 1997), although the term has often been used interchangeably with reflection, the self, self-care, and self-awareness.[2] Reflective practice is a distinct aspect of professional practice that embodies a compilation of knowing, being, and doing processes that are developed over time and through awareness of self, experiences with others, theory, and knowledge that leads to new understandings to improve practice.

My hope is that you will develop a greater understanding and appreciation for reflective practice as you progress through the exercises and theoretical concepts within each chapter. Additionally, it is my hope that you become more aware of your own thinking about self, others, and the profession, and that you will identify key points in your learning that warrant questioning and further exploration as you achieve greater independence in this learning process.

HOW TO USE THIS BOOK

This book is designed to guide your developmental learning as reflective practitioners throughout the entirety of your academic program. The theoretical concepts and experiential exercises build from the previous chapters' content, which promotes a deeper level of learning. Because of the progressive learning structure, the book is intended to be used in a sequential manner; however, there are distinct chapters of the book that can be used interchangeably with other material to reinforce different concepts in the text (e.g., Chapter 5: Mindfulness, Chapter 10: Reflective Tools).

Acquiring the skills of reflective practice is a process and evolves over time and through experiences (Allard et al., 2007; Brookfield, 2012; Coulson & Harvey, 2013; D'Cruz, Gillinham, & Melendez, 2007; Lyons, 2010). The concepts in each chapter are meant to align with the student's developmental learning journey and have been organized as follows.

Initial Stages of Student Learning: Chapters 1–3

The initial stages of student learning prepare you to reflect for action (Coulson & Harvey, 2013) as you explore the distinct concepts of self and key characteristics of Child and Youth Care practice as the beginning aspects of reflective practice. The focus of these initial chapters is on exploring self and raising awareness of how *this self* influences your actions.

Developing Stages of Student Learning: Chapters 3–6

You will be introduced to the processes of reflexivity and reflection that will guide you in your thinking about your professional identity and the impact on practice. You will further your observational skills to reflect on the underlying needs of others, which will guide your practice. Observation logs, models of reflection, and reflective journals will be introduced at this stage of learning.

Advanced Learning Stages: Chapters 7–13

The advanced stages of learning focuses on the higher-ordered learning of reflective thinking and critical thinking. At this stage, you are required to assume a higher level of responsibility for your learning as you bring forth your cases and experiences from practice as a focus for your learning and through independently run reflective group discussions.

The fundamental concepts introduced to you in the first six chapters lay the foundation for acquiring the advanced learning concepts of critical thinking, reflective writing, and collaborative reflection. You are encouraged to complete the exercises directly in this book as it aligns with one aspect of being in the moment and applying learning to practice. However, students may also wish to make copies of the templates included in the appendices. Later, when reflective journals are introduced, students will have the option to engage digital technology as an alternative.

Case scenarios will be featured throughout the text to support you in thinking reflectively and critically about your practice as you become more proficient at recognizing assumptions and interpretations as barriers to Child and Youth Care reflective practice. It is recommended that you reflect on the case scenarios individually before discussing them as a group. While working with others is a significant part of professional Child and Youth Care, it is important that practitioners identify and develop their own ways of thinking. Exploring your own way of thinking is actually one of the first steps in reflective practice.

Group and class discussions will provide further value to this process. As you develop the necessary skills to support your learning of reflective practice, more emphasis will be placed on group reflections. Interactions with others support the learning journey.

The inclusion of the Code of Ethics and the core competencies of Child and Youth Care practice is intended to support your ways of thinking about practice, along with a standardized way of engaging in practice. While they represent the overarching principles and guidelines that govern professional practice, as you will discover from the case scenarios, these principles and guidelines do not offer definitive solutions or "right ways" to engage in practice; rather, they will support your thinking and learning as reflective practitioners. These are listed in the appendices in the back of the book.

Many of the concepts introduced in early chapters will be reintroduced in the following chapters. While this may seem repetitive, it is intentional to support your learning. Learning relies on experience. Your learning will influence your experiences and your experiences will influence your learning. As you build on previous knowledge, acquire new knowledge, and engage in new experiences, your ways of thinking about your practice, self, and others will evolve. Building on previous knowledge and concepts while having the opportunities to apply them to experiences is essential for developing reflective practice.

A note on the case scenarios and reports featured in the book: these are based on this author's professional experiences. The individuals' names and content of the reports have been altered to respect confidentiality and privacy.

The case scenarios, experiences from your own practice, and learning concepts can trigger memories from past experiences that invariably evoke a range of different feelings. While this is a common experience, this can impede your learning experience and it is recommended that you access campus counselling services or counselling services in your community as issues arise. Seeking support from your class peers can interfere with your ability to establish and maintain the necessary professional attitudes and boundaries required for learning to occur.

The following attitudes are essential to your practice and will assist you in thinking about the diverse case scenarios and the children, youth, and families you will engage with during practice.

FOUNDATIONAL ATTITUDES OF PROFESSIONAL CHILD AND YOUTH CARE PRACTICE[3]

- Accepts the moral and ethical responsibility inherent in the practice
- Promotes the well-being of children, youth, and families in a context of respect and collaboration
- Celebrates the strengths generated from cultural and human diversity
- Values individual uniqueness
- Values family, community, culture, and human diversity as integral to the developmental and interventive process
- Believes in the potential and empowerment of children, youth, family, and community
- Advocates for the rights of children, youth, and families
- Promotes the contribution of professional Child and Youth Care to society

The only source of knowledge is experience.
    —Albert Einstein

I wish you a harmonious journey that is filled with many meaning-making moments.
May peace be with you.
—Donicka Budd

NOTES

1. For simplicity, I will use the term "professional practice" throughout the text to reference the Code of Ethics and core competencies that underlie Child and Youth Care practice.
2. Self-awareness for professional practice reflects the core competency of Professionalism that outlines the practitioners' responsibility to recognize personal strengths and limitations, feelings and needs (CYCCB, 2018).
3. "Foundational Attitudes of Child and Youth Care Practice" is taken directly from the Child and Youth Care Certification Board (CYCCB) website (www.cyccb.org).

CHAPTER 1

Reflective Practice

We do not learn from experience … we learn from reflecting on experience.

—John Dewey

LEARNING OBJECTIVES

In this chapter, you will:

- define reflective practice and the implications of practice
- describe the reflective practice radial
- communicate the Standards of Practice and their connection to reflective practice
- explain the concept of thinking about thinking that precedes self-awareness

The Child and Youth Care profession has evolved significantly over the past 20 years because of political and social influences. The focus of intervention now embodies a holistic approach where all systems in a child's life play a role in creating change. This has reflected a significant shift in a Child and Youth Care Practitioner's role and responsibilities. Where they once focused solely on children and youth, practitioners now work with families (Garfat & Charles, 2012) and other community professionals to support a child's psychological, social, and spiritual growth (CYCCB, 2018; VanderVen, 1992). Working with vulnerable children, youth, and families and the diverse systems they are connected to can at times raise complex uncertainties about the effectiveness of one's practice. With these uncertainties and the additional foci in the role comes a greater responsibility for practitioners to engage in reflective practice.

REFLECTIVE PRACTICE

Reflective practice is an approach to practice that requires Child and Youth Care Practitioners to examine their thoughts and experiences: What do I know, what do I think I know, and what is there to know? It asks practitioners to contemplate how this perceived knowing impacts their practice (Bolton, 2005; Anning, Cottrell, & Frost, 2010). Johns (2009) defines reflective practice as a process of learning through and from moment-to-moment experiences to improve in practice. Through this process, practitioners will consider the aspects of their work that they need to improve to align with professional practice (Hargreaves & Page, 2013).[1]

You will learn throughout your academic journey and beyond that the decisions you make will impact practice in various ways and must be grounded in theory (your reasons for why you do what you do; Garfat & Fulcher, 2012). This process of self-evaluation is essential to becoming reflective practitioners. Yet, that is only one aspect of reflective practice. Later in this chapter, you will learn about the different elements essential to becoming reflective practitioners. You will continue to develop and cultivate these skills over the course of your learning and beyond. It is important to point out that number of years of experience in the field does not equate a reflective practitioner. Reflective practice continues throughout your career as a practitioner.

Implications for Reflective Practice

Reflective practice requires an awareness and understanding of the Standards of Practice and core competencies of Child and Youth Care. As reflective practitioners, you need always to consider the best interests of the child, and your responsibility to self, the profession, and community as barometers for the decisions you make. This ability to reflect on practice requires just that: practice, time, and a commitment to look within oneself to determine the approach that is for the good of the individual and not for the convenience of the Child and Youth Care Practitioner.

Skill Development

Your greatest learning will come from your experiences with others, notably the children, youth, and families you will work with. Mistakes, or *errors in judgement*, are inevitable. It is from these experiences that you can learn in order to understand and develop your skills (Moon, 2008). Reflective practice provides the opportunity for practitioners to think back to an experience, evaluate their actions, contemplate why they did what they did, think about the impact on practice, and consider how practice can be improved. An awareness of theory and its application to practice requires that you have a comprehensive way of knowing others and the distinct factors that influence these others (Boud, 1999; Dewey, as cited in O'Connell & Dyment, 2011; Schon, 1983), and a commitment to improving your practice.

Improving Practice

Engaging in experiences with others and learning from these experiences will lead to developing your practice when you can acknowledge the barriers that may be impeding the work. You will be required to acknowledge gaps in your learning while being open to different approaches to practice. However, in order to do this, practitioners need to set aside their own values and beliefs to work with others. To do this requires an awareness of the values and beliefs that can impact practice. You will be introduced to opportunities for learning about your ways of thinking in the next chapter.

Professional practice necessitates that you differentiate your experiences from others' while assuming responsibility for your actions (Krueger, 2011; Mantzoukas & Watkinson, as cited in Hargreaves & Page, 2013). This can be exceedingly difficult for some practitioners. The ability to take responsibility for one's actions requires in part maturity, a certain degree of vulnerability, and awareness of self. In order to develop the skill of awareness, one needs to engage in the use of self and reflect on those internal processes that can impact practice. This concept—use of self—will be explored in further depth in the following chapter.

Philosophy to Practice

Reflective practice assists practitioners in learning about themselves, their work, their interactions, and the wider society and culture through experiences (Bellefeuille et al., 2008; Boud, 1999; Gharabaghi, 2008a; Mezirow, 1991; Moon, 2004; Scott, 2010; Stuart, 2013). Through these experiences, practitioners gain new insights to question and address circumstances through processes of inquiry[2] (Bellefeuille & Ricks, 2010; Bolton, 2009; Ricks, 1997); the aspect of questioning one's understanding, assumptions, experiences, and perceived knowledge demonstrates accountability for one's actions. Failure to do this, to engage in this process of inquiry, risks practitioners' ability to hold others responsible for their actions.

Engaging in reflective practice is similar to using a compass. The compass provides individuals with a sense of direction, a course to navigate toward; reflective practice provides a framework for practitioners to navigate their learning (Brookfield, 1995) and to direct one's action through insight (Dewey, 1971). The course both the compass and reflective practice lead to will be based on context (circumstances), location (identity), perspective (understanding), and practice.

The field of Child and Youth Care is rich in experiences that can be wrought with challenges and uncertainty. A willingness to explore these challenges and uncertainties creates the path from which reflective practice unfolds. Acquiring the essential skills and engaging in the distinct process of reflective practice takes time, awareness, and experiences (Bellefeuille et al., 2008; Scott, 2010) from daily interactions and field experiences. There is an innate knowing that comes with practice and experience, which Aristotle referred to as the practical wisdom that evolves from experiential learning (Kakkori & Huttuenen, 2007). These experiences are the catalyst for reflective practice to occur.

The practical wisdom Aristotle speaks of also relates to the idea that not all situations will have a text-based solution. This will require students to apply their learning in situations and use their judgement based on their relationships with children and families and the Code of Ethics that governs their practice.

Consider the Following Statements

- There isn't one right way of responding to vulnerable children and youth and families.
- The code of ethics does not determine one right way of practice.
- Working with vulnerable children, youth, and families requires an openness to learning about their lived experiences.
- Learning about self takes precedence to learning about others.

The concepts above highlight the complexity of Child and Youth Care practice and working with others. Complex situations provide practitioners with opportunities to think about their current ways of thinking. From the concepts above, select one to serve as a point of reference to think further about. In your thinking, consider what the point means for you and your learning, and identify your comments and questions that come from this thinking. Use the space below to respond.

_____

_____

_____

_____

The Child and Youth Care Way

In the following chapter, you will be introduced to the knowing, being, and doing framework of Child and Youth Care (White, 2007) as a means to construct your thinking about the field. Ways of knowing relate to your ways of thinking about a practice that evolves from past experiences, your feelings, values, beliefs, and social location (your position in history and society; Bellefeuille & Ricks, 2010; Gharabaghi, 2008b; Ricks, 1997; White, 2007). Ways of knowing also include the knowledge you will acquire in your learning. One way of knowing involves the Standards of Practice of Child and Youth Care that will be discussed later in this chapter.

Ways of being involve the fundamental skills and characteristics that underlie relational practice, the philosophy that underpins interactions between Child and Youth Care Practitioners and others. This will be discussed at further length in the following chapter.

Ways of doing involve the concept of reflective practice, which is the basis for this book. Reflective practice is a multi-dimensional, dynamic process that underlies effective Child and Youth Care practice that will be explored further in this chapter.

A Note on Insights

Insight refers to the connections individuals make from their learning experiences and often occurs from engaging in reflective practice. Through knowledge and experiences and one's ability to look back to reflect on practice, new learning and new ways of knowing develop. The process of achieving this insight can involve areas of uncertainty that enable practitioners to rethink and further examine their understanding of right ways of practice (Moon, 2004). We will continue to explore the concept of the "right way" of doing practice throughout the text.

Reflective practice provides the impetus for a vast array of rich learning opportunities that occur in the moment-to-moment experiences that each day brings. There is learning in every moment, both within and beyond the confines of the learning environment. Learning is not limited to the work and academic environments—learning occurs through experiences (Bellefeuille et al., 2008; Bellefeuille & Ricks, 2010; Garfat & Ricks, 1995). Sitting with these experiences to acknowledge the learning opportunities as opposed to criticizing or engaging in judgement is an experience in itself.

It is through these experiences, challenges, and uncertainties that practitioners learn about themselves: how they think, feel about, and view the world. As part of a relation-centred profession, there is value and necessity in knowing how ways of thinking can influence interactions with others. Exploring the distinct aspects of self, values, beliefs, assumptions, emotions, thought processes, and others' perspectives prepares students for the distinct processes required for reflective practice. This *reflection for action*[3] will foster greater awareness of your ways of thinking and the impact this can have on practice and will assist you in developing the deeper levels of reflection and learning that underlie reflective practice (Hatcher, Bringle, & Mathiah, as cited in Coulson & Harvey, 2013).

Something to Think About

Think about a recent experience you encountered that you described as "the worst ever." Maybe it was a class you attended where you believed you learned nothing, or perhaps an event you described as a waste of time. Spend a few moments and describe key aspects of that experience, in short or point form. Acknowledge the emotional tone in the writing and the emotions thinking about this experience brings up. Leave it for now and come back to it later in the day to review what you wrote. Think about the learning opportunities within this experience. If this seems difficult, then think about what your role was in maintaining this perception of the experience.

Use the space provided to respond to the following questions.

What did you do at that time? If you respond that you did nothing, think about this some more.

_____

_____

_____

_____

How did you benefit from doing nothing?

_____

_____

_____

_____

What are the alternatives to doing nothing?

_____

_____

_____

_____

What have you learned about yourself from this exercise?

_____

_____

_____

_____

Use the space below to include any additional comments or questions that you have.

_____

_____

_____

_____

Exploring these key questions that exist in every opportunity is learning.

The Characteristics and Rationale for Reflective Practice[4]

Reflective practice enables practitioners to:

- monitor, evaluate, and rethink their approach in practice
- learn from experiences related to practice, self, and experiences
- be intentional in decisions
- develop awareness of risks and benefits of decisions
- achieve greater accountability in their practice
- achieve a greater understanding of the experiences of others
- explore ethical dilemmas
- apply learning to future practice
- challenge personal and sociocultural assumptions that directly/indirectly impact the well-being of children, youth, and families
- question the uncertainties in practice

When you reflect on practice, you allow yourself the space to consider other ways of thinking and knowing (Bellefeuille & Ricks, 2010) and step outside the paradigm of your position that implicitly conveys power and privilege[5] (Lareau & McNamar Horvat, 1999). In doing so, practitioners assume responsibility for doing what they do (Bellefeuille et al., 2008; Bellefeuille & Ricks, 2010; White, 2007). Reflective practice embodies a way of knowing, being, and doing that informs ethical and competent practice (Bellefeuille et al., 2008; Bellefeuille & Ricks, 2010; Bolton, 2009; Garfat & Ricks, 1995; Ricks, 1997; White, 2007).

Child and Youth Care represents a philosophy for working with others that focuses on strengths, potential, and diversity as opposed to deficits and pathology (Garfat & Fulcher, 2012; McCammon, 2012). However, the practitioner's ability to realize these strengths can be clouded with judgement when others present challenging behaviours. It is these times that necessitate a shift in the practitioner's perspective, from a deficit (pathologizing) view of the other's to their own internal reaction and the circumstances for these behaviours. This ability to reflect on the experience and to create a new meaning (interpretatin) of the behaviours is fundamental to reflective practice.

It is by thinking about experiences and identifying the meaning one creates about those experiences that the practitioner's ways of thinking shift from a deficit-focused, *what is wrong* lens to a *what is there to be learned about this other* that underlies the Child and Youth Care philosophy (Garfat & Fulcher, 2012). Knowledge and experiences aside, however, there is a responsibility for the practitioner to develop the skills for introspection. Introspection enables practitioners to notice their internal reaction without letting it influence actions with others. This, however, requires a commitment to look inward and acknowledge feelings, ways of thinking, and position in history and society (social location) as factors that influence one's ways of thinking about and doing Child and Youth Care practice (Bellefeuille & Ricks, 2010; Ricks, 1997; White, 2007).

Practitioners who are challenged in embracing an introspective approach to practice risk viewing their experiences from a narrow lens that negates the diverse experiences and sociocultural influences that impact the children, youth, and families they work with. This rigid way of knowing risks practitioners demonstrating routine-based approaches (Dewey, as cited in Rodgers, 2002; Gharabaghi, 2008a; Schon, 1983) that invariably impede the potential emotional, cognitive, and spiritual developmental growth of others.

Going Inward

What is the connection between going inward and Child and Youth Care practice? You will hear this many times throughout your academic journey: you must first learn about yourself before you can learn about others. Learning about self involves understanding how you think, your perspectives, ways of thinking and feeling, and the values, beliefs, and assumptions you carry. From this learning evolves awareness, and from this awareness comes an ability to acknowledge the impact your behaviours and ways of thinking can have on others. From this thinking-feeling stuff, the journey in reflective practice begins.

Learning about self will uncover ways you think about Child and Youth Care practice. Many learning professionals focus on the right action, the right thing to say. They want the magic formula to guarantee best outcomes and will question their ways of doing things. "Am I doing this right? Is this the right way? What is the best way?" It is the nature of these questions that have plagued practitioners since the inception of the Child and Youth Care profession (Bellefeuille & Ricks, 2010; Garfat & Ricks, 1995; Gharabaghi, 2008b).

No simple answers exist to these complex questions, and it is the ambiguous meaning of "the right thing" that calls for reflective practice. We will continue to revisit the concept of right action throughout the book; however, for a moment, consider the meaning of "doing the right thing." You will discover that each person will have their own understanding of what "doing the right thing" means, which provides opportunities for further reflection and discussion. When deciding what the right thing is, practitioners are required to consider the best interests of the child at the heart of their practice and will realize that the best interests of the child will have different meanings based on the situation and individual needs of others. Adopting "the right" solution-based way of thinking implies an absolute method of practice that negates the uniqueness of children, youth, and families.

No one will perceive a situation the same way, as each person brings their own experiences and ways of thinking and ways of knowing to situations that will influence action (Bellefeuille & Ricks, 2010; Garfat & Ricks, 1995; Gharabaghi, 2008a; Ricks, 1997; White, 2007). It is the process of interacting with others, noticing, examining the context, and considering diverse perspectives that challenge this right way of thinking. Right action is not dependent upon what you do, but rather how you consider and decide what to do (Bellefeuille & Ricks, 2010; Garfat & Ricks, 1995; Gharabaghi, 2008b).

Considering these risks allows the space to challenge one's way of thinking and to consider alternative ways of thinking, a skill essential to Child and Youth Care reflective practice. When practitioners consider the lived experiences, sociocultural influences, and

Something to Think About

- Describe your interpretation of the "right" approach to practice.
- Identify the risks in adopting a "right" approach to practice. How might this approach influence your interactions with others in practice?

Use the space below to respond to the questions above and share with a partner.

_____

_____

_____

_____

_____

_____

_____

diverse perspectives of others and the values and beliefs that underlie these perspectives, their ability to reflect and improve in practice develops. Their ways of thinking and knowing expand beyond their own lens of experience and create the necessary space for new learning. In reading this, some might ask, does this determine a right way for engaging in practice? A right way of action implies either-or thinking; however, adopting this curious, individualized reflective approach to practice, which evolves from the interactions between the practitioner and others, reinforces the Child and Youth Care approach to practice.

When practitioners consider the unique developmental, historical, and cultural influences and needs of children, youth, and families (Gharabaghi, 2008b; Ricks, 1997) their thinking shifts from a right, absolute way of thinking to think critically about situations and experiences. Critical thinking is an advanced process of reflective practice, which will be explored in Chapter 8.

Let us consider the meaning of the term "the best interests of the child," as this will be referenced throughout the book. How might you understand this? Snow (2006) raises an important question for consideration: "How does one determine what is in the best interests of another and who determines this?" Your experiences and interactions with others will influence your meaning and response and will be the basis for further reflection as you proceed through the book. For now, however, think about what meaning "the best interest of the child" has for you and discuss with a partner.

When you have finished, select another statement below and discuss the meaning for you and its implications for practice. It is not the intention to determine one response, but to create the space for establishing the meaning of these important questions and their relevance to practice. Write your responses in the space provided.

What is Child and Youth Care practice? The roles and responsibilities?

_____

_____

_____

What does it mean to help others?

_____

_____

_____

Identify other questions you may have about Child and Youth Care practice and list them in the space below.

_____

_____

_____

When you have completed this exercise, share and discuss with a partner. How do you determine whose response reflects the "right" answer?

_____

_____

As you progress in your learning, you will recognize that some of the material will make you think, question, and rethink the impact this learning has on your practice. This thinking about thinking is a precursor to reflective practice and is essential to your learning potential.

Reflective practice as a dynamic, transitional, learning process involves five distinct processes that will be explored in more depth in following chapters. Collectively, each of these processes contributes to the overarching philosophy of reflective practice. The radial (Figure 1) provides a way to represent the different, though overlapping, processes of reflective practice. They can be described as a building of competencies to becoming reflective practitioners, the first of which starts with the self. Without an understanding and awareness of self, the practitioner's ways of being and doing are limited, the potential for developing optimal relationships that nurture and foster growth in others is limited, and reflective practice cannot occur.

As there are distinct elements of reflective practice, there are distinct characteristics that exemplify Child and Youth Care practice (Garfat & Fulcher, 2012). While it is not this author's intention to describe each of the characteristics identified in the literature

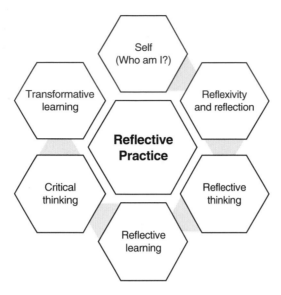

Figure 1: Reflective Practice Radial

Source: Recreated by author.

(Fewster, 1990a; Garfat, 2002; Garfat & Fulcher, 2012; Krueger, 2011), there are those distinctive to reflective practice that will be discussed in later chapters: intentionality, presence, noticing and curiosity, examining context, and meaning-making. These characteristics are woven throughout the text to reinforce your learning and will be presented through the knowing, being, doing framework of Child and Youth Care practice in Chapter 3.

In the following chapters, you will be introduced to the concepts of self and relationship as the foundations of Child and Youth Care (Fewster, 1990a; Krueger, 2011; Stuart, 2013). One aspect of knowing is the legislation[6] and standards of practice[7] that govern your work (White, 2007). For the purpose of the text, legislation will not be addressed as other courses will explore this at greater length; however, various legislative processes are referenced in the appendices.

The other aspect of knowing relates to the self—who you are in relation to your values, beliefs, assumptions, and social location; the being and doing components of this framework will be explored in depth in Chapter 3.

THE STANDARDS OF PRACTICE FOR CHILD AND YOUTH CARE

The Standards of Practice provide a foundation from which reflective practice evolves. They are guidelines to ensure that accountability for the practitioner's actions and responsibility for others occurs and encompasses the Code of Ethics and core competencies of Child and Youth Care. The standards of practice can guide students in managing uncertainties and ethical dilemmas (see Chapters 4 and 8) that arise in practice, but they do not represent absolute solutions. At times, ethical dilemmas will arise where learning professionals are challenged by the systemic policies that govern their practice and ways to address the needs and best interest of the child. This will provide opportunities for students to question, challenge, and engage in learning that will pose further questions for practice—the heart of reflective practice.

The Code of Ethics is determined by the provincial associations of Child and Youth Care practice and so vary between provinces. As such, the Code of Ethics listed in Appendix I reflects those listed in the Association for Child and Youth Care Practice (2017) and the Child and Youth Care Certification Board. A summary of the code has been listed below. It is not the intention of this text that learning professionals memorize these, but rather familiarize themselves with the guiding principles that govern the practice of Child and Youth Care and to acknowledge the distinct responsibilities they have as practitioners.

THE CODE OF ETHICS FOR CHILD AND YOUTH CARE PROFESSIONALS[8]

Child and Youth Care Practitioners have responsibility for self, to the client, the employer, the profession, and to society. The Code of Ethics does not represent ready-made solutions for which to respond to situations (Gharabaghi, 2008b; Ricks, 1997; White, 2007), yet they do allow space to think about the uncertainties that lie within these standards of practice. As you proceed through the book, these uncertainties will become more clear to you as you engage with the different case scenarios. As you review these standards of practice, highlight any aspects that may not make sense to you or you have a question about.

1. Responsibility for Self

Practitioners maintain competency by taking responsibility for identifying, developing, and fully utilizing the knowledge and abilities for professional practice: obtaining training, education, supervision, and experience to assure competent service. Responsibility for self also means maintaining high standards of professional conduct and maintaining physical and emotional well-being by being aware of personal values and their implication for practice and also by being aware of self as a growing and developing professional. This latter point reinforces the importance of engaging in a reflective practice, which will be explained further in subsequent chapters.

2. Responsibility to the Child, Youth, and Family

Practitioners shall do no harm to the child, youth, or family by refraining from demonstrating practices that are disrespectful, degrading, dangerous, exploitive, intimidating, psychologically damaging, or physically harmful to clients. They have a professional responsibility to recognize, respect, and advocate for the rights of the child, youth, and family and to ensure that services are sensitive to and non-discriminatory of clients regardless of race, colour, ethnicity, national origin, national ancestry, age, gender, sexual orientation, marital status, religion, abilities, health, political belief, political affiliation, and socioeconomic status. The Child and Youth Care Practitioner has a responsibility to obtain training, education, supervision, experience, and/or counsel to assure that they are demonstrating competent service.

They are responsible for developing individualized programs to meet the emotional, psychological, physical, social, cultural, and spiritual needs of the clients, and that address the child's developmental status, understanding, capacity, and age. Practitioners will recognize that competent service often requires collaboration, and such service is a cooperative effort that draws on the expertise of many. They will refer children, youth, and families to other professionals and/or seek assistance to ensure that appropriate services can be accessed. Practitioners will administer medication prescribed by the lawful prescribing practitioner in accordance with the directions and only for medical purposes and seek consultation when necessary. The Child and Youth Care Practitioner will observe, assess, and evaluate services/treatments prescribed or designed by other professionals.

The Child and Youth Practitioner recognizes the client's membership within a family and facilitates the participation of significant others in service to the client. They will foster client self-determination and respect the privacy of clients by holding in confidence information obtained in the course of professional service and will ensure that the boundaries between professional and personal relationships with clients are explicitly understood and respected and that the practitioner's behaviour is appropriate to this difference. It is understood that sexual intimacy with a client or the family member of a client is unethical.

Something to Think About

Responsibility to the child, youth, and family—*Do no harm.* What does this mean to you, this concept of harm? What is your understanding based on? Include influences from social media, past experiences, previous knowledge, or others. Use the space below to record your answer and any other questions or comments you have.

_____

_____

_____

_____

_____

_____

_____

3. Responsibility to the Employer/Employing Organization

Child and Youth Care Practitioners will treat colleagues with respect, courtesy, fairness, and good faith and they will relate to the clients of a colleague with professional consideration, and respect the commitments made to the employer/employing organization.

Something to Think About

Responsibility to the employer and/or employing organization states that practitioners are to treat their colleagues with respect, courtesy, and equity. Identify aspects of working in teams that would challenge this. Use the space below to respond to this question.

_____

_____

_____

_____

_____

_____

_____

4. Responsibility to the Profession

The Child and Youth Care Practitioner will recognize that in situations of professional practice the standards in the code shall guide the resolution of ethical conflicts. The Child and Youth Care Practitioner will promote ethical conduct by members of the profession and will seek arbitrations or mediation when conflicts with colleagues require consultation and if an informal resolution seems appropriate. The Child and Youth Care Practitioner will report ethical violations to appropriate persons and/or bodies when an informal resolution is not appropriate. They will encourage collaborative participation by professionals, client, family, and community to share responsibility for client outcomes. The Child and Youth Care Practitioner will ensure that research is designed, conducted, and reported in accordance with high-quality Child and Youth Care practice, and recognized standards of scholarship and research ethics.

The Child and Youth Care Practitioner will ensure that education and training programs are competently designed and delivered. These programs will meet the requirements/claims set forth by the program and the experiences provided will be properly supervised. The Child and Youth Care Practitioner will ensure that administrators and supervisors lead programs in high quality and ethical practice in relation to clients, staff, governing bodies, and the community. The Child and Youth Care practitioner will provide support for professional growth and evaluate staff on the basis of performance on established requirements.

5. Responsibility to the Community

The Child and Youth Care Practitioner will contribute to the profession in making services available to the public, promote understanding and facilitate acceptance of diversity in society, demonstrate the standards of the code with students and volunteers, and encourage informed participation by the public in shaping social policies and decisions that affect children, youth, and families.

The Child and Youth Care Practitioner will recognize that in situations of professional practice the standards in the code shall guide the resolution of ethical conflicts. The Child and Youth Care Practitioner will promote ethical conduct by members of the profession and will seek arbitrations or mediation when conflicts with colleagues require consultation and if an informal resolution seems appropriate. The Child and Youth Care Practitioner will report ethical violations to appropriate persons and/or bodies when an informal resolution is not appropriate.

They will encourage collaborative participation by professionals, client, family, and community to share responsibility for client outcomes. The Child and Youth Care Practitioner will ensure that research is designed, conducted, and reported in accordance with high-quality Child and Youth Care practice, and recognized standards of scholarship, and research ethics.

The Child and Youth Care Practitioner will ensure that education and training programs are competently designed and delivered. These programs will meet the requirements/claims set forth by the program and the experiences provided will be properly supervised. The Child and Youth Care Practitioner will ensure that administrators and supervisors lead programs in high-quality and ethical practice in relation to clients, staff, governing bodies, and the community. The Child and Youth Care Practitioner will provide support for professional growth and evaluate staff on the basis of performance on established requirements.

The importance and necessity of providing learning opportunities for learning professionals to integrate the Code of Ethics into their practice has been reinforced throughout the literature (Bellefeuille & Ricks, 2010; Garfat & Ricks, 2010; Gharabaghi, 2008b; Ricks, 1997).

Checking In

Where are you with understanding the concepts in this chapter thus far? Are they making sense to you? Are there areas you require further clarification about? What questions do you have that warrant further exploration to support your thinking about this chapter?

THE CORE COMPETENCIES OF CHILD AND YOUTH CARE

The core competencies of Child and Youth Care practice[9] are a set of principles that outline the essential skills and knowledge required of Child and Youth Care Practitioners and is comprised of five distinct competencies that underpin effective practice: Professionalism, Cultural and Human Diversity, Applied Human Development,

Relationship and Communication, and Developmental Practice Methods. The full list of the core competencies outlining the practitioner's responsibilities is in Appendix II. The following summaries will provide you with a brief overview of each domain in order to familiarize yourself with the content.

I. Professionalism

Professional practitioners are creative and flexible; they are self-directed and have a high degree of personal initiative. They demonstrate consistency in their tasks. They function effectively both independently and as a team member. Professional practitioners engage in professional and personal development and self-care. The professional practitioner is knowledgeable about the Code of Ethics and uses professional ethics to guide and improve their practice. They advocate effectively for children, youth, families, and the profession.

II. Cultural and Human Diversity

Professional practitioners actively promote respect for cultural and human diversity. They seek self-understanding and have the ability to access and evaluate information related to cultural and human diversity. They integrate their current and relevant knowledge into developing respectful, effective relationships, communication, and developmental practice methods. Knowledge and skills are employed in planning, implementing, and evaluating respectful programs and services, and workplaces.

III. Applied Human Development

Professional practitioners promote the optimal development of children, youth, and their families in a variety of settings and consider the developmental-ecological perspective that emphasizes the interaction between individuals and their diverse settings, which they are a part of. The everyday lives of children and youth, including those at risk and with special needs, within the family, neighbourhood, school, and larger sociocultural context is the focus of Child and Youth Care practice. Professional practitioners integrate current knowledge of human development with the skills, expertise, objectivity, and self-awareness essential for developing, implementing, and evaluating effective programs and services.

IV. Relationship and Communication

Practitioners recognize the significant importance of relationships and communication in the practice of ethical and competent Child and Youth Care. They work in collaboration with the individual (child, youth, family) to achieve growth and change. Ethical and competent practitioners develop genuine relationships based on empathy and positive regard. They actively demonstrate clear communication with others and document objective and respectful notes and reports. Relationships and communication occur and develop in the context of the diverse environments that impact children, youth, and families.

V. Developmental Practice Methods

Practitioners recognize the critical importance of developmental practice methods that are designed to promote optimal development for children, youth, and families including those at-risk and with special needs within the context of the family, community, and the lifespan. Developmental practice methods include Genuine Relationships, Health and Safety, Intervention Planning, Environmental Design and Maintenance, Program Planning and Activity Programming, Activities of Daily Living, Group Work, Counselling, Behavioural Guidance, Family (Caregiver) Engagement, and Community Engagement.

Table 1 outlines the connections between the Standards of Practice and reflective practice.

Table 1: Reflective Practice to Standards of Practice, Code of Ethics Connection

Reflective Practice Element	Code of Ethics	Core Competency
Self: Who Am I? • Values, beliefs, social location, assumptions • Child and Youth Care characteristics of intentionality, presence, curiosity, noticing, context and meaning-making, mindfulness	**Responsibility to Self** • Develops knowledge and skills necessary to benefit children, youth, and families • Aware of personal values and their implication for practice • Mindful of self • Awareness of the importance of self-care and the responsibility to seek guidance **Responsibility to Child, Youth, and Families** • Does not cause harm • Culturally sensitive practices • Encourages safe and ethical practice • Ensures services are culturally sensitive • Affirms that there are differences in individual and family needs and meets those needs on an individual basis • Ensures interactions reflect developmental age, status, understanding, and capacity • Recognizes and adjusts for dynamics related to power, authority, and position	**Professionalism** • Value orientation • Self-awareness • Recognition of personal strengths, limitations, feelings, and needs • Self-care **Cultural and Human Diversity** • Awareness of own bias • Awareness of social location, impact of power and privilege • Demonstrates anti-oppressive approach in practice **Applied Human Development** • Theory to practice • Developmental theory, attachment theory, Bronfenbrenner's ecological systems theory **Relationship and Communication** • Building relationships • Writing daily logs • Reports

(continued)

Table 1: Reflective Practice to Standards of Practice, Code of Ethics Connection (*continued*)

Reflective Practice Element	Code of Ethics	Core Competency
Reflexivity • Awareness of impact of values, beliefs, assumptions, and social location on others	**Responsibility to Child, Youth, and Families** • Does not cause harm • Ensures services are culturally sensitive • Affirms that there are differences in individual and family needs and meets those needs on an individual basis • Ensures interactions reflect developmental age, status, understanding, and capacity • Recognizes and adjusts for dynamics related to power, authority, and position	**Professionalism** • Recognize and assess own needs and feelings and keep them in perspective when professionally engaged **Cultural and Human Diversity** • Awareness of social location, impact of power and privilege • Demonstrates anti-oppressive approach in practice • Adjusts for effects of age, culture, background, experience, and developmental status on verbal and non-verbal communication
Reflection • What is required for me to improve?	**Responsibility to Child, Youth, and Families** • Encourages safe and ethical practice • Ensures appropriate boundaries between professional and personal relationships	**Professionalism** • Reflect on one's practice and performance • Evaluate own performance to identify needs for professional growth **Applied Human Development** • Recognizes the influence of the child/youth's relationship history on the development of current relationship • Assess quality of relationship through ongoing process of self-reflection **Developmental Practice Methods** • Approaches align with the developmental, individual needs of the child, youth, and families • Bronfenbrenner's ecological systems theory • Assess quality of relationship in process of self-reflection and impact of self in relationship

Reflective Practice Element	Code of Ethics	Core Competency
Reflective Thinking • Reflective Process Model; Schon's models of reflection • Ability to give and receive feedback	**Responsibility to Child, Youth, and Families** • Affirms that there are differences in individual and family needs and meets those needs on an individual basis • Ensures interactions reflect developmental age, status, understanding, and capacity	**Professionalism** • Evaluating on practice and performance **Applied Human Development** • Well-versed in current research and theory in human development with emphasis on developmental ecological perspective
Reflective Learning • Reflective journals • Reflective dialogues • Collaborative reflections	**Responsibility to Self** • Engages in ongoing supervision and/or counsel as appropriate **Responsibility to Child, Youth, and Families** • Values collaboration with colleagues and those from other disciplines **Responsibility to the Employer and/or Employing Organization** • Responds to employer in a professional manner and seeks to resolve differences collaboratively • Treats colleagues with respect, courtesy, and equity • Models flexibility and inclusiveness in working with colleagues and family members **Responsibility to the Profession** • Acts in a professional manner toward colleagues	**Cultural and Human Diversity** • Establish and maintain effective relationship within team environment **Relationships and Communication** • Establish and maintain effective relationships within team environment • Giving and receiving constructive feedback **Developmental Practice Methods** • Develop and sustain collaborative relationships
Critical Thinking • What is in the best interest of this child, and how does this align with or contrast existing agency/societal policies? • Awareness of ethical dilemmas	**Responsibility to Self** • Engages in ongoing supervision and/or counsel as appropriate **Responsibility to Child, Youth, and Families** • Recognizes, respects, and advocates for the rights of the child, youth, and family	**Professionalism** • Advocacy • Relationships and communication • Giving and receiving feedback **Cultural and Human Diversity** • Supports children, youth, and families to overcome culturally based barriers to services

(*continued*)

Table 1: Reflective Practice to Standards of Practice, Code of Ethics Connection (*continued*)

Reflective Practice Element	Code of Ethics	Core Competency
Critical Thinking (*continued*)	**Responsibility to the Profession** • Acts in a professional manner toward colleagues • Ensures that practitioners, supervisors, and administrators lead programs according to high-quality and ethical practice	**Applied Human Development** • Applies process of ethical decision-making in a proactive manner
Transformational • Demonstrates learning and acquisition of skills into practice	**Responsibility to Self** • Develops knowledge and skills necessary to benefit children, youth, and families • Participates in education and training for ongoing professional development **Responsibility to Child, Youth, and Families** • Fosters self-determination and personal agency • Encourages a child or youth's participation within a family and community, and facilitates the development of social networks • Observes, assesses, and evaluates services/treatments prescribed or designed by other professionals **Responsibility to the Community** • Promotes awareness of the profession and the needs of children, youth, and families to the community • Participates in education and training for ongoing professional development	**Professionalism** • Awareness of law and regulations • Demonstrate knowledge and skills in use of advocacy • Describe the rights of children, youth, and families in relevant settings **Cultural and Human Diversity** • Recognize and prevent stereotyping while accessing and using cultural information • Establish and maintain effective relationship within a team environment • Design and implement group work, counselling, and behavioural guidance with sensitivity to the client's individuality, age, developmental, culture, and human diversity **Applied Human Development** • Well-versed in current research and theory in human development with emphasis on developmental ecological perspective • Create and maintain safe and growth-promoting environment • Skilled at communication with others • Report writing • Observations are objective and respective of clients • Interpersonal communication

These core competencies are achieved over time and through experiences with others. The responsibility of promoting emotional, social, and spiritual development of others (CYCCB, 2018; White, 2007) necessitates practitioners possess an awareness of self that underlines professional practice. The following chapter will examine this concept of self more closely, however, it is important for learning professionals to realize that self is not a fixed concept and is ever-changing and evolving (Gharabaghi, 2008a) through and in relation to experiences with others (Fewster, 1990b; Krueger, 2004).

> Awareness is the greatest agent for change.
> —Eckhart Tolle

CLOSING THOUGHTS[11]

When did you feel most engaged? Least engaged?

_____

_____

_____

What is the most important information you have learned thus far?

_____

_____

_____

What questions remain for you from this learning?

_____

_____

_____

NOTES

1. Professional practice involves the distinct skills and knowledge of Child and Youth Care as outlined in the Standards of Practice.
2. Inquiry relates to the process of questioning one's internal experiences and the experiences of others. This will be discussed in Chapter 3.
3. Reflection for action is a concept based on Schon's (1983) reflective models and prepares students to engage in experience-based learning and to explore the expectations of experiences they will encounter, which can assist with improving or changing one's way of doing things (Coulson & Harvey, 2013; Killion & Todnem, 1991).
4. The characteristics of reflective practice were adapted from Ash and Clayton (2009); Pollard and Anderson (2008).

5. Power and privilege are terms to represent one's professional identity and one aspect of your social location (Gharabaghi, 2008a; Lareau & McNamara Horvat, 1999).
6. Legislation in Child and Youth Care involves the distinct laws that relate to the rights of children.
7. The Standards of Practice is a term to refer to the Code of Ethics and core competencies of Child and Youth Care practice and have been taken directly from the Child and Youth Certification Board (www.cyccb).
8. The Code of Ethics has been taken directly from the Child and Youth Care Certification Board (www.cyccb).
9. The core competencies of Child and Youth Care have been taken directly from the Child and Youth Care Certification Board (www.cyccb).
10. The Reflective Practice to Standards of Practice, Core Competency table was adapted from White (2007). Code of Ethics content and core competencies content taken directly from the Child and Youth Care Certification Board (2018). Association for Child & Youth Care Practice. https://cyccb.org/CYCcertification@youthworkacademy.org. © 2017 the Child and Youth Care Certification Board.
11. The closing thoughts reflection is adapted from the CIQ—Critical Incident Questionnaires in Keefer (2009).

CHAPTER 2

Starting Where You Are

Self-awareness is a key to self-mastery.

—Gretchen Rubin

LEARNING OBJECTIVES

In this chapter, you will:

- explore individual perspectives
- learn to identify personal strengths

In the previous chapter, you were introduced to the concept of reflective practice and its connection to professional practice. Reflective practice as a dynamic process of thinking about, learning, and exploring new ways for improving practice is a life-long skill that requires practice and experiences to cultivate. Practitioners need an awareness of who they are, which begins with acknowledging personal perspectives and individual strengths. This chapter will take you through different exercises to develop this awareness.

Reflective practice begins from within. This introspective process involves exploring the self, which involves one's values, beliefs, identities, and assumptions (Bellefeuille & Ricks, 2010; Fewster, 1990a; Garfat & Ricks, 1995). These aspects will be explored further in the next chapter. For the purpose of this chapter, you will explore your ways of thinking about self by completing a number of exercises.

The use of metaphors and symbols can assist individuals in creating meaning about themselves (Di Fabio & Bernard, 2014) while providing a different way of thinking (Stevens & Cooper, 2009) about self. Engaging opportunities such as these can prepare professionals to learn methods for expanding their ways of thinking, which is necessary for reflective practice.

As you progress through the remainder of the chapter, notice your internal reactions (thoughts, emotions). List them in the space provided below each activity. The purpose is merely to be aware of how emotions and assumptions can emerge. The activities are designed to familiarize you with the thinking aspect of reflection.

Exercise 1: Tap into Your Creative Potential

Refrain from overthinking this exercise and let go of the idea that there is a right or wrong way of completing it. If you notice you get stuck on doing this "right," come back to the exercise at a later time. Use the time to think about what the "right way" of thinking means to you, where this originates from, and how this might influence further ways of thinking and doing.

Think about an object you own that holds special meaning for you. As you think about this object, consider its unique features and attributes as extensions of your personality. How do these characteristics influence your relationships with others? What assumptions (beliefs) have others made about you based on these characteristics? Capture the object in the space below by drawing or taking a picture to print and paste. If you feel blocked during this creative process, imagine walking into a store and seeing something that said "YOU" all over it; what would that be? Find a picture of this item or draw it in the space below. You can select an image from the Internet or other media.

In the space surrounding the image, write three words that describe how this item personifies you. These can be emotive or descriptive words. Once you have completed this part of the exercise, consider how you can incorporate these aspects of self into your studies and your interactions and relationships with others.

Exercise 2: All in a Song

Think of your favourite song, one that you most identify with or best describes you. Create an image or select one from the Internet (remember to cite its source) or among your personal photographs that represents the message this song conveys about you.

In the space below, identify the feelings and thoughts that this song brings up for you. Which part of the song speaks to you or relates to your life?

_____

_____

_____

_____

_____

_____

_____

Something to Think About

When you have completed the creative exercises above, identify any new insights you have discovered about yourself. Use the space below to write about this.

_____

_____

_____

_____

_____

_____

_____

_____

_____

_____

_____

The Me-o-meter[1] is a tool created to allow adolescent clients to explore their sense of self and their meaning of the exercise. Pen-and-paper exercises can create a distance from having to share openly during sessions and, in this author's experiences, provide opportunities for adolescents to be present and focus on the moment. When adolescents have challenges identifying different aspects of themselves, it has been helpful to ask them what others in their world would say about them. This exercise is only intended to raise your awareness about who you perceive yourself to be and way of thinking.

Select one strength and one limitation you have identified and think about how these influence your interactions with others (your expectations of self and others, for instance). If you identified adventurousness as one of your strengths, for example, you may expect others to be open to trying new things and feel bothered if they are not. If you identified communication as a challenge because you are easily distracted or worry about saying the right thing, you may have a difficult time paying attention to conversations. If, however, you identified communication as a strength, you may expect that others will be as open to communicating and addressing conflict as you are. (As you identify additional strengths in your learning, you are encouraged to add them.)

Exercise 3: The Me-o-meter

Fill in the Me-o-meter below and follow the steps listed here:

1. In the centre circle, write your name.
2. In the second circle, write words to describe you. List as many words as you can to describe yourself.
3. In the third circle, list your strengths (the skills you possess that enable you to achieve goals, develop relationships, and complete other tasks in life).
4. In the fourth circle, list those actions/behaviours you engage in that underlie the strengths you listed above (the evidence). This provides a sense of ownership and acknowledgement of your own strengths.
5. In the fifth circle, list those challenges or limitations you possess (characteristics that may prevent you from achieving your goals).

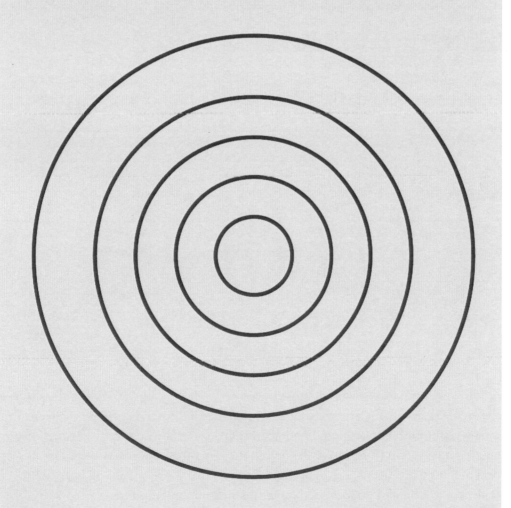

Something to Think About

What thoughts or feelings did you experience from completing the Me-o-meter exercise?

_____

_____

_____

What aspects of this exercise were challenging or easy for you?

_____

_____

_____

If you were challenged in identifying strengths, consider what factors made it difficult. Was this related to your current beliefs about self—that you lack in strengths—or because it was simply difficult to identify what you do well, beyond being caring, kind, and friendly?

_____

_____

_____

_____

_____

_____

_____

_____

This will reinforce the idea that through experiences and your ability to reflect on these experiences, your awareness of self (strengths and limitations) will increase. Your awareness of both strengths and limitations provides opportunities for further learning and requires you to think about the impact these will have on practice (an essential aspect of reflective practice is recognizing the impact that your actions will have on others). Include any insights you discovered about yourself from this exercise.

_____

_____

_____

_____

_____

_____

_____

_____

_____

_____

Learning professionals enter this field for different reasons, which are often based on past experiences. Irrespective of the nature of your experiences, these will invariably influence your understanding of Child and Youth Care Practitioners' roles and responsibilities. The following exercise provides an opportunity to think about your perspectives of Child and Youth Care.

Exercise 4: Pursuing Child and Youth Care

Use the space below to describe what influenced you to pursue this field. It is not necessary to describe in detail past experiences, but the aspects of those experiences that influenced your decision to pursue Child and Youth Care. In the space below, describe your reasons for pursuing this field. The following questions will guide you in your writing:

- What influenced your decision to pursue Child and Youth Care?
- What is it about becoming a Child and Youth Care Practitioner that interests or inspires you?
- What hopes and fears do you have about this role?

_____

_____

_____

_____

_____

_____

_____

_____

_____

_____

_____

Using the space below, you may also wish to create a collage (e.g., art, imagery, poetry) that captures your thinking in this exercise.

The previous exercises provide opportunities for you to contemplate your ways of thinking and seeing self as a frame of reference for your experience of self.

Something to Think About

What connections are there between the strengths and challenges you listed and your interest in pursuing Child and Youth Care?

The ability to acknowledge the strengths of others is reflective of a strength-based approach (Garfat & Fulcher, 2012) to practice. A strength-based approach considers the inherent resources and strengths of individuals as a catalyst for change (McCammon, 2012). Practitioners, however, need to demonstrate the ability to recognize their own strengths, which is an essential aspect of self-awareness for professional practice. Recognizing your own strengths enables you to recognize strengths in others.

The following strengths inventory exercise provides an opportunity to identify the strengths you possess. This list is by no means exhaustive and is intended to provide you with an awareness of the language used to describe strengths. This will be beneficial to you when you are required to write about the strengths that children, youth, and families present. The strengths inventory can provide a valuable resource in your future practice.

Exercise 5: Strengths Inventory[2]

Review Table 2 and identify those qualities that relate to you. The purpose of this exercise is not to identify as many strengths as you can; rather, it provides you the opportunity to consider the uniqueness and resources that exist within you. When you have finished, review the list again to determine if these are developing strengths, current strengths, or potential strengths to develop. This will provide you the opportunity to identify those strengths you actively demonstrate and those strengths requiring further development. What is necessary for you to develop in these areas? Which aspects of your academic journey and life beyond academia would enable you to develop these strengths? Return to the Me-o-meter exercise and notice how the two lists of strengths compare. What similarities and differences are there? Add any new strengths identified in Table 2 to your Me-o-meter. When you have finished, respond to the questions that follow.

Checking In

Where are you with understanding the concepts and exercises in this chapter in relation to reflective practice? What have you learned that you may not have been aware of before? What questions do you have that warrant further exploration to support your thinking about and learning in this chapter?

Table 2: Strengths Inventory

Accountable	Analytical	Assertive	Creativity
Maintain responsibility to self and others.	Thinking things through and considering different ways of thinking.	Self-awareness. Ability to assert your needs with others without fear of rejection.	Ability to perceive problems from a range of perspectives; thinking of new ways to do things.
Empathic	**Engaging**	**Fair**	**Honesty**
Ability to consider the emotional experience of another.	Ability to form relationships with others.	Providing people opportunities that reflect their individual needs. Separating your personal feelings while working with others.	Ability to be truthful about your intentions and motives with others.
Inclusive	**Individuality**	**Inquisitive**	**Insightful**
Focusing on similarities and strengths of people while working together.	Ability to define your own style and unique way of being in the world without influence from others.	Openness to learning new things, independently or in groups. Every experience provides an opportunity for learning.	Ability to perceive messages beyond presenting behaviours.
Integrity	**Leadership**	**Observant**	**Open-minded**
Ability to do what is right without denying your own or others' values.	Ability to organize and encourage groups of people to work together to accomplish tasks.	Attentive to what is occurring around you. Ability to notice subtleties of others.	Consider perspectives of others; receptive to new learning.
Organized	**Perseverance**	**Perspective**	**Responsive**
Ability to prioritize tasks. Maintain orderly environment.	Ability to complete tasks regardless of the obstacles that may exist.	A way of looking at the world that considers the unique circumstances of people.	Ability to adapt approach to meet the needs of others.
Self-aware	**Self-directed**	**Spiritual**	**Strength-based**
Maintain awareness of the impact of your behaviour on others and areas you require further growth and development.	Take responsibility and ownership for own learning. Seeking out support from others as required.	Committed to defining meaning and purpose in what you do.	Ability to identify the strengths and potential in others. Seeking opportunities that foster learning.

Thinking about Your Strengths

In reviewing these strengths, did you identify some that you had not considered before?

_____

_____

_____

Which strengths do you demonstrate more frequently or actively?

_____

_____

_____

Which strengths come naturally to you?

_____

_____

_____

Which strengths would you like to further develop?

_____

_____

_____

How have these strengths influenced your interactions with others?

_____

_____

_____

Identifying strengths in others is not simply acknowledging what they are good at, nor is it about praising them for their efforts and accomplishments. Assuming a strengths perspective involves viewing others' potential and the inherent resources they possess as factors for creating change (Garfat & Fulcher, 2012; McCammon, 2012). The value in identifying and understanding the different strengths that individuals possess will assist you in perceiving those children, youth, and families you work with from a strengths perspective rather than from a problem or deficit perspective. You will learn throughout your program that everything Child and Youth Care Practitioners do is intentional and purposeful (Garfat & Fulcher, 2012). Each of the exercises in this book is designed to prepare you for the next concept. It is important that practitioners develop an awareness and understanding of self before attempting to understand others.

As you think back to your experiences of the previous exercises, contemplate your initial reactions. When individuals are asked to do something that is unfamiliar to them or outside of their comfort zone, it may be perceived to offer little to the learning experience. Continue to explore the nature of these comments and the judgement that underlies them. How might this way of thinking influence your actions or your receptivity to new experiences. As you have learned, and will continue to learn, the self (beliefs, values, assumptions, experiences, social location) has a significant bearing on your practice.

Consider the Following Scenario: Daria

Daria, a first-year student, attended an orientation at a community program that provides groups for children and youth who have experienced loss. The facilitator asked everyone to create an image that best represented themselves and to give this image a voice. Daria rolled her eyes and expressed her opinion of this activity, muttering, "Stupid exercise." From that point on, she took the mindset that this was a waste of time and determined she would not make the children do any of these activities. "What," she thought, "does this have to do with loss?" At the end of the orientation, the facilitator approached her to share her observations of Daria's disinterest in the group and suggested that she pursue another group to support children in the community.

This scenario illustrates the impact that one's thoughts can have on their actions (body language; unwillingness to participate in new experiences) and provides opportunities to give further thought to the reaction as a focus for reflection as opposed to the activity itself. The following chapter will introduce you to the key characteristics of Child and Youth Care that are essential for adopting a reflective mindset: intentionality, presence, noticing, curiosity, context, and meaning-making. You will discover that, through adopting these characteristics, your ways of thinking about others and situations will take on a much more comprehensive outlook.

Exercise 6: Thinking about Thinking

Pay attention to the thoughts that arise for you in your reactions to different exercises or situations and how these are conveyed through your body language and behaviours. Briefly write about these in the space below and be sure to date the entries. The more you do this, the more your thinking will evolve. Repeat these exercises over the span of a week. The more you attend to these thoughts, the more you become aware of how your thoughts impact your actions. The first one has been completed for you as an example.

Situation: Class lecture   **Date:** xxx. xx, xxxx

In class today, the professor asked Daria to put away her phone. "She has no right," Daria thought, "I pay for my education and will use my phone as I choose" (thought). For the remainder of the class, Daria spent time updating her Facebook. She had disengaged from the class lecture (impact on behaviour).

Situation: **Date:**

_____

_____

_____

Situation: **Date:**

_____

_____

_____

Situation: **Date:**

_____

_____

_____

Situation: **Date:**

_____

_____

_____

The above exercises provide you with opportunities to think about and share your ways of thinking in the immediate moment. As indicated above, thinking about how one thinks is one aspect of the self—you in practice with others. These exercises also reinforce the idea that each person will have a different experience of a situation that will further influence their ways of thinking about and doing Child and Youth Care practice.

In the following chapters, you will continue to become more aware of the prevalence of your thinking. This awareness is essential to your role as a Child and Youth Care Practitioner as it provides many opportunities to distinguish the origins of your thinking (beliefs, past experiences, values, assumptions, social location). Thinking about the origins of your thinking raises your awareness of how you think about situations and others and the influences that inform your thinking. Until such awareness is established, however, practitioners risk framing this thinking as fact or as justification for their behaviours and creating the potential to blame others.

The following exercises are designed to provide you with additional opportunities to increase your awareness.

Something to Think About

A co-worker at your part-time job asks you what a Child and Youth Care Practitioner does. How might you explain this? Do not be concerned with saying "the right thing"; merely describe your understanding of the Child and Youth Care role and write your response below.

_____

_____

_____

_____

_____

_____

_____

_____

_____

_____

After you have finished, review your response. Notice the words you used and the emotional tone of your words. What perspective might the co-worker have based on your explanation? Where did you obtain your information about the role of Child and Youth Care: your own ideas and opinions? Your earlier experiences with Child and Youth Care Practitioners? Share and discuss with a partner. This will give you the opportunity to consider how your language may be perceived by others.

In the next chapter, you will learn about the different aspects of self and how these influence your interactions and the decisions you make.

CLOSING THOUGHTS[3]

When did you feel most engaged? Least engaged?

_____

_____

_____

What is the most important information you have learned thus far?

_____

_____

_____

What questions remain for you from this learning?

_____

_____

_____

NOTES

1. The Me-o-meter is a tool developed to foster awareness in adolescents and was created by Budd (2014).
2. The strengths inventory exercise was adapted from the VIA Character Strengths (2004–2014), and Peterson and Seligman (2004).
3. The closing thoughts reflection is adapted from the CIQ—Critical Incident Questionnaires in Keefer (2009).

CHAPTER 3

The Knowing, Being, and Doing of Child and Youth Care Practice

The only true wisdom is in knowing you know nothing.

—Socrates

LEARNING OBJECTIVES

In this chapter, you will:

- be introduced to the knowing, being, doing framework
- explore the concept of self through experiential exercises
- identify values, beliefs, assumptions
- explore social location
- explore the impact of self on practice through case scenarios
- be introduced to relational practice as the essence of Child and Youth Care practice
- be introduced to the Child and Youth Care characteristics of intentionality, presence, noticing, and curiosity

In the previous chapter, you began to consider your ways of thinking, which is one aspect of reflective practice. In this chapter, you will further your learning to explore other aspects of self through different experiential exercises, which will assist you in developing the awareness and understanding of how self can influence your interactions with others.

KNOWING, BEING, DOING FRAMEWORK

The knowing, being, doing framework provides a way to understand Child and Youth Care reflective practice (Mann, Gordon, & MacLeod, 2009; White, 2007) and has been discussed across the literature (Garfat & Ricks, 1995; Krueger, 2011; Ricks & Bellefeuille, 2003; Stuart, 2013; White, 2007). Within this framework evolves a means for exploring

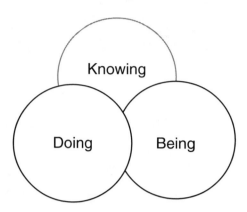

Figure 2: Knowing, Being, Doing
Source: Adapted from White, 2007.

self, others, and the theoretical principles that underlie Child and Youth Care practice. It is through this interconnected process of knowing, being in, and doing professional practice that reflective practice develops.

For the purpose of this chapter, an overview of the framework is provided, with more focus on knowing self and an introduction to being with others. Bellefeuille et al. (2011) assert that the concept of self is not to be understood as a separate individual construct, but rather as a result of a relational process that has developed through relationship and continues to evolve and shift throughout the practitioner's experiences (Fewster, 1990b; Garfat, 1992; Gharabaghi, 2008a; White, 2007).

Knowing embodies the self and the standards of practice that govern professional practice. As discussed in Chapter 1, the standards of practice are the principles to guide professional conduct and assist in making ethical choices (Ricks & Bellefeuille, 2003). The guidelines and core competencies are the principles that govern Child and Youth Care practice. This chapter will focus on knowing self and an awareness of how self both impacts (Fewster, 1990a; Ricks, 1997; Ricks & Bellefeuille, 2003; White, 2007) and is impacted by others (Ricks & Bellefeuille, 2003). This knowing relates to the use of self—the practitioner's ability to engage in thinking about their beliefs, values, assumptions, and their social location that can impact practice (Garfat & Fulcher, 2012; Krueger, 2004; White, 2007). When practitioners are not grounded in their own sense of self, they risk practicing from a place of reactivity and impulse rather than the intentional, reflective position of professional practice (Gharabaghi, 2008a). Further to this, however, is the awareness of the potential impact that values, beliefs, and assumptions can have on others. This is not to suggest that one's ways of thinking are wrong, but to provide an opportunity to determine how these implicit ways of thinking can impact one's ways of being and doing.

As you develop your awareness, you will begin to notice that your reactions are less about others' behaviours and more about what is triggered within you. This awareness is a precursor to the concepts of doing Child and Youth Care practice that will be explored in the latter part of this chapter. You cannot demonstrate the capacity to be present, notice, and be curious about others if you are not attuned to self, who you are. Attuning to oneself and others relates to the concept of conscious awareness. Fewster (2002) describes attunement as the process by which practitioners acknowledge and respond to their own and to others' inner experiences.

Professional Practice

Many learning professionals will profess their commitment to demonstrating a genuine, empathetic, and non-judgemental approach in their practice; however, this necessitates an awareness of their own emotions and thought process that can influence the potential for judgement. Practitioners are required to develop self-awareness and maintain appropriate professional boundaries so that their own experiences do not impact practice (CYCCB, 2018).

> The effective child and youth care practitioner is one who is self-aware.
> —Fewster, 1990a

Achieving this awareness requires you to explore your use of self by identifying your feelings, beliefs, values, assumptions, and social location. It is experiences with others that challenge your ability to separate your own reactions and perceive how they are influencing how you respond to others; this is impossible if you are not aware of your own internal experiences (Bellefeuille & Ricks, 2010; Garfat & Fulcher, 2010). It takes time, practice, and concerted effort to engage in self-inquiry as a means to achieve greater awareness of self that will expand your ways of thinking and knowing, leading to professional practice with others. From these experiences, you will discover that it is the meaning you have created of experiences with others that fuels the potential for judgement and difficulties in presenting an empathetic, genuine, and non-judgemental approach to others.

Self

> Self is the vehicle for which relationships develop.
> —Gharabaghi, 2008; Krueger, 1990

Both Child and Youth Care Practitioners and the others they interact with in practice bring their own experiences, ways of thinking, seeing, and being in the world (Krueger, 2004; Garfat & Ricks, 1995), which are influenced by one's feelings, thoughts, values, beliefs, assumptions, and social location (Garfat & Ricks, 1995; Ricks & Bellefeuille, 2003). These aspects of self are often implicit (hidden), in that they are not always at the forefront of one's consciousness. Yet, they can have a profound influence on one's interactions with others. Becoming more aware of these implicit aspects of self can make explicit the underlying expectations practitioners have of others. In the following sections, you will be introduced to different exercises that will reveal these aspects of self, which will support you in

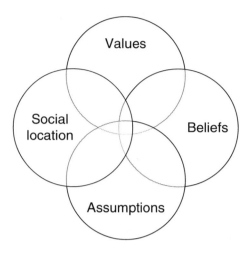

Figure 3: Aspects of the Self
Source: Created by author.

becoming more aware of why you do the things that you do. You will work on expanding your ways of knowing to enhance your understanding of the individual needs of others as separate from your own, the decisions you make, and actions you demonstrate in practice, all of which represent distinct aspects of professional practice (Garfat & Ricks, 1995). This is important when interacting with others who may not share similar ways of thinking.

What is of significance is the interaction between self and others and their experiences of one another. This in-between space, the interpersonal that exists under the conditions of security, vulnerability, caring, and engagement between the practitioner and the child, youth, or family, is referred to as the co-created space (Bellefeuille & Jamieson, 2008; Garfat & Fulcher, 2013; Fewster, 1990b; Mann-Feder, 1999); this is the *being with* dimension. We will return to the concept of the co-created space in the following chapter, as it is important to give meaning to the other before we proceed in exploring those distinct aspects of self that contribute to this co-created space.

Who Is the Other(s)?

The term other(s) is used throughout this book to mean children, youth, families, colleagues, and other professionals. These others possess inherent unique qualities, strengths, and their own realities (Anglin, 1999), which are distinctive from those of the practitioner, although not from an us-versus-them perspective. Rather, practitioners adopt a "here I am, and here you are" lens that parallels (Garfat & Fulcher, 2013) the co-created space, the in-between space that defines one experience from another. This is in contrast to the position of exclusion, oppression, superiority, or "othering" that is well-documented in the anti-oppression literature (Dominelli, 1998; Kumashiro, 2000; Ngo, 2008; Snow, 2009). The perspective functions by creating the space for emotionally and intellectually responsive relationships to develop (Curry et al., 2011). Further to this is recognition and appreciation for cultural diversity in creating inclusive environments.[1]

Many of the children, youth, and families you will work with have experienced traumatic events that include, but are not limited to, abuse, neglect, death, separation, loss, mental and/or physical illness, domestic violence, and war. These diverse experiences can negatively impact an individual's sense of self, and one's ability to relate to others and the world. While it is not the intention of this book to go into detail about supporting others in managing these experiences, it is important to note the manner in which practitioners acknowledge other realities will guide their actions (Anglin, 1999; Bellefeuille & Ricks, 2010; Garfat & Charles, 2012; Ricks & Bellefeuille, 2003). In order to objectively understand the other's experiences, Child and Youth Care Practitioners need to establish a strong sense of who they are as practitioners, as distinct from the other, who comes with their own ways of thinking, seeing, and being in the world (White, 2007).

The following exercises will provide you with experiences to explore aspects of self, notably your beliefs, values, assumptions, and social location, and the potential implications on practice.

What lies behind us and what lies ahead of us are tiny matters compared to what lies within us.

—Ralph Waldo Emerson

Exercise 7: Your Beliefs

Beliefs are those ideas we accept as true based on past experiences, knowledge, and the sociocultural environment we exist in. An awareness of beliefs can assist you in understanding why you do the things you do, which is fundamental to reflective practice.

Table 3 provides examples of personal, professional, and faith-based beliefs. Review the table to identify which beliefs align with your current way of thinking. These should not be shared with others. Be open to completing this honestly and not from a place of what you think you "should" identify with. This exercise is intended to raise your awareness of the beliefs that guide your way of being in the world.

Table 3: Beliefs

The future is determined by one's past.	Children, youth, and families do the best they can with the resources they have.	When I am upset, it is because of something someone has said or done.
The future is determined by experiences yet to occur.	Children, youth, and families are our greatest teachers.	Behaviours are good or bad.

(continued)

I am responsible for my actions and …	The higher the grade, the better the CYCP you will be.	Behaviours represent an unmet need the child is attempting to meet.
Others are responsible for how I think and act.	Education is the most important asset anyone can have.	The more friends one has, the more likeable they are.
When you trust others, you will experience disappointment.	Showing emotions is a sign of weakness.	Children, youth, and families who argue with the CYCP should be transferred to another practitioner.
Everything happens for a reason.	Family shapes who we become.	The past defines who you are.
When others are nice to you, they usually want something from you.	When we do nice things for others, others will do nice things in return.	Mistakes are opportunities in disguise.
I am responsible for how others feel.	Creativity is about artistic expression.	Children and youth have a right to express how they feel.
Life is meaningful when accomplishments are achieved.	It is the parent's responsibility to teach children right from wrong.	Children should know right from wrong.
Experiences are meaningful regardless of the outcome.	Children do the best that they can with what they have.	When people struggle, it is because of a lack of faith.
Rules should be the same for everyone in order to be fair.	Children and youth should listen to adults.	Individuals' struggles are a result of a disconnection from others.

When you have completed this exercise, return to the beliefs that fit for you and identify the origins of the beliefs by indicating: **E** (past experiences), **SC** (sociocultural environment: e.g., family, school, neighbourhood), **SM** (social media), or **O** (other).

You may discover that some beliefs have evolved from more than one place. Select one of the beliefs that you identified with and connect it to the respective sources that support this belief. Consider the potential expectations that may underlie this belief, which could impact your interactions with others. See the exercise below.

A word on writing about past experiences: it is not necessary to go into specific detail. You may choose to state, "My earlier childhood experiences led me to believe that …" or "my previous experiences at …"

_____

_____

_____

_____

_____

_____

_____

_____

_____

_____

Sample Exercise in Thinking about Beliefs

Gilles's past employment experiences as a sales manager (origin) led him to adopt an "every man for himself" mentality. The job was competitive and isolating. Co-workers and management were not to be trusted. He remembered a time when he shared his ideas with a co-worker, who then used them to their own advantage. Gilles believed that co-workers could not be trusted and that it was better to work alone (belief). This way of working could be challenging in a professional environment that required trust and communication. He realized that he may have a harder time trusting others and that it may be difficult for others to connect with him (potential impacts).

Identify any thoughts or questions that come up from reading this and add them to the space below.

_____

_____

_____

_____

_____

Review the following scenario and notice your thinking and feelings that emerge.

Consider the Following Scenario: Indiana

Indiana is a first-year student in the Child and Youth Care Program. When asked why she wanted to pursue Child and Youth Care as a profession, she explained that she wanted to change the system so kids in care have a better experience, adding that she had a lot to offer kids in care because of her own past experiences.

Indiana appears to believe that:

- The system for kids in care needs to change
- Kids in care can have a better experience
- She has a lot to offer to kids in care as a Child and Youth Care Practitioner
- Her beliefs (what she considers to be true) are based on her past experiences

Acknowledging your beliefs can help you realize what expectations you may have of yourself, others, and the situation. While expectations can be well intentioned, they can also set you up for anticipating that they will be achieved, without considering other important details. For instance, consider Indiana's belief that the system for kids in care needs to change. How might this influence her ways of being with others in care, such as the children and youth, her supervisors, or child welfare workers? Will she advocate for the rights of children and youth in care without involving the other professionals in this thinking? Will she be challenged in considering her limits as a practitioner? Are there limits for what can be advocated for, from a systems perspective? Discuss and share with a partner.

Values

Values are those things that individuals consider important to them and are similar to beliefs and assumptions, in that they influence the decisions people make (Bolton, 2009; Gharabaghi, 2008b). The values one holds invariably impact the way one thinks about and interacts with others. An exploration and awareness of values (what you consider to be important) will assist new practitioners in thinking more about why they do what they do (Bellefeuille & Ricks, 2010; Garfat & Fulcher, 2012; Ricks, 1997).

There are two versions of the values exercise, Exercise 8 and Exercise 9. You may choose to complete one or both. The blank spaces at the end of the list are for you to write in additional values that you identify as important to you.

Exercise 8: My Values

Review Appendix IV, Values Exercise, Version 1 and select the values you identify with. Next, categorize them into the four columns listed in the table provided and select the top five from your most important column. Consider where these originated from: past experiences, family culture, current experiences, or other. Provide your response in the space below. There are no right or wrong answers, nor is there a right or wrong way of completing this exercise. The purpose is simply to raise awareness and learn more about self and why you may do what you do.

What is most important to me	What is important to me	What is not important to me	What is neither/nor

Exercise 9: Determining Your Values Assessment

This version of identifying values is an adaptation of an existing values assessment (Demartinis, 2013) that encourages learning professionals to consider the meaning of different areas of their life that have significance to them. It is by making sense of this meaning that practitioners can acknowledge what is important to them. When you have finished, compare your values between the two exercises. Are they similar or different? If different, why do you think that may be?

On a piece of paper, make three columns. Create 13 rows and number each (the numbers do not determine an order of importance).

The first column will indicate your first choice, the second your second choice, and the third column your third choice. Respond to each question below using the columns (1, 2, 3) to list your responses. When you are finished, review your list and circle each repeating or similar word with a different coloured marker. Select the three most common (indicated by the number of similarities).

1. What do you fill your personal or professional space with most? What types of items stand out in these spaces? We tend to keep items of meaning close to us or where they can be seen (pictures, certificates, metaphorical symbols, trophies, work tools [toys, paintings, books, etc.]). Identify three types of items that fill your space most.

2. How do you spend your time? What most occupies your time within a 16-hour day? We tend to make time for things that are important to us (working, studying, self-care, working out, recreational activities, sports, etc.). Identify three things you spend your time on most.

3. What energizes you most? We tend to have the energy for the things that are important to us and inspire us (acts of service [e.g., volunteering], working, working out, socializing, shopping, cooking, entertaining, reading, researching, etc.). Identify the three things that you find energy for most often.

4. What do you spend your money on that has meaning for you (events, books, courses, trips, home, appearance, etc.)? We tend to find money for those things that are important to us. Identify three things you tend to spend your money on or find ways to afford these items that are meaningful to you.

Questions 1–4 may yield similar responses, and that is okay.

5. What areas of your life do you feel most organized or structured in? While it may be easier to identify areas where you are disorganized, focus only on the areas of your life that are structured and organized (social events, workout regime, appearance, self-care practices, meal or dietary regime, agenda, specific spaces in your home [clothes and shoes closet, office, bedroom, workout room]). We tend to demonstrate order and structure in the areas of our life that have the most meaning for us. Identify three things/areas that you are most organized in.

6. What areas of your life are you most disciplined and focused in? We tend to be the most dedicated and motivated in those areas that are important to us (studies, workout routine, social or social media interactions, appearance, meal or dietary regime, work or social activities, family). Identify three areas you are most disciplined and focused in.

7. What aspirations do you think about most often? We tend to think most about things that we aspire to and that currently exist or are beginning to materialize in our lives and not simply what we desire or unrealistic expectations. These are often things or experiences that have significant meaning (family, lifestyle, financial gain, freedom, travel, specific experiences, expanding education, meeting new people, building a business idea or project). Identify three things that you think most about that are currently occurring in your life.

8. What goals or aspirations do you have for your life that are reflected by your current lifestyle (family, financial freedom, travel, education, meeting new people)? We tend to envision a life that we are currently making strides toward. Identify the three things that you visualize, envision, or daydream about most for bringing about.

9. What does your dialogue with self consist of that is meaningful to you? What are you planning, creating, building, or narrating that is important to you? We tend to plan and talk over with ourselves things that are meaningful and currently present in our lives. Identify three things that you dialogue with yourself that are meaningful to you.

10. What does your dialogue with others (friends, family, co-workers) consist of that is meaningful to you? We tend to discuss topics of importance with others in social settings. Identify three things you talk about most with others, or experience joy when talking about, that are meaningful to you and beginning to materialize in your life.

11. What or who inspires you most? Consider the similarities between experiences, people, and things that have inspired you (specific moments, yours or others' accomplishments, specific songs, presentations, experiences). We tend to be most inspired by people and experiences that hold great meaning for us. Identify three things that inspire you. If you think of an individual, consider what they *do* that inspires you.

12. Which goals do you commit to working on each day? We tend to work on goals that have the most meaning for us. Identify three goals that you are bringing into reality (e.g., writing a book, attending college, organization and time management, advancing in your job, etc.). Identify the three most persistent goals that you have focused on and that you are definitely and gradually bringing into reality.

13. Which topics inspire you most, that you are most interested in learning more about? We tend to look for these topics that inspire us most in bookstores, newspapers, or magazines, or ask questions about (social issues, politics, financial issues, relationships, self-improvement, faith, spirituality, travel, family, etc.). Identify three things that inspire you the most.

When you review your list to identify common themes, consider the meaning behind experiences or symbols that you may have included on your lists. For instance, in the first question, if you listed your cellphone as something of importance, consider the purpose this serves for you (e.g., connections with others).

The following is an example of Exercise 9.

	1	2	3
1	Buddha statues	Crystals	Positive affirmations
2	Writing	Working	Working out
3	Writing	Researching	Attending spiritual events
4	Work tools (games, toys, art supplies)	**Courses**	Books
5	Social events	Work	Gym routine
6	Work	Writing	Self-care practices (meditating)
7	Spirituality (events, leaders)	Book project	**Education**
8	Book publication	**Completing master's**	Connecting to others
9	Spiritual topics	Ways to engage children and students	Book project
10	Spirituality	Work	Social issues
11	Collette Baron Reid	Gabor Maté	Children, youth, and families I work with
12	Book completion	**Completing master's program**	Spirituality
13	Spirituality	**Indigenous traditions**	**Current issues in Child and Youth Care practice**

There are similarities in each of the columns that reveal the top three values: work, spirituality, education. If you notice line 11, the names of people relate to spirituality and work. You will also notice that lines 3 and 11 have different shading, which represent the two value systems they represent.

Review your values and identify the connection of these to Child and Youth Care practice. For instance, if you selected independence as something you value, how does this relate to being a Child and Youth Care Practitioner?

Where did these values originate from (family, culture, past experiences, faith, previous knowledge, learning, significant people, etc.)?

Use the space below to respond to the questions above.

_____

_____

_____

_____

_____

_____

_____

_____

_____

_____

_____

_____

_____

_____

_____

> There is value in knowing your highest values. If you live aligned and congruent to your highest value, you will achieve the most out of life, you will experience fulfillment.
> —Dr. John Demartinis

Identifying the values that underlie your behaviours takes practice and the ability to step back from your familiar way of doing things to develop an understanding of why you do what you do. This will assist you in understanding the reasons for the behaviours of others, which can minimize the risk of personalizing those behaviours and responding from a reactive position. As you engage in the scenarios in the following chapters, you will become more proficient at identifying the values that underlie the actions of individuals in the scenarios, in addition to your own.

To prepare you for those scenarios, review the following scenarios and identify the values that underlie the manager's actions. Pay attention to your initial reactions as you read these.

Exercise 10: Pair and Share—Identify the Values

In pairs, read through each of the following scenarios and identify the values (see Appendix IV, Values Exercise, Version 1) that influenced the manager's responses.

Case Scenario A

You walked into work late one shift. There was a traffic accident that held you up and you were unable to access your phone to call work. When you arrive, your manager approaches you and tells you that you're fired for being late. He puts up his hand as you attempt to explain and reminds you that, as per your contract, there is zero tolerance for tardiness.

Case Scenario B

Imagine this very same scenario with the exception of the manager's response. When you arrive, he asks that you meet with him. He demonstrates concern for your wellbeing and asks what happened. When you explain, he asks what you could have done and what you will need to do for future similar occurrences. He asks that you consider this and directs you to start work.

The same scenario resulted in two different responses. While you could say that the different personalities resulted in different outcomes, there is more to a person's response than that. Discuss and share with a partner.

Something to Think About

How did your responses compare with your partner's?

_____

_____

_____

_____

Were they similar or different? Were you tempted to change your response to appease your partner? If so, consider the value that influenced your need to be "like the others."

_____

_____

_____

Self and relationship represent the tools practitioners employ to engage and connect with vulnerable children, youth, and families (Bellefeuille et al., 2008; Garfat, 1992; Gharabaghi, 2008a; Mann-Feder, 1999). However, they are to be understood as distinct components that have profound implications for practice. One must know oneself to be in a relationship with others (Garfat & Charles, 2012; Stuart, 2013). This knowing, you learned, involves a strong awareness of self, since self influences the very manner in which relationships develop (Garfat & Ricks, 1995). One cannot do Child and Youth Care practice without the presence of relationships, since relationships are at the heart of Child and Youth Care practice. Without relationships, Child and Youth Care risks being perceived as just another helping profession with textbook solutions to address complex life issues.

Consider the Following Scenario: Mya

Mya recently began her practicum at John Marshal's Home for Troubled Teens. She recalled feeling unsettled by the reference to "troubled teens" listed in the agency's name but realized she wanted to start building her experience, so she didn't think she should be picky. During her first shift, the other staff barely spoke to her. They told her to spend time reviewing the policy and procedure book. She sat in the office from 9 a.m. to 12 p.m. reviewing the manual and writing out questions to discuss with staff later. When she finished and entered the floor to ask about lunch, a few of the girls from the home were sitting in the living room eating lunch, while staff sat in the kitchen eating their lunch together. She felt perplexed by this and did not understand why everyone would not be eating together. When she asked about the girls in the living room, the staff replied, "That's how it is around here." Mya expressed her interest in joining the girls to eat her lunch and staff laughed, saying, "Yeah, no. That would make us look bad and the girls would think you were just trying to get into their business." The staff explained that her role was to supervise the girls and to ensure that they weren't getting into trouble.

When they observed her chatting with the girls and playing cards, staff pulled her aside and reminded her again her role was just to supervise. This went against everything that Mya had learned and believed in as a practitioner. She thought about the experiences with the girls and believed that she could make a positive influence. When she returned the following day, she engaged with the youth and initiated baking with them. Interested and eager to do something more than watch TV, the girls responded in agreement. Staff intervened and reminded the girls about the off-limits kitchen rule and redirected them back to the living room. Mya was spoken to again and reminded that if she did not follow through on the agency expectations, her practicum would be terminated.

When Mya discussed the situation with her peers at school, they told her she needed to just push through, as she could be terminated from the practicum if she did not abide by the agency rules. For Mya, this us-vs.-them mindset reflected an oppressive power dynamic that went against her values for connections. She explained that the culture of the agency that reflected this us-vs.-them did not align with her values about equality and creating experiences to establish relationships. What should she do?

This scenario illustrates an example of when the practioner's values are different from the agency values. Explore the implications for Mya if she were to remain at this practicum and list them below. Are there implications for the youth if she remains? How will she decide the best course of action (refer to the Code of Ethics to support your decision)?

_____

_____

_____

_____

_____

Child and Youth Care, as introduced in Chapter 1, requires more than an understanding of your interests, strengths, and challenges; it also relates to your day-to-day experiences with others as they live their lives (Kiffiak, 1994), which can include community, residential settings, hosptials, the family home, day programs, youth justice settings, and schools (Kiffiak, 1994; Stuart, 2013). The importance of your awareness of your beliefs and values and the assumptions you hold about others cannot be overstated. This awareness has significant implications for your practice if you are not aware of these influential aspects of self.

You are responsible for your actions, and while you may not always know what to do or what is the best course of action at the time, it is important that you consider your reasons for the decisions. This is important, as you will discover that others may not share your views of situations, nor will they always respond in the manner you anticipated. Think about this more. How might you respond to others who may not support or share your ideas? Will you surrender your ideas to appease them? Will you argue your point to challenge them in seeing your idea your way? Irrespective of the position you take, consider the impact this can have on the others you work with and your responsibility to developing as a professional practitioner.

ASSUMPTIONS

Assumptions are ideas that are accepted as truth without proof or evidence to support them, whereas beliefs are ideas that are accepted as truth and have evolved over time. Assumptions and beliefs are aspects of self that can and invariably have influenced the practitioner's thinking and actions in practice. Learning to question the source of information about others is essential to professional practice. The exercises and case scenarios presented in this text will provide you with opportunities to distinguish between what you think you know, what you don't know, and what there is to know (Garfat, 1992). Let us begin with assumptions about Child and Youth Care practice.

Exercise 11: Assumptions about Child and Youth Care

The following exercise will support you in identifying those assumptions you hold about situations related to Child and Youth Care practice. There is no wrong way or right way of completing these. Refrain from overthinking the statements and check off those that you assume to be true.

- There is no money in the Child and Youth Care profession.
- Child and Youth Care professionals are glorified babysitters.
- People enter this field to resolve their own past experiences.
- Child and Youth Care professionals only work in group homes.
- Child and Youth Care involves working with troubled children.

Use the space below to include additional assumptions you may have heard.

_____

_____

_____

_____

_____

Pay attention to the internal reactions (feelings, thoughts) you experience after reviewing these assumptions.

How do you know these to be true?

_____

_____

_____

What is the source that confirms these to be true?

_____

_____

_____

How might these assumptions impact your interest in becoming a Child and Youth Care Practitioner?

_____

_____

_____

What is your role in challenging these assumptions?

_____

_____

_____

Assumptions can influence one's actions if they are not challenged. However, in order for such assumptions to be challenged, practitioners need to be open to considering a different way of thinking, an alternative perspective that will foster new ways of knowing.

Consider the Following Scenario: Dina

Dina is a third-year student who has been contacted by an agency to interview for a potential job. Upon arriving to the interview, she was told the interviews were running late. As she waited, she observed other individuals in the waiting room leaving to be interviewed. She wondered if they were interviewing for the same position she was. Thirty minutes later, Dina was still waiting. She determined that the position had already been filled and that they had forgotten about her. She considered inquiring at the front desk about what was taking so long, then determined that they would have let her know. She waited another 10 minutes and decided to leave. Dina's assumption that the position had been filled influenced her decision to leave.

Consider the Following Questions

Assumption: The position had been filled.

- How does Dina know this to be true?
- What is the evidence to support this assumption?
- What did Dina base this assumption on? Fact? Previous experience?
- Was there more for Dina to know about this situation to confirm or deny this assumption?

This scenario illustrates how assumptions can impact one's actions and the importance of seeking further information to challenge such assumptions. However, in order to challenge this assumption, it would be necessary for Dina to consider alternative perspectives of why the supervisor did not arrive for the interview.

Exercise 12: Challenging Your Assumptions

As events and experiences occur in your day-to-day interactions, pay attention to the assumptions you make about these experiences. Complete this exercise over a few weeks' time as practice for noticing and challenging your assumptions. Use the space below to describe the situation and the assumption you have identified, then respond to the questions that follow.

Briefly describe the situation:

_____

_____

_____

Identify the assumption:

_____

_____

_____

How do you know this to be true? (Social media, experience, previous or current knowledge, beliefs, or values?)

_____

_____

_____

What is the evidence to support this assumption?

_____

_____

_____

Is there more for you to know about this situation to confirm or deny this assumption?

_____

_____

_____

Briefly describe the situation:

_____

_____

_____

Identify the assumption:

_____

_____

_____

How do you know this to be true? (Social media, experience, previous or current knowledge, beliefs, or values?)

_____

_____

_____

Is there more for you to know about this situation to confirm or deny this assumption?

_____

_____

_____

IMPLICATIONS FOR PRACTICE

When practitioners try to establish a relationship with others without having engaged in self-inquiry, there is a greater risk for the practitioner to make assumptions and decisions in practice that do not consider the lived experiences or individual needs of others (Ricks & Bellefeuille, 2003).

Many learning professionals believe that they will be better practitioners if they share similar experiences with the people they work with. This way of thinking often evolves from an intent to connect and establish relationships with others. They believe that if children and youth can see how they have overcome adversity, children and youth may be inspired to do so as well. There are risks to this way of thinking that warrant consideration of the potential impacts of their actions on others (White, 2007).

Consider the Following Scenario: Jalari

Jalari worked in an adolescent residential home. Eager to prove to the youth that he could relate to them, he initiated a discussion about the challenges of being a youth in present-day society. What began as an honest attempt to connect with others became a recollection of Jalari's personal experiences as a survivor of abuse. He immersed himself in the memories and anger that still consumed him. Unaware of his emotions in sharing his story, it became clear to the youth that Jalari seemed more interested in sharing his painful experiences than learning about them as individuals, separate from their trauma and painful pasts. Jalari's efforts to connect with these youth evolved into a personal account of unresolved torment. Triggered by these memories, Jalari struggled to remain present and available to the youth's emotional needs. For some of these youth, Jalari had mirrored other emotionally unavailable adults they had been disappointed by. Jalari's inability to perceive and understand the impact his actions had on these youth interfered with his ability to build relationships with them. He had become another "self-serving" adult who would only disappoint them.

Use the space below to note the thoughts or feelings you had in response to this scenario.

_____

_____

_____

_____

_____

_____

Consider the Following Scenario: Rory

Rory was a 15-year-old youth who had just been brought into foster care. Her parents requested support for managing Rory's behaviours and had agreed to foster care as a temporary solution. Rory remained in her room for most of the two days. Despite the foster parent's efforts, she was not interested in being with the others. Concerned and in an effort to support her, the agency director agreed to meet with her and took her out for a drive. He thought she may feel more comfortable and most teens preferred drives to just sitting and conversing. In Tom's effort to connect with Rory, he spoke of his own experiences in care and the challenges he experienced. From that point forward, Rory would only agree to meet and talk with Tom. When she threatened to harm herself, she demanded that Tom come as she perceived him to be the only one who understood and cared for her.

Use the space below to list any reactions, thoughts, or questions you have.

_____

_____

_____

_____

_____

_____

_____

_____

As you read over the two scenarios, you will notice that both the student's and the director's values for connections and relationships influenced their actions. However, their good intentions had a significant impact on the youth and the scenarios illustrate the way that one's interpretations of an experience can influence one's ways of thinking, seeing, and being. In the first scenario, the youth's interpretation that Jalari was only concerned with himself may have been influenced by past experiences.

In the second scenario, the director did not anticipate the potential impact of his well-intended actions (sharing past personal experiences). His actions may have reinforced for Rory that only people who lived through what she had could understand. Her dependence on Tom for emotional support limited her ability to accept help from others in the foster home.

As you learned from the previous scenarios, the practitioner's way of thinking is often based on their beliefs, values (Bellefeuille & Ricks, 2003; Gharabaghi, 2008b; Ricks, 1997), assumptions (Bellefeuille & Ricks, 2010), and past and present experiences (Gharabaghi, 2008a). These can have significant impacts on their practice if they are unaware of self and who they are as individuals. The next exercise provides you with opportunities to consider how your beliefs, values, and ways of thinking could impact your interactions with others and impact your practice. Review the statements listed in Table 4 and identify those that stand out for you.

The awareness of what is influencing one's practice and the implications of this underlies professional practice. As Garfat (2003d) states, knowing why we do what we do is reflective of knowing self. This raises another question: Is it ever okay to share past personal experiences with children, youth, and families? Although this is outlined in the Code of Ethics as a responsibility to children, youth, and families to ensure appropriate boundaries between professional and personal relationships, the answer to this question is not a simple one, and as such there is no single, direct answer. This does, however, lead to further questions to consider:

- What is the reason for sharing?
- What potential impact does sharing have on the relationship?

Exercise 13: Implications for Practice

This is an exercise to consider the potential impact that your ways of thinking may have on your interactions with others. Return to your beliefs and values exercises and select two or three from each, then list them in Table 4. Record your responses in the respective columns. For instance, if you value communication, you might expect that others would be as open to engaging in communication and conflict resolution as you. This is not to suggest these expectations are wrong; rather, it is simply an opportunity for you to be aware how this might further influence your actions.

Table 4: Implications for Practice

My beliefs		Assumptions underlying beliefs	My values	Potential expectations of others	Potential perspectives of others toward me	Potential impact on the relationship
Example:	Parents should never hit their children.	Parent who hit their children are bad parents.	Problem-solving Communication Relationships	I might expect that all parents value communication and understand the difference between punishment and discipline.	Parents might find me judgemental.	Parents may not find me supportive or approachable.

Something to Think About

Think back to the reflective exercise you completed in Chapter 2—your reasons for entering this program. Identify the values that influenced your decision to pursue this program. What have you discovered from this new learning that you were not familiar with before? Use the space below to include your responses.

_____

_____

_____

_____

_____

_____

_____

_____

_____

_____

_____

Consider the Following Scenario: June

June recently began working at a female adolescent residential home. As much as she was excited about this new opportunity, she was feeling quite uncertain of herself as well. She remembered what she was like as a youth and grimaced thinking about this. One particular night, June was watching a television show with two youths as a reference to discuss sensitive topics. At that moment, another staff member, Betty, entered the room and turned the television off, announcing the program was inappropriate. June sat there motionless, uncertain of what to do. In her uncertainty, she did nothing and both youths left, seemingly upset by this. June avoided staff for the remainder of the night, feeling ashamed and humiliated. However, as she was driving home, she realized how angry she was at Betty's actions. "Whatever," she thought; she would just ignore Betty and request not to work with her. When June arrived at the home the following day, she greeted everyone with the exception of Betty. June greeted the youths as they sat down to snack and chatted about the night's events, without a mention of the previous night.

Give some thought to what might have underlined the anger and humiliation June experienced, considering her actions the following day. Use the space below to record your responses.

_____

_____

_____

This scenario illustrates the impact that emotions can have on one's actions. The potential to avoid addressing these situations with the individual involved will have an impact on practice. Identify the impact that June's actions could have on the evening shift and the youth.

_____

_____

_____

As you progress through this book, you will discover the importance of questioning your decisions and actions as essential to the reflective practice process. The key characteristics of Child and Youth Care practice introduced later in this chapter will support your understanding of why you may do the things you do.

The Child and Youth Care profession has existed for over 20 years (Garfat & Charles, 2009). The professional title has changed over that time; where once professionals were Child Care Workers, then Child and Youth Workers, the present title is now Child and Youth Care Practitioners. Despite the changes this field has experienced, there still appears to be a lack of recognition for professional identity (Gharabaghi, 2008b; White, 2007), and confusion over what it is Child and Youth Care professionals do allows negative assumptions about the profession (Garfat & Charles, 2009; Gharabaghi, 2008b).

Social Location

Another aspect of self is identifying and understanding the potential impact of your social location. Social location represents the different sociocultural groups individuals belong to (gender, race, class, age, ability, religion, sexual orientation, culture, education, profession, and geographic location) as a result of their position in history and society (Garfat & Ricks, 1995; Lareau & McNamara Horvat, 1999). Embedded in these groups are the rules and roles that influences one's ways of thinking about others (Garfat & Ricks, 1995; Lareau & McNamara Horvat, 1999).

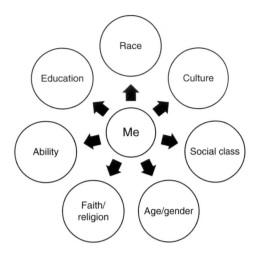

Figure 4: Social Location

Source: Created by author.

Exercise 14: Social Location: Who Am I in Relation to the Other?

The purpose of this exercise is to provide you with an opportunity to identify those distinct aspects of your social location using the template (Figure 5). Use the template as a reference for completing your social location. Alternatively, you can use your own format for presenting your social location In the space provided on the next page. Feel free to omit the locations that do not relate to you and add other identifying aspects of your social location that are not included above. Then identify (in point form) the distinct roles and rules that exist within each group and list these beside the corresponding spaces. When you have finished, review the different aspects of your social location to identify those that have influenced your decision to pursue Child and Youth Care practice.

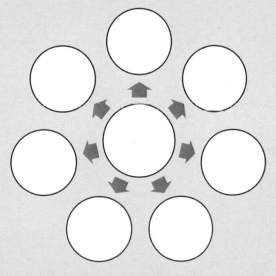

Figure 5: Social Location Template

Source: Created by author.

An important aspect of social location is the power and privilege you hold as a Child and Youth Care Practitioner.

—Gharabaghi, 2008a

Identify any three aspects of your social location (family role, race, social class, age, religion, sexual orientation, ability, geographic location, etc.) and describe how they might influence one of the following: interactions with others, your work ethic, your philosophy as a learning professional, relationships. Provide examples to support your thinking. Consider the rules that relate to your roles within these aspects of your social location. For instance, if you identify as a middle child, what rules have been established in your family role? Perhaps you are the peacekeeper who is responsible for settling disagreements between your siblings. Perhaps your role is to ensure your parents do not worry about you as the self-sufficient child. Rules can be implicit (hidden) or explicit (overt). How might the distinct roles and rules influence your decision and interactions with others?

You may wish to respond to these questions in the space below or you can note this on the respective areas of your social location chart.

_____

_____

_____

_____

_____

_____

_____

_____

_____

_____

_____

_____

_____

_____

_____

_____

_____

_____

_____

_____

_____

_____

_____

_____

_____

_____

Checking In

Where are you with the concepts and exercises you have learned about so far? What is making sense? What is not? What questions do you have that warrant further exploration to support your thinking? Take pause to think about your learning thus far.

If you practice solely from your social location, your ways of knowing others will be based on the rules and roles within the group you identify with. There are risks to this thinking in that you consider your way of knowing is *the* way to understand others. What impact will this have on your practice? Your *ways of being* with others? These are important questions to consider and will be revisited in Chapter 6 when you are introduced to the concepts of reflexivity and reflection.

As you become more aware of your beliefs, values, assumptions, and professional identity, you will begin to realize the influence these (self) have on your ways of knowing, seeing, and being in the world (Ricks & Bellefeuille, 2003; Lareau & McNamara Horvat, 1999; Ricks, 1997; White, 2007). As you become more attuned to the internal process of self, the ability to engage in self inquiry develops, which will enable you to recognize the impact of your thinking on others (Garfat & Charles, 2012; Gharabaghi, 2008a; Ricks, 1997; White, 2007).

Having an awareness of your own social location can assist you in understanding how your professional identity both impacts and is impacted by society (Hernandez-Wolfe & McDowell, 2010). Consider for a moment, how are you perceived by others? What aspects of your social location influences other perspectives of you? How might these perspectives influence your interactions with others?

_____

_____

_____

How have others perceived you in the past (based on these aspects of your social location)?

_____

_____

_____

How have their perspectives influenced your interactions in the past?

_____

_____

_____

What is the connection between your professional identity and your position of privilege and power?

_____

_____

_____

Include any questions or comments you have in the space below.

_____

_____

_____

Knowing What You Know

Professional practitioners are required to establish how they know what they know, the basis of their knowledge (Garfat & Ricks, 1995; Ricks & Bellefeuille, 2003; White, 2007), while considering larger sociocultural, historical, and political contexts in which they and others exist (White, 2007). Practitioners need to consider the impact their beliefs and assumptions (Bellefeuille & Ricks, 2010; Garfat & Ricks, 1995; Gharabaghi, 2008a; Ricks, 1997) and social location (Lareau & McNamara Horvat, 1999; White, 2007) can have in both their interactions with others and how their ways of thinking about others can influence larger organizational system (schools, Child Welfare, justice, etc.) practices toward children (Lareau & McNamara Horvat, 1999) who present with complex behaviours (Bolton, 2009). It then becomes important for practitioners to be aware of the limits of their knowledge and how this limited knowledge might further discount the other's experiences (Bellefeuille & Ricks, 2010; Lareau & McNamara Horvat, 1999; Ricks & Bellefeuille, 2003).

Review the scenario below to consider the potential implications for practice when practitioners are operating from their assumptions and the privilege and power position of their professional identity.

Consider the Following Scenario: Phoebe

Phoebe is a seven-year-old child in Grade 1. Over the past few weeks, she has begun to scream and cry upon her arrival to the classroom. She throws her papers and books when she is asked to complete a task. She has been unable to sit for long periods of time and has complained frequently of stomachaches. Liana, the Child and Youth Care Practitioner, has called the parents several times to pick Phoebe up, as her behaviours have been too difficult to manage in class. Her parents have not responded to the school's messages nor have they come to pick Phoebe up. Phoebe leaves with her older sister every day after school. In meeting with the teacher, Liana expressed concerns that something was going on at home and referred to the parents as negligent, not caring about Phoebe. Liana commented if she was a mom, she would drop everything for her child.

To understand Liana's comments and assumptions, it is important to identify the privilege and power she maintains in her professional identity as a Child and Youth Care Practitioner.

Liana is a middle-aged, white female who has been married for five years. She lives in an upper-class neighbourhood and has no children. She has worked in the schools as a practitioner for 10 years and maintains a strict approach for responding to behaviours. Her efforts to manage Phoebe's behaviours through planned ignoring and consequences have not been successful. She believes that Phoebe's behaviours are related to her need for attention and control. She has never met the parents and believes that parents are responsible for their children's behaviours. Review Table 5 to identify the aspects of self that influence Liana's thinking and actions. Use the space below to include additional thoughts or questions you may have.

_____

_____

_____

Table 5: Phoebe

Liana's beliefs	Liana's assumptions	Liana's values	Social location (identities, memberships; roles and rules embedded in each)	Family/child's perspectives of Liana	Potential impact on Liana's interactions with the family/child
• Parents should be supportive of the school. • Parents should trust my judgement and be willing to collaborate with me. • Parents should take responsibility for their child's behaviours.	• Phoebe's parents don't care about her. • The parents are negligent. • Phoebe is seeking attention.	• Order • Discipline • Respect • Responsibility	• White, privileged • Upper-class • Professional identity: CYC Practitioner (power position) • Membership: School board • Roles: Maintain control of classroom • Rules: Academic focus • Personal identity: Partner without dependents • Membership: Home; adult-oriented • Rules: Children are seen and not heard; adults are accountable to others	• The child may believe the CYC Practitioner does not care. • She may feel responsible for her parents' actions (they're not calling). • May not be willing to collaborate or consider change when they experience judgement and blaming attitudes from the school. • The CYC Practitioner is blaming us. • The teacher is the cause for the behaviours.	• She may provide additional attention to compensate for what she believes the parents are not providing the child. • May assume a blaming, defensive attitude toward the parents. • Expectations for Phoebe may exceed what she can do. • Attempts to seek control of the situation. • Knowledge is limited to practitioner's own professional and personal lens about children's behaviours. • Perceives self as expert on children's learning needs. • Perspectives of the family will not consider their lived experiences.

The connections between the practitioner's self and the potential implications on practice are well presented in the example above, which brings to light the importance of knowing one's self and others in practice. Consider for a moment how different Liana's approach might be toward Phoebe and her parents had she demonstrated a strong awareness of self and the implications on practice. How might these differences have presented in her practice?

_____

_____

_____

The importance of considering others' perspectives, in addition to an awareness of self and being open to learning about what underlies experience and meaning and the connection to practice, is addressed in the second part of this chapter.

Something to Think About

During class, the topic of spanking was raised to determine if this was considered abuse. Jenisse, a first-year Child and Youth Care student, spoke up and asserted that every parent should be charged for hitting their child. When the professor asked her to explain her thinking, Jenisse shared her beliefs that spanking was a form of abuse. "Spanking," she asserted, "always turns into hitting." "That's abuse," she said loudly, "and parents always get away with this."

Let us consider the beliefs, values, and assumptions that underlie Jenisse's comments. _Parents should be charged for hitting their child (value). Spanking leads to abuse (belief/assumption). Parents always get away with stuff (belief/assumption)._ It would be important for Jenisse to consider the origins of these comments. Are these based on past experiences (beliefs), what she considers important (values of justice and fairness), or knowledge (past and current learning)? Professional practitioners are required to defend their thinking in conveying how they know what they know.[2] If her comments are based on her own experiences, Jenisse risks assuming that this happens or has happened to others.

How might Jenisse's beliefs, values, and assumptions affect her ability to support a family whose beliefs and values differ from hers? Discuss and share with a partner and explain your thinking in the space below.

_____

_____

_____

_____

_____

_____

_____

_____

_____

_____

_____

_____

_____

The following scenario provides you with the opportunity to consider the perspectives of others through exploring their values, assumptions, beliefs, and social location. Review the scenario below and respond to the questions that follow.

Exercise 15: Expanding Your Ways of Knowing

Janella is a first-year student who possesses strong religious values. One day during a class discussion, one of her peers was sharing her earlier experiences of residing in care. This individual was known for her colourful use of language, and she did not spare any formalities during class. Janella grimaced, and she experienced a knot in her stomach. She thought to herself, "Shut up already," and couldn't stand to hear her peer's voice when she spoke. Janella had determined that she did not like her peer and often engaged in behaviours that demonstrated this. She would speak over her classmate or distract herself with her phone. If we consider Janella's beliefs, values, and assumptions that influenced her behaviours toward her peer, what might these be?

Assumptions: What has Janella believed to be fact where no supporting evidence exists?

_____

_____

_____

Beliefs: What beliefs might underlie Janella's behaviours?

_____

_____

_____

Values: What is important to Janella?

_____

_____

_____

What aspects of Janella's social location may be influencing her reactions toward her peer?

_____

_____

_____

Now consider the other student.
Assumptions: What assumptions may have influenced her sharing of personal past experiences?

_____

_____

_____

Beliefs: What does she think is true?

_____

_____

_____

Values: What might she consider to be important? Consider her potential reasons for sharing her experiences in care.

_____

_____

_____

Social location: What aspect of her social location might influence her openness to sharing her experiences?

_____

_____

_____

An experience is not an experience unless it involves interaction between the self and another person, the material world, the natural world, an idea …
   —Carol Rodgers

Fostering this greater sense of knowing others necessitates practitioners query how others know what they know. Is there evidence to support what they know? Have the others' larger sociocultural and historical contexts been considered? What more is there to know? This last point requires openness and curiosity to learn about the other beyond the surface behaviours presented by them. Learning to know others allows practitioners to develop a greater understanding of others and their lived experiences. In the following chapter, you will be introduced to the concept of worldviews[3] and the important questions to ask for leaning about the others.

Checking In

Where are you at with the concepts you have learned so far? What is making sense? What is not? What questions do you have that warrant further exploration to support your thinking? Take pause to think about your learning and respond to the questions using the space below.

_____

_____

_____

As you continue through the remainder of the chapter's case scenarios, pay attention to thoughts, emotional reactions, and questions that arise. In addition to listing them in the spaces provided for you, be sure that you address these in class or with your professor. This aspect of thinking and doing are essential to your learning.

The following case scenario will provide you opportunities to explore the assumptions, values, beliefs, and perspectives of the practitioner as a means to consider the perspective of Ji. We will revisit this case scenario again in the following chapter to support your learning about the Child and Youth Care characteristics that relate to reflective practice.

Consider the Following Scenario: Ty, Debbie, and Ji

Ty, a second-year Child and Youth Care student, recently secured a practicum at a community residential home for youth. As part of his orientation, he was given a file on a youth he would be working with on an individual basis. When he finished reading the file, he experienced an overwhelming sense of fear and anxiety and determined that the youth was dangerous and that he could be hurt. He told his professor that he felt unprepared to work in such a dangerous place and feared for his safety. Review the following case note and notice the assumptions you make.

Residential Home Case Note

Child: Ji McDougal   **Date:** Jan. xx, xxxx

Staff: Debbie Lou, CYCP

Ji had another difficult evening tonight. He refused to clean his room and join the group for dinner. He was quiet throughout dinner and did not respond to staff's attempts to engage him. He did not complete his chores and when reminded of the potential consequences, he punched a hole in the wall. Staff directed him upstairs to his room. He refused and told staff he was going out. Staff told him to stop and pointed out that there would be further consequences. He responded by throwing books off the bookshelf, telling staff to leave him alone. He gathered his coat and shoes and began walking toward the front door and pushed staff out of the way as she attempted to prevent him from leaving. He told her if she tried to stop him again, he would punch her out and left the home. Ji returned home two hours later and spent the remainder of the night in his room.

Ji's volatile and hostile behaviour seemed to come out of nowhere. He may be at risk of hurting others.

Consequence: Ji is to be off program for 24 hours.

Debbie Lou

Figure 6: Ty's Case Note

Source: Adapted from American Counseling Association. https://www.counseling.org › ethics-columns › ethics_december_2018_notes.

Imagine that you were Ty reading this report. What questions might you have that would support your understanding of what occurred? For instance, is there a history of conflict between this staff member and Ji? Use the space below to write down your own questions.

_____

_____

_____

_____

_____

_____

_____

_____

_____

_____

_____

_____

_____

Identify the assumptions, beliefs, and values that have influenced Ty's decision to withdraw from this practicum. Challenge the assumptions you have identified. How might these influence his interactions with Ji? As you have learned earlier in this chapter, learning to challenge assumptions is an important part of professional practice.[4] Use the space below to record your responses.

Ty's assumptions about the residential home:

_____

_____

_____

Ty's assumptions about Debbie:

_____

_____

_____

Ty's assumptions about Ji:

- Ji is dangerous.

Add in two more of your own.

_____

_____

_____

Ty's beliefs about his lack of skill and readiness to work in a residential home may be related to his lack of experience. Within this belief, however, lies another assumption: that he will not receive the support or necessary training to fulfill his role. Recall that an individual's own past experiences in similar situations can influence their current ways of thinking.

Ty's values for safety and structure might speak to his need for predictability and order. While this is not to suggest that this will not be provided at his practicum, this does highlight a learning opportunity for Ty to explore—learning to manage unpredictability in different settings. Identify other values that may underlie Ty's desire to withdraw from this practicum (refer to Appendix IV, Values Exercise, Version 1).

_____

_____

_____

In meeting with his professor the following day, Ty was encouraged to challenge his assumptions, which may provide him a different perspective of Debbie, Ji, and the residential home.

When challenging assumptions, it is important to ask:

- How do you know this to be true? (Social media, experience, previous or current knowledge, beliefs, or values?)
- What is the evidence to support this assumption?
- Is there more to know about this situation to confirm or deny this assumption?

Ty's professor reminded him that situations that present as unfamiliar can create uncertainty and doubt; however, it is important to consider the circumstances (context) to develop a better understanding of the situation. He encouraged Ty to create a list of questions based on the assumptions, values, and beliefs he presented about the residential program.

Assuming the position of Ty, create a list of questions you might have based on what you have read from the scenario and Ty's values, beliefs, and assumptions.

_____

_____

_____

_____

These questions will provide you with opportunities to seek out the necessary additional information that will support you in:

- Challenging your assumptions
- Developing a better understanding of the program rules
- Being aware of different contexts and perspectives
- Remaining in the present

Doing and Being

White (2007) asserts that there are many ways of doing and being in Child and Youth Care practice that relate to the diverse skill sets practitioners possess. The *doing* of Child and Youth Care practice involves *being with* others, which involves distinct analytical skills (White, 2007) and characteristics of Child and Youth Care practice that will support you in learning different ways of understanding the experiences of others. These skills, all of which connect to reflective practice, include practicing noticing/attending, interpreting/meaning-making, and collaborating/deliberating[5] (White, 2007). Characteristics of intentionality, presence, noticing, curiosity, examining context, and meaning-making (Garfat & Fulcher, 2012) will assist learning professionals in establishing the connections that are necessary for developing relationships in their practice (Brendtro & du Toit, as cited in Garfat & Ricks, 2012). These skills and characteristics will be referenced throughout the text as defining features of reflective practice. As you engage in the different case scenarios in this book, these key characteristics will assist you in developing a greater understanding of the issues within the case scenarios. You will discover the value in integrating these skills and characteristics into both your daily practice and understanding the case scenarios takes precedence over the solutions you may wish to suggest.

Self and the awareness of it in relation to working with others has provided one aspect of the foundation from which reflective practice evolves. The other aspect involves the interactions between the practitioner and others (children, youth, families, colleagues, supervisors, professors, other community professionals).

RELATIONAL PRACTICE

Relational practice is defined as a dynamic, rich, flexible, and continually evolving co-constructed process, where meaning evolves between individuals, family, or community

(Bellefeuille & Jamieson, 2008; Fewster, 1990b; Garfat & Fulcher, 2012; Mann-Feder, 1999). Relational practice embodies a person-centered approach that considers the unique needs and experiences of others (Bellefeuille & Ricks, 2010; Garfat & Ricks, 1995; Garfat & Fulcher, 2012).

> Time is of the essence in all relationships.
> —Jerry Acuff

Knowing self and the impact this self has on others is fundamental to relational practice that involves ways of knowing, being, and doing (Gharabaghi, 2008a; White, 2007) and occurs through your experiences with others. If self is the vehicle from which relationships develop (Gharabaghi, 2008a; Krueger, 1990), then reflective practice can be understood as the path from which professional practice evolves. Through self or, more aptly, through the use of self, relational practice evolves.

Relationship is the heart of the practice of Child and Youth Care (Anglin, 1999; Bellefeuille & Ricks, 2010; Garfat, 2003c; Garfat & Fulcher, 2012; Krueger, 2005). It is the focus on relationship as an intervention that distinguishes Child and Youth Care practice from other disciplines (Anglin, 1999; Garfat & Fulcher, 2012; Krueger, 2004; Maier, as cited in Mann-Feder, 1999; Stuart, 2013). However, it needs to be clarified that relationships don't just happen as a result of your interactions. They evolve through "integration of a complex constellation of knowledge, skills, and elements of self" (Anglin, 1999, p. 146) and the willingness of the practitioner to co-create new experiences (Anglin, 1999; Garfat & Fulcher, 2012) with others that foster autonomy, trust, and safety. It is the distinct characteristics of Child and Youth Care (intentionality, presence, noticing, curiosity, examining context, and meaning-making) that allow for greater understanding of others.

Intentionality

Intentionality implies that each decision you make in practice is deliberate and purposeful (Garfat & Fulcher, 2012) and considers the best interests of the child, youth, and family and is not made out of haste, judgement, or as means to conform to systemic standards or rules that do not consider the best interests of others (Dewey, 1933). Practitioners establish the purpose of each interaction as an opportunity to demonstrate presence through noticing and curiosity as precursors to fostering connections with others.

We return to the concept of the co-created space (Bellefeuille & Jamieson, 2008; Garfat, 2003b; Fewster, 1990b; Garfat & Fulcher, 2012; Mann-Feder, 1999) as the space between the practitioner and the other where the practitioner establishes connection with the other through presence, noticing, curiosity, examining context, and meaning-making (Garfat & Fulcher, 2012). The shift from *what I think I know* to *what is there to know* embodies this co-created space. Being with others in their day-to-day interactions requires practitioners to step outside of their habitual ways of thinking, to consider alternative ways of knowing, being, and doing with others (Bellefeuille & Ricks, 2010; Ricks & Bellefeuille, 2003; White, 2007).

These connections are fundamental to promoting the emotional, social, and spiritual development of children, youth, and families (Garfat, 2003c; Garfat & Charles, 2012; Krueger, 2011; Stuart, 2013).

This experience of co-creation conveys interest and acceptance of others as unique individuals with their own experiences and ways of thinking and being (Bellefeuille & Jamieson, 2008). Experiencing the other as the other experiences you is reflective of this co-created space (Garfat, 2008). Within this space, practitioners remain aware of self as distinct from the other (Garfat, as cited in Garfat & Ricks, 1995), in that their own internal experiences are not influencing or impeding their ability to *be* with the other.

While relationships are at the heart of CYC work, the connection is the foundation of the relationship (Brendtro & du Toit, as cited in Garfat & Ricks, 1995; Krueger, 2005, 2011). It is through the co-constructed space that connections are established (Bellefeuille & Jamieson, 2008; Fewster, 1990b; Garfat, 2008; Garfat & Fulcher, 2012; Mann-Feder, 1999). Practitioners need to be present and fully in the moment for these connections to occur.

Being Present

Being present is a central feature of Child and Youth Care practice (Garfat & Fulcher, 2012, p. 19) that involves the practitioner seeing the other in the immediacy of the present moment (Fewster, 1990a; Garfat & Fulcher, 2012; Krueger, 2005) without judgement, while at the same time being present with self (Fewster, 1990a; Ricks & Bellefeuille, 2003). Doing so conveys a genuine interest and regard for others.

Being present enables you to notice both what is occurring within (internal dialogue, emotional reactions, physical reactions) and outside of you (environmental influences including others). In being present, you attune yourself to the emotions that may be influencing the other's behaviours without engaging in your own internal experiences. When you are truly present, you are attuned to the individual's experience, seeing the other beyond their presenting behaviours (Bellefeuille & Ricks, 2010) and acknowledging the implicit (hidden) meaning behind their behaviours; you are more attentive to and aware of what is happening for the other.

The sensitivity to the other's experience strengthens the necessary connections (Kabat-Zinn, 1997) that are at the root of Child and Youth Care practice. Attuning to the emotional effect of others conveys "I see you and I am with you"; this message is pivotal to relational practice (Garfat & Fulcher, 2012; Ricks, 1997). This can be challenging for practitioners when they are consumed with *what they think they should say*, *what they think they should have said*, or situations from the previous day.

Presence and noticing often occur simultaneously. When you are present, *fully in the here and the now*, you are more aware of what is occurring around and within you. Paying attention to who sits before you as separate unique individuals, each of whom bring their own way of thinking and being in the world (Garfat & Fulcher, 2012), requires the practitioner to see beyond the surface behaviours they present and to consciously attend to the moment-to-moment experience (Kabat-Zinn & Kabat-Zinn, 1997; Krueger, 2005; Nhat Hanh, 1987).

Noticing

Being with vulnerable children and families requires practitioners to demonstrate presence and notice the diverse circumstances that influence behaviours. This occurs through a process of observing and becoming aware (Dewey, as cited in Rodgers, 2002). It requires time, effort, and a commitment to disengage from secondary distractions; if you are like many who profess to multitasking, I challenge you. Multitasking is a myth and is actually counterproductive and detrimental to personal and professional practice (Crenshaw, 2008; Orsillo & Roemer, 2011). Multitasking impedes one's ability to notice and demonstrate curiosity (Orsillo & Roemer, 2011) and presence.

The following exercise is practice in noticing and experiencing self.

Exercise 16: A Practice in Noticing[6]

Commit to this practice twice a day for now; in the morning when you wake and at night when you settle for bed. As you develop in this practice, you can engage in it at any time or in any place.

Sit quietly in your room without any distractions from your phone, television, radio, or computer.

Focus on yourself and ask yourself:

- What physical sensations am I noticing in my body right now? Notice any tension or heaviness in your body.
- What am I feeling right now? Notice your emotional affect: anger, joy, stress, nervousness. Note fatigue, hunger, cold, and warm are states, not feelings.
- What am I thinking right now? Notice the thoughts that come up for you at this present time. Simply notice; do not engage, do not judge, do not shift to solutions—just notice.

This exercise will assist you in noticing internal reactions as they occur. It is this process of noticing that will assist you in slowing down your reactions toward others. Use the space below to respond to the questions above.

_____

_____

_____

The purpose of this exercise is to familiarize you with the concept of noticing without engaging in the internal experiences that arise from the experience.

As practitioners, you will encounter different experiences that will evoke strong reactions. How will you carry yourself in that moment in a way that is reflective of professional practice, not responding from this reactive place?

When you are with others, notice where your attention is drawn. What do you notice when you first meet someone? What do their facial expressions, body language tell you; what do you notice is happening for them? Does their body language align with their verbal expressions? Does their tone of voice align with their verbal messages? What are they not saying that captures your attention?

In learning to observe others through an intentional, curious lens, the potential to make assumptions and judgements about others will lessen. Brockbank and McGill (2007) highlight the importance of practicing the skills of observation as a precursor to the more advanced processes of reflective practice. It is from these observations that the potential for learning and purposeful action occurs.

Opportunities to cultivate your observational skills will be introduced throughout the different exercises and case scenarios. Observation logs can be used at any time in your practice to reinforce the importance of being present, noticing, and demonstrating curiosity. We will revisit the observation logs in Chapter 6.

Consider the Following Scenario: Kilarni

Kilarni has worked as a Child and Youth Care Practitioner for two years and recently started a position at a children's mental health agency providing outreach services to families. He has been working with an eight-year-old boy, Gavin, who has been struggling in managing his behaviours at school and home. The mother reported that she and the father recently separated, and this had been hard on Gavin and his brother, and she was also struggling to manage the demands of a single parent. She was open to having someone to speak with, and for the next session, Kilarni brought along a colleague, Jade, to meet with the mother. As Kilarni and his colleague entered the living room and introductions proceeded, Gavin jumped up from his seat and ran under the table and sat. Jade, who was meeting the family for the first time, instructed Gavin to be a big boy and sit with his mother, adding that this was a safe space. In response, Gavin buried his head under his arms on the floor, at which time she said, "You are being very rude." Kilarni, having worked with the family for the past month, had previously observed Gavin's discomfort in meeting new people (often standing behind his mom or colouring when new people attempted to speak with him). At this, Kilarni commented, "Gavin is just letting us know he's feeling strange with new people" (noticing/presence). "He'll come out when he is ready."

Kilarni's understanding of Gavin (from past interactions) enabled him to interpret Gavin's behaviour as a reflection of the fear and uncertainty he felt at meeting a new person, as opposed to judging Gavin's behaviours as rude or defiant. Kilarni's awareness of self (in recognizing his own values of respect for other individual experiences) enabled him to be present and attend to Gavin's fears of meeting new people. This scenario exemplifies the idea that safety is a co-created experience. Kilarni, acknowledging Gavin's discomfort, indirectly conveyed, *I get you, bud. It can be scary meeting new people.*

This noticing and attending to the other's felt experience can foster a sense of safety (Garfat & Fulcher, 2012). Many practitioners attest to providing a safe space upon first meeting children, youth, and families to support individuals; however, "safety" includes more than the physical environment. Safety represents an experience that is created and shared by both practitioner and others and is a highly subjective experience. It is important for practitioners to be mindful of the implicit message conveyed through *this is a safe space*, which suggests the power and authority practitioners have over others (Fewster, 1990b; Gharabaghi, 2008a). This threatens the very essence of what Child and Youth Care does: fostering environments that promote the emotional, social, and spiritual development of others (CYCCB, 2018; White, 2007).

Safety is a co-constructed experience, involving both the practitioner and the other, who are influenced by each other (Fewster, 1990b). The practitioner and the other each determine the conditions for which they experience safety through this co-created space.

Judgement, on the other hand, diminishes one's ability to be present and notice what is occurring for the other. Therefore, it becomes even more important that the practitioner act as an observer (Brookfield, 2012) and interpreter of the other's behaviours and disengage from their internal dialogue or habitual ways of knowing.

Practice in Observing
Observing others in your immediate environment will provide you with opportunities to demonstrate presence, noticing, and curiosity before you begin your practice. Observe their body language and facial expressions; consider context and paying attention to the emotional tone of their comments (noticing). *Does this align with what they say?* What implicit message is conveyed through their body language and facial expressions? It is not necessary to comment or point this out to others; this is simply an exercise for you to practice over the next few weeks.

In the section above, you learned about the characteristics of being present. It is important to highlight that being present involves practice, practice, and more practice. Similar to learning any new skill, the more you do something, the better you become. Your learning of these key CYC characteristics cannot be confined to reading one chapter. There is practice involved in order for these characteristics to become second nature to you. As you have and will continue to learn, adopting the characteristics discussed in this and the proceeding chapter is fundamental to becoming reflective practitioners. Hence, experience, a commitment to practice, and a willingness to risk being vulnerable (Brookfield, 2012) are required to cultivate this practice. In the following section, you will learn about the remaining characteristics to reinforce your learning of relational practice, which will assist you in becoming reflective in your practice with others.

The following exercise is to be completed individually and in the community, and requires your full presence (refrain from using your phone, tablet, or laptop during this time).

Exercise 17: A Practice in Presence and Noticing

Find a comfortable spot in a public place: for example, a park, the coffee shop, or the library. Wear headphones as you sit and let your attention drift to a particular scene that captures your interest. This can involve an individual person, a group of people, a store, a scenic image, or anything within your peripheral. Just notice where your attention is drawn and sit in this space and observe what is happening. Pay attention to your internal reactions (emotions, thoughts). The following questions are to guide your observations.

What aspects of this scene capture your attention?

_____

_____

_____

If there are people present, what do you notice about their body language and facial expressions?

_____

_____

_____

Simply sit and be present and observe. Do not focus on any discussions or other distractions. Add any questions or additional thoughts you may have in the space below.

_____

_____

_____

Thinking about Your Experience

What did you notice about your internal reactions during this time? Note, for example, emotions of restlessness, boredom, curiosity.

_____

_____

_____

What, if any, internal dialogue was occurring within you? Consider the thoughts that emerged or the comments you said to yourself about this exercise or your observations of others.

_____

_____

_____

What assumptions did you make of the others you observed?

_____

_____

_____

Did you attempt to interpret what you were observing?

_____

_____

_____

Use the space below to include any additional comments or questions that you have about this exercise.

_____

_____

_____

This exercise provides an opportunity to practice presence and to notice where you focus your attention when observing others. Continue this practice of noticing when you first meet others. What do you notice? Do you focus on their physical traits, the way they carry themselves? What are your initial thoughts when meeting someone? What is this influenced by? Judgements, assumptions, curiosity? Commit to practicing this exercise for the next two weeks and notice if your focus shifts.

> Be patient. Everything comes to you at the right moment.
> —Buddha

Noticing and Curiosity

The concept of noticing and curiosity is well-documented in Child and Youth Care (Garfat & Fulcher, 2012; Stuart, 2013) and the reflective practice literature (Dewey, 1933; Dewey, as cited in Rodgers, 2002; Moon, 2004). Noticing is not limited to a simple idea, yet presents an important element in the process of reflection; it is the foundation on which the act of reflection is based. Reflection cannot occur without first noticing:

- Your internal reactions (thoughts, emotions) to situations
- Aspects of the interaction with others
- Aspects of the others' actions

Working with others who bring their own ways of knowing and being can challenge the practitioner and may require them to abandon their assumptions (Gharabaghi, 2008b; Bellefeuille & Ricks, 2010; White, 2007) and the lens through which they may perceive others. Noticing their own reactions and thought process and the meaning they have created of their experience can assist practitioners in rethinking their ways of thinking and being with the other.

Consider the chapter exercises you have engaged in. Think about your assumptions toward these. How did these assumptions influence your willingness to engage in these exercises? Which aspects of the exercise influenced your assumptions?

In questioning your experiences, you invite opportunities for further understanding and different ways of thinking. What might be another way to think about these exercises that connects to your learning? Perhaps a practice in suspending judgement?

Curiosity arises from noticing and allows practitioners to suspend judgement of others (Gharabaghi, 2008a). By being curious, you contemplate the uncertainties that enable you to better understand self, others, and their experiences. Being with others requires a curiosity about the sociocultural and historical influences that impact others' experiences (Melton, as cited in Garfat & Ricks, 1995). In being curious, you allow for new ways of knowing and seeing others. Your perspectives of others begin to shift. They are no longer based on what you observe, but rather what there is to know (Garfat & Fulcher, 2012; Garfat & Ricks, 1995).

Recall the exercise in presence and observation you completed earlier in the chapter. What was your experience of this exercise? What did you feel and think about this exercise? For instance, if you noticed that you felt restless from sitting and observing others, consider why. Was the restlessness related to your need to be busy and do something? What does being busy mean for you? A sense of accomplishment? Time well spent?

Curiosity allows for the consideration of a different perspective, which is essential to reflective practice.
　　—Donicka Budd

Reflective and Self-inquiry

The concept of inquiry as a significant aspect of reflective practice is woven throughout much of the literature in Child and Youth Care practice (Bellefeuille et al., 2008; Garfat 2002; Garfat & Fulcher, 2012; Ricks & Bellefeuille, 2003; Stuart, 2013; White, 2007). It represents the process by which practitioners question their thinking about their experiences and the meaning and potential impact on practice. When engaging in inquiry, practitioners seek understanding in the moment by asking questions, challenging assumptions, and examining the implications of actions and choices in practice (Bellefeuille & Jamieson, 2008), in order to achieve greater awareness (Bellefeuille & Ricks, 2010; Garfat & Fulcher, 2012; White, 2007). It involves practitioners reflecting on their actions in situations by asking, "What was my role in this? How did I contribute to this situation?" (Bellefeuille & Jamieson, 2008) and inquiring about others' experiences.

Many terms, however, have been used to describe this sort of inquiry: self-inquiry, relational inquiry, and reflective inquiry. For the purpose of this book, we will refer to *self-inquiry* as the process of examining the internal reactions of experiences and *reflective inquiry* as the process for achieving understanding about others (Lyons, 2010, p. 35).

All inquiry represents an intention for learning, for establishing new ways of knowing.

Reflective Inquiry

Bellefeuille and Ricks (2010) describe Child and Youth Care as a continual process of reflective inquiry that involves questioning with colleagues and supervisors or about others to obtain clarity and understanding about situations or issues of concern. Engaging in reflective inquiry creates the necessary space to suspend judgement and expand one's own ways of knowing to consider what *else* might be happening or what is yet to be known. Ricks and Bellefeuille (2003) highlight the importance of establishing what is true and what forms the basis for this truth. This understanding informs more purposeful reflective action (Bellefeuille & Jamieson, 2008; Bellefeuille & Ricks, 2010; Dewey, as cited in Rodgers, 2002; Garfat & Fulcher, 2013) in the practitioner's approach toward others.

Lyons (2010) asserts that reflective questions represent an intention for learning and establishing new ways of knowing. These questions that guide the practitioner's thinking and understanding about others, however, are what practitioners reflect on with themselves or with colleagues as opposed to asking the children, youth, and families. This marks a great distinction between asking children *why they did what they did* and considering the meaning of others' actions. For instance, consider the last time you asked a child why they did what they did. Typically, the response is "I don't know."

Reflective practitioners engage in their own form of inquiry as a means to establish the reasons. This is not to suggest that practitioners are all-knowing; what they do is create room to consider the possibilities. These, of course, will depend on the context (circumstances) and how you have created the meaning of the situation based on what has occurred (meaning-making). These will be explored at length in the following section.

Self-inquiry

Self-inquiry involves exploring aspects of self in relation to experiences to achieve greater awareness through a process of questioning (Bellefeuille & Ricks, 2010: Garfat & Fulcher, 2010; Gharabaghi, 2008a; White, 2007). Through self-inquiry, practitioners consider: *What am I basing this knowledge on: my values, beliefs, social location? What previous experiences have contributed to my thinking this way? What role do I play in contributing to this experience?* The focus of the inquiry is on self, whereas the focus of inquiry on others is reflective inquiry.

The list included in Appendix V represents some of the many ways to engage in inquiry and will be influenced by your experiences (Bellefeuille & Ricks, 2010; Krueger, 2011; White, 2007). It is only to provide you a reference point to begin. As you become more proficient with engaging in inquiry, you will formulate your own questions about self and others. Note: When engaging in reflective inquiry, ensure your questions are intentional and align with the situation.

You will discover that what you think you know is less important than what there is to know. Engaging in reflective inquiry requires practitioners to be open to this process of inquiry through presence, noticing/attending, and curiosity.

Return to the scenario involving Liana and Phoebe to engage in a process of reflective inquiry. What questions does Liana need to consider to gain further understanding of Phoebe and her family? List these in the space below. (Refer to the template above to guide you in your thinking.) What other questions might you consider through inquiry?

_____

_____

_____

When practitioners do not query the basis of their knowledge they run the risk of making decisions that can significantly impact others. Assumptions represent more of a way of not knowing than knowing, until further exploration determines these assumptions to be valid or inaccurate. How one determines such assumptions to be true or not will depend on the practitioner's ability to engage in inquiry. Engaging in a process of inquiry is necessary to determine how practitioners know what they know

(Bellefeuille & Ricks, 2010; Ricks, 1997) as it provides one way of challenging assumptions about others. This requires an intentional approach to practice that embodies presence through noticing and curiosity.

For instance, recall the case scenario involving Kilarni, Gavin, and Jade. To engage in reflective inquiry, you would consider the circumstances that contributed to Gavin's hiding under the table by asking, "What about this space is threatening Gavin's sense of security and safety?" Reflective inquiry seeks to understand the circumstances for Gavin's behaviours as opposed to asking, "Why he is being rude?", which indicates judgement and the practitioner's own way of knowing.

> What we notice can influence what we see.
> —Garfat, 2003b

Return to Exercise 17, the practice in presence and noticing. Where did your attention go during these exercises in terms of noticing others?

_____

_____

_____

What did you notice?

_____

_____

_____

If you didn't capture this in your notes above, I would encourage you to repeat the exercise in a similar location or take 10 minutes of your day to engage in the practice of noticing. This is a silent exercise to be completed individually and independent of any external distractions.

Exercise 18: Daily Practice

Observe the individuals around you on a daily basis. Pay attention to their body language and facial expressions and tone of voice. What do you notice?

_____

_____

_____

What do they appear to be saying?

_____

_____

_____

_____

_____

Does their non-verbal expression (e.g., gestures) align with what they are say-ing? Practice will help you discern between the subtle changes of tone, body and facial gestures. This attuning to the other supports the co-created space of relational practice.

_____

_____

_____

_____

_____

You will discover in the upcoming case studies, and your interactions with children, youth, and families, that actions can have many meanings. There is a tendency for practitioners to judge such actions as "bad," "intentional," "manip-ulative," or "attention-seeking"; however, it is important to keep in mind that all behaviours occur as a result of circumstances (context; Garfat & Fulcher, 2012). It is the practitioner's responsibility to consider these circumstances. We will re-visit this in the following chapter when the characteristic of context is introduced.

Exercise 19: Practice in Curiosity and Noticing

Observing others will provide you with practice for reflective inquiry through attending/noticing and demonstrating curiosity. As indicated above, noticing creates opportunities to demonstrate curiosity and curiosity diminishes the po-tential for judgement. What might you be curious about when observing others? Their mannerisms, their overt expressions? Their quiet demeanour? What ques-tions might you ask yourself to guide you in the process of understanding others' behaviours? Remember that the questions you ask need to be intentional and will involve asking what, when, how, and where questions.

For instance, if you notice that one of your peers is quiet during a group discussion, be curious and refrain from assuming they are not interested in the discussion. What questions might you consider? *What about this discussion is contributing to her quiet demeanour? What about the day, the dynamics, etc. is contributing to her quiet demeanour? What is my role to engage her? How might I encourage her involvement?* These are just a few ideas to support you in practicing reflective inquiry, which begins with the process of noticing and demonstrating curiosity.

Knowing Others

Practicing from one way of knowing without considering the potential to know more limits ways of knowing and being with others (Bellefeuille & Ricks, 2003, 2010). The ability to learn about others through reflective inquiry provides practitioners opportunities to expand their ways of knowing and being with others. These others, however, can also include other professionals (psychiatrists, psychologists, doctors, lawyers, teachers, principals, social workers, and psychotherapists) who provide services to the children, youth, and families you work with, all of whom will share their own ideas and perspectives of the others.

More often than not, you will discover that others' perspectives will differ from your understanding of the children, youth, and families. How do you determine which perspective is *right* or whose perspective holds more value? Some practitioners may believe that the level of education might privilege one's way of knowing, yet this assumption risks negating their own knowledge, skills, and experiences of engaging with vulnerable children, youth, and families.

Exercise 20: Location, Location, Location

Consider where you locate yourself as a professional within the perceived hierarchical domains of helping professions. From the list of community professionals above, position these in a hierarchy of professional services in the space provided. Where do you place yourself in relation to these professional others? There is no right or wrong way of completing this exercise; it is another exercise to get you thinking about your ways of thinking that foster further awareness. The top of the list represents who you perceive as the all-knowing expert of children, youth, and families, while the bottom of the list represents who you perceive to be the least knowing expert.

Be curious in your thinking here. What previous or current knowledge has to lead you to believe this? Notice where you have located yourself. *What might this imply about your role and the field of Child and Youth Care? What evidence supports your thinking?*

I now invite you to consider the following.

You will, if you have not already, learn about the different settings that employ Child and Youth Care professionals: school settings, residential settings, justice settings, community-based settings (e.g., day treatment programs, mental health programs, recreational programs). Within school and residential settings, practitioners are with the child or youth from five to eight (sometimes longer, depending on the nature of the program) hours a day over a five-day period. In spending this amount of time with the child or youth, albeit perhaps not as intensively all the time, you will have opportunities to develop an understanding of others through daily observations, reflective inquiry, and daily interactions.

What might you come to know from the frequency and consistency of your interactions?

_____

_____

How might this knowing influence your interactions with others?

_____

_____

How might this knowing influence other community professionals' perspectives? Their understanding of others?

_____

_____

What value might there be in attending meetings and case conferences to share your knowledge and perspectives of others?

_____

_____

How do you understand the reasons for not attending these meetings to share your perspectives of others with whom you engage on a daily basis? As you respond, pay attention to your internal reactions and any judgement that may occur.

_____

_____

How often do the other community professionals interact with these others? Where do they base their knowing of these others?

_____

_____

Having considered this, has your position on the ladder changed? If not, explore your thinking further here through reflective inquiry.

_____

_____

How might my thinking influence others' thinking? What responsibility do I have to ensure my professional voice is considered with other community professionals? How might thinking, "I am just a student; I am just a Child and Youth Care Practitioner" influence others' perspective of me?

_____

_____

In considering the perspectives of others, you need always consider others' perspectives of you, as this will further influence your thinking and actions in practice. The knowing, doing, and being framework offers a succinct way of exploring self and others. This chapter provided you with an overview of the distinct skills and characteristics of this framework that are related to reflective practice. In the following chapter, you will be introduced to the remaining characteristics of Child and Youth Care and their implications for practice. These skills and characteristics provide a foundation for the reflective processes to evolve. One cannot engage in reflection without embracing the distinct characteristics of Child and Youth Care practice.

> What we don't know is much more than what we know.
> —Albert Einstein

CLOSING THOUGHTS[7]

When did you feel most engaged? Least engaged?

_____

_____

_____

What is the most important information you have learned thus far?

_____

_____

_____

What questions remain for you from this learning?

_____

_____

_____

NOTES

1. Creating an inclusive environment is reflective of the Culture and Diversity domain of the core competencies. Awareness and Inquiry and Developmental Practice Methods Sensitive to Cultural Human Diversity (CYCCB, 2018).
2. Sociocultural and historical influences relate to the aspects of social location and the diverse systems of an individual's life. You will learn more about these systems when you are introduced to Bronfenbrenner's ecological systems theory in the following chapters.
3. Worldviews are a set of interconnected beliefs and assumptions that individuals hold about human nature, the world, and their experiences in the world (Koltko-Rivera, 2004).

4. Defending what you know is reflective of the Professionalism domain (professional boundaries) of the core competencies and Applied Developmental Practice Methods domain (interventions planning) of the core competencies.

5. Deliberating and collaborating with others will be explored in Chapters 7 (reflective thinking) and 8 (critical thinking).

6. The practice in noticing exercise has been adopted from Germer, Siegel, and Fulton (2014).

7. The closing thoughts reflection is adapted from the CIQ—Critical Incident Questionnaire in Keefer (2009).

CHAPTER 4

Making Meaning of Experiences

The journey of a thousand miles begins with one step.

—Lao Tzu

LEARNING OBJECTIVES

In this chapter, you will:

- explore the Child and Youth Care characteristics of context and meaning-making
- learn about Bronfenbrenner's ecological systems theory
- be introduced to the concept of worldviews and its relation to reflective practice
- define and distinguish ethical issues from ethical dilemmas

In the previous chapter, we explored the co-constructed space and the characteristics of Child and Youth Care practice that influence relationships and are essential to becoming reflective practitioners: intentionality, presence, noticing, and curiosity. Presence through noticing and curiosity will assist practitioners in suspending judgement of others as they engage in the process of reflective inquiry. Reflective inquiry will assist practitioners in seeking understanding about others. You will continue to expand your ways of thinking, seeing, and being by considering context and through a meaning-making process that is central to relational practice (Bellefeuille & Ricks, 2010; Krueger, 2005).

The use of self will always remain an integral part of one's approach to practice and will shift and evolve with each new experience.

—Gharabaghi, 2008a

WHAT IS CONTEXT

Context is an oft-misunderstood aspect of reflective practice (Boud, 1999), as it is not considered an active process or skill to be developed. Yet, it holds significant importance for understanding the decisions and actions of others. Context involves circumstances or variables unique to the individual and is influenced by both internal and external factors. Internal influences include the developmental stages, illness, psychological and medical issues, beliefs, values, and previous and current experiences. External influences include elements from the sociocultural environments (relationships, policy, community, etc.; Boud, 1999; Dewey, 1933; Garfat & Fulcher, 2012; O'Connell & Dyment, 2013; Rodgers, 2002). Both influence the meaning of a situation. In saying that, everything occurs in context and no two contexts are ever the same (Garfat & Fulcher, 2012), which reinforces the earlier point about the interconnectedness of the characteristics of Child and Youth Care.

Considering the context of a situation requires practitioners to pay attention (presence) to the minutia of the interactions (Garfat & Fulcher, 2012; noticing) and the surrounding environment to engage in inquiry (curiosity) and establish meaning (meaning-making) of the situation that is unique to the individual (Krueger, 2011). In this sense, every situation needs to be understood as an experience distinct to the individual and cannot be perceived through the same lens as other experiences. Everything occurs in context, and everything shifts and changes in response to context (Garfat & Fulcher, 2012). It is the concept of context that underlies the uncertainties that arise when practitioners consider a *right way* of doing something when they hold the Code of Ethics as the determinant in what is considered the *right action*.

Consider the Following Scenario: Javier

After staying up all night to prepare for two tests and to complete an assignment, Javier arrived to class late and kept to himself for the remainder of the day. He refrained from joining in class discussions and declined his peers' request to join them for lunch. His peers were confused by this change in behaviours, as Javier is often engaging and actively participates in class. One of his peers commented to him that he may need medication for his drastic mood change.

There is always more to know than the surface behaviour presented before you. When you consider that all behaviours serve a purpose (Garfat, 1992), you expand your ways of knowing to invite curiosity and a willingness to consider different perspectives that underlie context to create new meaning, all of which provides the foundation for reflective practice to occur. Through inquiry and the consideration of context, the potential for assumptions to occur decreases.

For instance, a child who has recently experienced the loss of a parent may express his grief through anger, whereas another child will express anger in response to transitions and changes in routine. This is not to suggest that one experience is more important than the other; however, it highlights the significance that meaning-making has in reflective practice. We need to appreciate the context in which the behaviours occurred since context will influence your understanding and the respective approach to supporting this child. In considering context, we acknowledge that each child requires a different approach and not the one-size-fits-all paradigm that underlies many behavioural management approaches (Bellefeuille & Ricks, 2010; Gharabaghi, 2008). Context involves a willingness to be curious about the diverse factors that influence behaviours.

BRONFENBRENNER'S ECOLOGICAL PERSPECTIVE: A CASE FOR CONTEXT

Bronfenbrenner's ecological perspective represents the social, political, and cultural environments to which individuals belong (Addison, 1992, Härkönen, 2007; White, 2007). Within these diverse interconnected systems, context can be seen as a dynamic, fluid concept for understanding the unique needs of individuals. Individuals cannot be understood in isolation from the diverse systems involved in a person's life (Bellefeuille et al., 2008; Garfat & Charles, 2012; Härkönen, 2007; Ricks & Bellefeuille, 2003; White, 2007); to do so risks presenting an inaccurate and biased perspective of the other (Bellefeuille et al., 2011; Ricks, 1997). These diverse systems influence the context in which complex issues develop (Ricks & Bellefeuille, 2003). Changes within each system will invariably change aspects of the others. When you relate this to the concept of examining context, it becomes evident that context is an ever-changing, dynamic construct (Kokinov, 1999) of meaning-making moments: your ways of knowing influence and are influenced by ways of being and doing (Bellefeuille & Ricks, 2010; Ricks & Bellefeuille, 2003; White, 2007).

While it is not the intention of this book to go into depth about Bronfenbrenner's ecological perspective, it is important to consider his contributions to the systemic approach for understanding the other's experiences, which can influence their ways of knowing, seeing, and being in the world (Bellefeuille et al., 2008).

Bronfenbrenner's ecological systems theory is based on five environmental elements that impact the other's development (Härkönen, 2007). Bronfenbrenner believed that changes in one system impacted other systems (Addison, 1992).

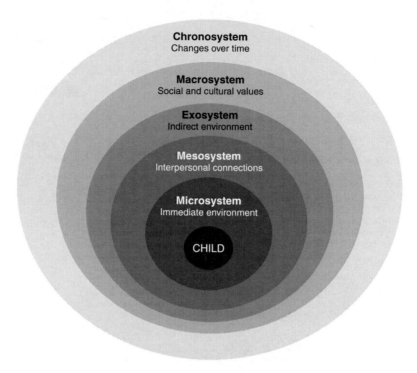

Figure 7: Bronfenbrenner's Ecological Systems

Source: The Psychology Notes Headquarters. https://www.PschyologyNotesHQ.com.

Microsystem

These are the environmental systems that are directly involved with an individual and that can impact their development; for example for a child, microsystems may include their home, school, peers, neighbourhood, and community, and the respective relationships within each space.

Mesosystem

It is the nature of the relationships between members of the child's microsystem.

Exosystem

They are the environmental systems that do not directly interact with the child yet still impact the child's development.

Macrosystem

They are the cultural attitudes and ideologies of society that impact the child.

Chronosystem

These are the significant life events and transitions that have directly impacted the child's development.

Exploring the distinct aspects of an individual's ecology will lead to further inquiry about the individual's lived experiences that provides context and creates new meaning, which leads to informed action.

Exercise 21: Bronfenbrenner and You

Identify the distinct aspects of Bronfenbrenner's five environmental elements that have influenced or are influencing your life. Recreate the template above in the space below and label each environmental element accordingly. There is no need to explain in detail what each means; simply identify and list the distinct aspects within each system.

When you are finished, select two aspects from each of the systems and consider how these have influenced who you are today. For instance, within your microsystem, you might identify that your family influenced the values and beliefs you possess. How might these distinct systems influence your practice?

_____

_____

_____

_____

_____

_____

_____

_____

_____

_____

_____

Checking In

Where are you with understanding the concepts and exercises in this chapter thus far? How are you connecting the concepts and exercises to your development as a Child and Youth Care Practitioner? What questions do you have that warrant further exploration to support your learning?

Context influences meaning and meaning influences action.
—Bellefeuille & Ricks, 2010

MEANING-MAKING

In the following chapter, you will be introduced to the processes of reflexivity and reflection, both of which involve thinking about the meanings (based on your interpretation) you create about experiences. The concept of meaning-making is prevalent in reflective practice (Garfat & Fulcher, 2012; Krueger, 2004) and will be discussed throughout the remaining chapters. For the purpose of enhancing your awareness of meaning-making, I encourage you to spend time at the end of your day to deconstruct experiences to establish the meaning you created from them.

Dewey (1933) believed that making meaning is the function of reflection: to make connections between the aspects of the experience (Dewey, as cited in Rodgers, 2002) in order to make sense of it. To make sense of one's experiences requires the use of self, examining the context to engage in reflective inquiry to establish an understanding of the situation while considering the diverse perspectives of others. The meaning one makes of experiences can impact how one thinks (Bellefeuille & Ricks, 2010; Garfat & Fulcher, 2012).

Consider the meaning you make from earning high grades. Do high grades reflect passion, commitment to learning, or effective Child and Youth Care practice?

The importance for understanding one's meaning of experiences has been documented extensively in the Child and Youth Care literature (Bellefeuille & Ricks, 2010; Bolton, 2009; Fewster, 1990a; Garfat, 1992; Garfat & Charles, 2012; Garfat & Fulcher, 2012; Gharabaghi, 2008a; Krueger, 2005, 2011; Moon, 2004). Creating meaning implies a willingness to explore alternative perspectives (Ricks, 1997) and the unique experiences of others that leads to new experiences (Kruger, 2011). Within every experience is an

Figure 8: Making Meaning from Imagery

Source: 8a: http://cute-pictures.blogspot.com/2008/07/sun-set-beautiful.html under CC BY, 8b: https://jaywalkingthroughlife.wordpress.com/2011/02/04/ under CC BY, 8c: created by author.

Exercise 22: Creating Meaning

Look at the images in Figure 8 and identify one or perhaps several aspects of each that stand out for you. Pay attention to your internal reactions (emotions and thoughts) and note them in the space below. Do not attempt to analyze or engage in judgement about these images or the exercise; simply notice the emotional reactions and thoughts you experience. In an effort to understand these reactions, I invite you to engage in self-inquiry. List the questions below. For instance, you might ask, "What was it about the scene that made me feel …" or "What about this image that leaves me feeling or thinking …?" Refrain from overthinking, as this is an exercise in establishing meaning or at least inquiring about the meaning these images hold for you. Notice when you engage in comments that imply judgement and set them aside.

This exercise is to assist you in further acknowledging the connection between experiences, thoughts, and actions and can present difficulties as it requires you to expand your usual way of thinking. Many practitioners will struggle with engaging in these abstract, meaning-making exercises for various reasons. However, consider if this is related to your need for structure or your expectations of how things should be. How might this way of thinking connect to Child and Youth Care practice?

_____

_____

_____

Irrespective of your experience above, I invite you to be open to this exercise to engage in the meaning-making moment. Of the three images above, which did you most identify with?

_____

_____

What aspects did you identify most with (in terms of mood, the message it conveyed, etc.)?

_____

_____

What meaning does this image hold for you (peace, calm, chaos, stress, hope, etc.)?

_____

_____

How will this meaning influence your interactions or ways of thinking moving forward in the day? For instance, if you thought that this was an entire waste of time, how might your thinking influence your emotions and actions throughout the day? If you thought this was a valuable exercise in exploring perspectives, consider how this might influence further thinking and your emotions as you move forward in your day.

_____

_____

_____

_____

opportunity to reflect. As you think back to your day, notice the thoughts and emotions that emerge for you. One can profess to having a bad day; however, can they identify the distinct experiences that contributed to this bad day? In doing so, you will begin to notice the meaning you create from those experiences. Many will focus on what did not go well, and others will focus on what did go well. The focus of one's attention can say a great deal about a person, yet the important question is "What does it mean to you?"

Creating meaning is influenced by one's beliefs, values, and assumptions and, as such, no two individuals will create similar meanings of experiences. Before we proceed into the meanings of experiences, let us begin with simply acknowledging experience and noticing the emotional reactions that experiences can evoke and the impact on one's thinking.

Sharing your experiences of this exercise with others will assist you in realizing the diverse perspectives that individuals have of the same situation. This awareness of the differences in others' thinking will support you in expanding beyond your immediate ways of thinking to allow for different perspectives.

> The meaning one creates from an experience is what gives the experience value.
> —Dewey, as cited in Rodgers, 2002, p. 848

Consider the Following Scenario

Person A is walking down the road and observes a group of people standing together and laughing. They look at person A and continue to laugh. Person A may consider that they are enjoying one another's company and laughing at a joke or situation that has occurred. Person A may think that they are looking to see who is approaching. Meaning: Person A has determined that people are enjoying each other's company.

Person B, however, perceives the situation differently. Person B often feels awkward in social settings. Zir discomfort is magnified when noticing the group of people laughing, and zi perceives that the group's laughter is directed toward zi. This current experience may reinforce zir difficulties in social settings and perspectives of self. Zi may continue to avoid further social settings. Meaning: Person B has determined zi has little to offer to social situations.

Something to Think About

Imagine you are in class and struggling to stay focused on the lecture that seems boring to you. As luck would have it, the professor calls on you. What is your reaction to this? Embarrassment that she caught you? Mortified that you have no idea what she is talking about? Notice any assumptions that emerge, such as "She did this on purpose to embarrass me," "She always does this to students. She likes showing us up," or "She only calls out students who are on their phones." The meaning you may have created here is that the professor is out to get you as opposed to seeing the professor's efforts to engage you in the class discussion.

Let us now consider the potential beliefs or values that may underlie the professor's decision to call on students who are on their phones. In considering the above, your meaning of the sitation may shift.

Take a mindful step back to consider the perspectives of the professor that influenced her actions. What might she believe is her responsibility to students in her class? To the profession? To the others whom the students will work with one day?

_____

_____

_____

Has the meaning you created in this situation shifted? If so, what contributed to this shift? Note any questions you may have.

_____

_____

_____

When you acknowledge the meaning that situations have for you, you can begin to inquire about the impact this has on you and your practice.

Exercise 23: Putting Experiences into Context

Kelly, a 15-year-old youth, was recently discharged from her 13th home. During a conversation with her, as you are explaining the routines and rules for the program, she tells you to zip it. "Blah, blah, blah," she continues when you tell her this can be a different experience for her. She then leaves the room.

What assumptions do you make about Kelly based on this interaction?

_____

_____

_____

Engage in reflective inquiry. (See Table 6 for the list of questions to guide you in your thinking.) What questions will you consider to establish an understanding of Kelly's experiences?

_____

_____

Consider the context that may be influencing her behaviours. How does the internal and external context you have identified influence the meaning you make about Kelly's behaviours?

_____

_____

_____

How might this awareness influence your response? How would you respond?

_____

_____

_____

Creating meaning and engaging in reflective inquiry takes practice and a concerted effort to refrain from jumping to problem-solving/solution mode as it requires you to slow down in your thinking (Dewey, 1933) to allow the opportunities for new thinking to occur.

Table 6: Reflective Inquiry Questions

Self-inquiry	Reflective Inquiry
Who am I?	Who is this person? What do I know about this other person?
Am I operating from an assumption or from cues I am observing in the other?	What do I know about this situation?
What am I basing this knowledge on? My values, beliefs, my social location?	What is the nature of their familial interactions? Interactions with others?
What previous experiences have contributed to my thinking this way?	What is important for me to know that will assist my understanding of their experiences?
What do I need to know that will enable me to better understand this situation?	What is the other's experience of me? How have their perspectives of me influenced their response?
How have I contributed to this other's experience?	What purpose does their behaviour serve them?
What is my role to engage her? How might I encourage her involvement?	What about this discussion is contributing to her behaviour?
What aspects of my presentation might be influencing the other's behaviours?	What about the day, the dynamics, the … is contributing to the behaviour?
How are aspects of self influencing my approach here?	What aspects of the other's self is influencing their behaviours?
What is another way for me to understand this situation?	What systems are involved with this individual that may be influencing their behaviours?
What aspects of this situation are similar to other situations I have encountered? What do these similarities mean for me?	How is this individual's sense of self influencing their interactions with others?
What shifts in my approach are necessary to influence a different outcome?	What do they require to have a different experience of helping professionals?
How will shifts in my approach benefit me?	How will shifts in my approach benefit the others?
What am I missing? What am I not seeing that is important to see?	How much of their past experiences/relationships are influencing their current interactions?

The following case scenario will provide you with opportunities to apply the learning concepts from this and previous chapters as a means to reinforce your learning. As indicated in Chapter 1, reflective practice and learning occur from experiences and such case scenarios are intended to provide you with these experiences. Let us revisit the scenario involving Debbie and Ji, presented earlier. As you re-read the scenario, consider doing so through the lens of curiosity, context, and meaning-making. In order to understand the staff's response to Ji, further context has been provided.

Consider the Following Scenario: Debbie and Ji

Debbie has worked at the residential home for teens for 10 years, most recently as a full-time employee. She believed she could have more impact if she was a regular influence on the floor and full-time allowed for this. She was still in the process of establishing relationships with the youth and familiarizing herself with their distinct personalities and individual needs. She struggled to connect with one of the youths, Ji. He was often away at his mother's for the weekend, which was when she had worked the most as a part-time employee, so she hadn't had the opportunity to interact with him. She had heard from other staff that he could be moody at times and that he had a conflicted relationship with his mom. Ji often kept to himself upon return to the residential home from these visits. Debbie decided she would take a no-nonsense approach with Ji. She did not do well with moody people and believed that firm limits could snap them out of their mood. They are so hard to read, she realized.

Ji returned home from a visit with his mother and spent the time between his return home and dinner in his room. Ji's relationship with his mother was conflicted and often ended in shortened visits because of their conflict. Ji was not one for talking or expressing his feelings and would not reach out to staff for support. Ji preferred to be left alone when he returned from his mother's, notably when visits did not go well.

In order for Debbie to consider context and create the meaning of Ji's behaviours, she will need to acknowledge her assumptions, beliefs, and values (use of self) first.

Debbie's Assumptions

- Debbie has interacted little with Ji and so has assumed that his anger is out of control. His angry behaviours do not align with her values and beliefs.
- Debbie's observations of Ji's aggressive behaviours have led her to assume that he doesn't care about others. His disregard for her attempts to seek control was evident and led her to believe he only cares for himself.

Debbie's Beliefs

- Debbie maintains strong ideals about what she considers appropriate respectful behaviour.
- Debbie believes that:
  - Youth should listen and follow through on direction
  - Youth should show respect to staff by not swearing or yelling

These beliefs are based on her earlier childhood experiences and from working front-line as a Child and Youth Care Practitioner. She has observed too many occasions where staff has presented inconsistent expectations and the impact of this on the youth. She believes that by maintaining a consistent, predictable approach, youth will always know what to expect from her.

Debbie's Values

- Respect: People should communicate their intentions and youth should abide by these intentions.
- Leadership: Having a strong presence in the home where youth know what to expect and who will oversee their safety.

As you read the above, you may get a sense of the reasons for Debbie's response to Ji's behaviours. She believes she is doing right to ensure his safety and the safety of others.

Residential Home Case Note

Child: Ji McDougal   **Date:** Jan. xx, xxxx

Staff: Debbie Lou, CYCP

Ji had another difficult evening tonight. He refused to clean his room and join the group for dinner. He was quiet throughout dinner and did not respond to staff's attempts to engage him. He did not complete his chores and when reminded of the potential consequences, he punched a hole in the wall. Staff directed him upstairs to his room. He refused and told staff he was going out. Staff told him to stop and pointed out that there would be further consequences. He responded by throwing books off the bookshelf, telling staff to leave him alone. He gathered his coat and shoes and began walking toward the front door and pushed staff out of the way as she attempted to prevent him from leaving. He told her if she tried to stop him again, he would punch her out and left the home. Ji returned home two hours later and spent the remainder of the night in his room.

Ji's volatile and hostile behaviour seemed to come out of nowhere. He may be at risk of hurting others.

Consequence: Ji is to be off program for 24 hours.

Debbie Lou

Figure 6: Ty's Case Note

Source: Adapted from American Counseling Association. https://www.counseling.org › ethics-columns › ethics_december_2018_notes.

Revisiting Debbie's Case Note

As you may have noticed from the case note, her well-intended efforts (driven by her beliefs, values, and assumptions) have not considered the unique needs and experiences of Ji. Knowing what you now know about context and meaning-making, what internal and external factors may have influenced Ji's behaviour?

_____

_____

_____

_____

How does your knowledge of the context shift your understanding of Ji's behaviours? What new meaning have you made about his behaviours while considering the context?

_____

_____

_____

_____

Considering the perspectives of others and creating meaning of others' behaviours, while intended to be highly objective, still suggests a level of subjectivity (Gharabaghi, 2008a) since these are based on your own perspectives of others—what you think the other is thinking or experiencing. This is not to suggest that there is no value to this; there is. However, if you are to take another step back, out of your way of thinking and seeing to consider the worldviews of others, you open yourselves up to learning so much more about them.

Exercise 24: Practice in Creating Meaning

Identify a situation that you spend considerable amount of time thinking about or perhaps a situation that evoked a strong reaction. Refrain from the _I/he/ she shouldn't have_ way of thinking, as this implies judgement, and refrain from solution finding. This is simply an exercise to engage in meaning-making. Think about the aspects of the experience that were most upsetting to you. How did you interpret this situation? What did you determine it to mean? How did your interpretation of this situation influence your thinking and actions?

Use the questions below as a reference to practice creating meaning of situations as they occur. Continue this for the next few weeks. Record your responses in the spaces below. Refer back to these as a means to measure your shifts in perspective over time.

Briefly describe the situation.   Date: _____

_____

_____

_____

What was your interpretation of the situation?

_____

_____

_____

How did your interpretation influence your thinking and actions?

_____

_____

_____

Briefly describe the situation.   Date: _____

_____

_____

_____

What was your interpretation of the situation?

_____

_____

_____

How did your interpretation influence your thinking and actions?

_____

_____

_____

Briefly describe the situation.   Date: _____

_____

_____

_____

What was your interpretation of the situation?

_____

_____

_____

How did your interpretation influence your thinking and actions?

_____

_____

_____

Briefly describe the situation.   Date: _____

_____

_____

_____

What was your interpretation of the situation?

_____

_____

_____

How did your interpretation influence your thinking and actions?

_____

_____

_____

EXPLORING THE WORLDVIEWS OF OTHERS

Worldviews are a set of interconnected beliefs and assumptions that individuals hold about human nature, the world, and their experiences in the world (Koltko-Rivera, 2004). Children, youth, and families come with their own unique experiences and histories; however, what you must remember is that these experiences can have devastating consequences for their abilities to develop and sustain healthy relationships and the capacity to cope with daily challenges (Krueger, 2011). An awareness of these worldviews will guide you in your practice (Koltko-Rivera, 2004) as they expand your ways of thinking about others, which can shift your ways of being with others.

An understanding of worldviews can assist you in looking beyond the presenting behaviours that are a manifestation of these worldviews. In doing so, we can perceive the individual from a significantly different lens, which will inform your approaches. In order for you to become familiar with the concept of worldviews, it will be beneficial for you to identify your personal worldviews and the potential impact on your ways of thinking, seeing, and being in the world.

> In understanding or in the least hypothesizing a child, youth or family's worldviews, practitioners demonstrate a more balanced perspective of the needs of the others.
> —Gharabaghi, 2008; Garfat & Fulcher, 2012

The behaviour iceberg is a popular metaphor to explore an individual's worldviews. The top of the iceberg represents those behaviours others see, while the bottom of the iceberg, beneath the water, represents those hidden aspects of the other—beliefs, values, experiences.

Figure 9: Behaviour Iceberg

Source: Adapted from https://commons.wikimedia.org/wiki/File:Iceberg.jpg under CC BY-SA.

Exercise 25: Examining Your Worldviews

Consider those aspects of yourself that are demonstrated through behaviours. It can be helpful to create a separate list of your characteristics that are noticeable to others and briefly identify the behavioural aspects of these characteristics. For instance, if you consider yourself friendly, what is it that you do? Do you initiate interactions with others? Do you offer your assistance or help others? If you were to describe yourself as impatient, which behaviours would others notice? Do you have a tendency to interrupt or mutter to yourself? If so, specify this. The bottom part of the iceberg reflects those hidden aspects of self that can include your beliefs, values, experiences, thoughts, and emotions. With respect to past experiences, there is no need to go into great detail; rather, define these in five words or less. For instance, if your past experiences include frequent moves or loss, indicate just that without describing these. The purpose of this exercise is to demonstrate the connection between past experiences and behaviours and how this impacts your ways of seeing the world.

The Top of the Iceberg: Behaviours Others See

List how you present yourself to others through your actions and behaviours in point form. There is no need to describe or explain these; just label them. Refrain from using personality traits, such as "nice" and "kind," as they are subjective terms.

_____

_____

_____

Think about how the distinct aspects of your personality are reflected through your interactions (what people see).

_____

_____

_____

Beneath the Iceberg: What Others Don't See

Beneath the iceberg lies the beliefs, values, and experiences unique to the individual.

Your values:

Include what you consider important. Values are often shaped by sociocultural influences (relationships, past and present experiences, family, culture, etc.).

Your beliefs:

Include what you consider to be true that is informed by sociocultural influences (relationships, past and present experiences, family, culture) and the evidence to support this.

Also include previous or current significant experiences that have influenced who you are today.

When you have finished, review your template and notice the connections between your experiences, behaviours, values, and beliefs. Consider how your behaviours have been influenced by your experiences and how your experiences have shaped your values and beliefs.

How have these (experiences, values, and beliefs) influenced your relationships and your interactions with others? For instance, if you described yourself as sociable and outgoing, "the life of the party," consider the values this may relate to. Perhaps you value family and relationships and you believe that people's success is based on the quality of connections they have; your worldviews (outlook toward life) may indicate an optimistic view that endeavours to maintain contact with others. On the flipside, you may rely heavily on the support of others to experience a sense of identity and success in the world. This is not to suggest that past experiences define us; rather they provide you with an understanding of how these different aspects of you are connected. Include any additional comments or questions that surface for you from this exercise in the space below.

_____

_____

_____

_____

_____

_____

_____

_____

Exercise 26: Revisiting Ji

Let us return to the case scenario involving Debbie and Ji. Drawing from key aspects of the case scenario, Ji's iceberg has been completed. As you review his iceberg, notice if there is anything you would like to add to his values, beliefs, or past experiences that influences how he may see and experience his world. Remember that each of you bring your own experiences and meanings to situations and, as such, may not always perceive others through the same lens. How one person views and contextualizes behaviours may be different from others. It is also important to consider that you will not always have all details of a child's history; however, observation invites the opportunity to engage in reflective inquiry to hypothesize about those hidden aspects—what the child may believe, value, or have experienced that may assist you in understanding their behaviours and their resulting worldviews.

Behaviours:

    Moody

    Isolated

    Aggressive

Beliefs:

    Adults want to be in control

    Adults can't be trusted

    He is not good enough

    Staff get paid to "care"

Values:

    Autonomy and
    independence

    Respect

    Privacy

Experiences:

    Conflict with adults

    Childhood abuse

Figure 10: Ji's Iceberg

Source: Adapted from https://commons.wikimedia.org/wiki/File:Iceberg.jpg under CC BY-SA.

For instance, Ji's conflict with his mom may pique your curiosity about the history of their relationship—has it always been conflicted, is this more recent, or did it evolve from a significant loss or event in their family? The behaviour iceberg template is a valuable resource in building an understanding and helping you to think about your approach with others.

How might Ji's worldviews assist Debbie in understanding Ji's behaviours?

_____

_____

_____

What new insights might Debbie have about Ji that she may not have been aware of before?

_____

_____

_____

How might these new insights shift her perceptions of Ji?

_____

_____

_____

How might this influence her future interactions with Ji?

_____

_____

_____

Share and discuss with a partner.

Let us return to the concept of meaning-making. Ji's worldviews have provided Debbie with context for understanding his behaviours. As she has become aware that his moodiness may be more related to his struggles with self-expression (meaning-making), she is more aware that he will require support in this area. Rather than leave him alone in his room when he returns home from visits, she will check in with him. She is also now aware that he may require space when his emotions become heightened and she can use this as an opportunity to label his feelings and encourage him to take some space (meaning-making). Debbie has created new meaning of Ji's behaviours that will continue to influence her interactions with him. This in turn will create a different experience for Ji, who may now begin to experience Debbie as a support rather than the adversary he once perceived her as.

The real voyage of discovery consists not in seeking new landscapes, but in having new eyes.
—Marcel Proust

As you begin to create meaning of experiences beyond your own way of thinking and seeing others (remember, this will require you to separate your values, beliefs, and assumptions), it is important to consider the potential meaning others may have made of you. This heightened awareness will further assist you in your interactions and approaches with others.

Let us consider Ji's perspectives of Debbie that may be based on his own beliefs and past experiences:

- Ji perceived Debbie as uncaring.
- Ji perceived Debbie as controlling.

What other perceptions might he have of Debbie, based on your interpretation of the case scenario?

_____

_____

_____

_____

While it may not have been Debbie's intention to come across this way, these were Ji's experiences. With the conflict that he experiences in his relationship with his mother, he may be more sensitive to others' reactions toward him, notably females. You will learn throughout the program that a child's perceived negative experiences with adults and peers can have an adverse impact on a child's sense of self and their ability to develop relationships with others (Golding & Hughes, 2012; Steele & Malchiodi, 2012).

DO NO HARM

At this time, I encourage you to consider the responsibility to the child, youth, and family: *Do no harm.* In Chapter 1, you were asked to think about your understanding of the concept of harm. Learning professionals will often reference any physical contact that causes harm to the child, but the concept of harm is context-dependent and subjective, in that harm is not always physical. Rather, it depends on the individual's experiences, their worldviews, and their sense of self. As with the concept of safety discussed previously, the concept of harm varies from person to person.

Phelan (2009) explains that the intention of the practitioner's actions is not always perceived in the same way by children, youth, and families. Their perspectives of the practitioner can evoke fear, resentment, and distrust that further exacerbate a need for safety and security that they currently lack. Doing no harm is about being deliberate and intentional in considering the needs of others (Phelan, 2009). When practitioners do not consider the individual needs of others, they risk inadvertently creating harm that exacerbates the existing struggles others are experiencing. *Do no harm* ensures that the practitioners' actions respond to the needs of others and not their own.

Debbie's intentions of establishing limits and holding Ji accountable for his behaviours did not consider his individual needs for safety and security. Debbie's seemingly routine-oriented response neglected the context for his behaviours. Could Ji have perceived Debbie's approach as a threat that would only exacerbate the insecurity and uncertainty he experienced with his mother? While this may not have been Debbie's intention, it does highlight the need for practitioners to be mindful of the impact their actions can have on others and how others perceive them (Bellefeuille et al., 2008; Bellefeuille & Ricks, 2010; Brookfield, 1987; Dewey, 1933; Garfat & Fulcher, 2010; Ranahan, Blanchet-Cohen, & Mann-Feder, 2015; Ricks & Bellefeuille, 2003).

The connection between meaning-making and issues of right or wrongdoing is significant. Many individuals will respond in ways familiar to them. These routine-oriented ways will be challenged during times of uncertainties. Such uncertainty of what to do or how one determines right from wrong action is common in Child and Youth Care practice (Ricks & Bellefeuille, 2003; Smith, 2006). When practitioners are faced with the task of determining right from wrong actions, more often than not, they are faced with an ethical issue.

ETHICAL ISSUES

Ethical issues are described as issues of concern about others' behaviours (family or community members) that conflict with the cultural norm (Ricks & Bellefeuille, 2003, p. 120), whereas ethical dilemmas involve situations where the practitioner's own values compete with the ethical principles outlined in codes of ethics (Ricks, 1997). Ethical dilemmas will be discussed at length in Chapter 8.

The scenario below illustrates an example of an ethical issue. There is no easy solution, and the process for determining the best course of action requires stepping back to consider all perspectives and potential options that are available to the practitioner. Note any questions or thoughts you have and monitor your impulse to find a solution.

> ### Consider the Following Scenario: Ted
>
> Ted worked at Bloom's Home for Teens as a part-time CYC and had been there for five years. Recently, one of the teens, Dee, had gone AWOL from the home and had been missing for four days. A police warrant was out for his arrest due to his involvement in a break-and-enter incident. Staff were instructed to contact the police should he return to the home. When Ted arrived for his afternoon

shift, he observed Dee sitting at the table with the supervisor, Maxine. On his way to greet Dee, Ted was pulled away by another staff member who wanted to update him. According to the other staff, Dee arrived at the home at lunch, feigning starvation. The supervisor fed him and spent the rest of that time with him. When Ted asked when the police would arrive, staff responded that Maxine had directed them not to call. Ted was notably confused, given the initial directives from the police to contact them. When he entered the dining room to question Maxine, she merely shook her head and held up her hand and continued to engage with Dee. He stood there dumbfounded. What should Ted do?

Note your reactions and identify any questions that come up for you.

_____

_____

_____

_____

> Ethical practice is achieved through and driven by the self as opposed to being driven by external variables.
> —Garfat & Ricks, 1995

This scenario represents an ethical issue that requires Ted to determine the most optimal course of action. Ethical issues, as you recall, are issues of concern about the other's behaviours (family or community members) that conflict with the cultural norm (Ricks & Bellefeuille, 2003, p. 120). They provide an opportunity for practitioners to consider the different elements/individuals that are involved in determining the available options and the best course of action. How do you determine what is the *right thing* to do in this situation?

Identify the potential options for Ted.

_____

_____

Identify the potential impact of these options.

_____

_____

Identify whose interests and needs are the basis for these options.

_____

_____

Refer to the Code of Ethics (Appendix I) as a reference for discussion and to assist you in narrowing down your options. Explain your process in the space below, including your internal reactions to this scenario.

_____

_____

_____

_____

_____

_____

_____

_____

_____

_____

_____

_____

Exercise 27: Ethical Issues Practice

Table 7 presents a list of scenarios that could be considered ethical issues. Review each scenario and highlight aspects of the scenario that stand out for you. Determine if this is an ethical issue (based on what seems wrong) and give the basis for your decision. Refer to the Code of Ethics (Appendix I) to support your decision.

The ethical issues listed in Table 7 provide you with other ways to expand your ways of thinking and doing through examining context, creating meaning, and engaging in reflective inquiry, with the Code of Ethics as principles to guide your actions as you continue to ask those essential questions to assist you in creating meaning and establishing an understanding of situations.

Table 7: Exploring Ethical Issues

Situation	Ethical issue	Ethical principle to support your argument (refer to Standards for Practice, Appendix I)
David is an eight-year-old child who resides in Keele Treatment Home for Boys. He returned home from his second overnight visit with his family. Access with his family was reinstated after five months of no contact. When he arrived home Saturday night, he refused to stay in his room and would not listen to staff directives. He was sent to his room for the remainder of the night, where his behaviour escalated.		
Camari has phone access with his mother every Sunday evening. Each time the mother calls, she demands to know what staff have done this week to "mess up" her son. She presents as angry and dismissive toward staff. The supervisor has suggested that further phone contact be discontinued until a meeting occurs with the mother about her behaviour toward staff.		
Kathy has been working at the group home for the past six months. During one shift, a youth, who often leaves on her own for the weekend, told staff she was staying put as she heard that people were looking to mess her up and she needed to stay at the home. Kathy took the youth out to have her nails done with one of the other youths, and they spent the remainder of the evening playing board games over take-out. On Monday morning, the supervisor questioned Kathy's weekend spending and reminded her that youth were expected to leave the home for the weekend and not use it as a "vacation spot."		
Deffrey, a 10-year-old child, attends Plars day-treatment program for school. When he was told that he would be moved to another home that day, he threw the art supplies off the table. Deffrey was sent to time-out and told to write a letter of apology to staff for breaking the art supplies.		
Campina, a 14-year-old youth, attempted to pull out her peer's hair weaves when the other youth made a comment about Campina's substance-using mother. Staff intervened and brought Campina into the kitchen to make smoothies.		

REFLECTIVE MOMENT

As you move forward in your learning journey, continue to think about the worldviews and environmental systems that impact your day-to-day interactions—both yours and others. Self-inquiry will guide you in this process. Practice will assist you in adopting a relational practice approach with others that will inevitably become a regular aspect of your day-to-day thinking. You will discover that as you do, your ways of thinking, seeing, and being in the world begin to shift.

CLOSING THOUGHTS[1]

When did you feel most engaged? Least engaged?

_____

_____

_____

What is the most important information you have learned thus far?

_____

_____

_____

What questions remain for you from this learning?

_____

_____

_____

NOTE

1. The closing thoughts reflection is adapted from the CIQ—Critical Incident Questionnaire in Keefer (2009).

CHAPTER 5

Mindfulness

The best way to take care of the future is to take care of the present moment.

—Thich Nhat Hanh

LEARNING OBJECTIVES

In this chapter, you will:

- be introduced to and define mindfulness as a form of self-care
- describe the connection between mindfulness and Child and Youth Care reflective practice
- check in and monitor the need for self-care
- explore different ways of engaging in mindfulness

This chapter is intended to provide you with a brief overview of mindfulness and its connection to Child and Youth Care reflective practice. It will by no means cover the vast information available.

The previous chapters have provided you with opportunities to engage in exploring self through identifying your strengths, perspectives, values, beliefs, and assumptions. This awareness of self will continue throughout your career as a Child and Youth Care Practitioner and is one of the key components of professional practice. Awareness of self enables you to embrace and apply the characteristics of Child and Youth Care practice through presence, noticing, demonstrating curiosity, examining context, and creating meaning of the situations you encounter. Everything you do as a practitioner is intentional and always to achieve greater understanding of others that will inform your actions in practice.

That being said, it is important to acknowledge that the field of Child and Youth Care, while rewarding, can also take a toll on you if you are not practicing self-care or have difficulties in "turning it off." Child and Youth Care practice requires that we invest much emotional energy in the children, youth, and families we interact with, all of whom bring their own way of thinking, seeing, and being. The need to slow down one's thinking and reactions becomes ever more apparent. In order to sustain the demands of practice and to create that much-needed balance to demonstrate effective practice, practitioners must know when and how to "turn down the volume" to create necessary emotional distance from the work.

TURNING IT OFF

With the intensity that Child and Youth Care work can bring, it can be difficult to "turn it off," to separate yourself from the emotions and overthinking that occurs. This turning off is beneficial for entering into the next experience. Turning it off, however, does not suggest you stop caring or you become desensitized to the experiences of the other; it simply means creating distance from your internal experiences to begin anew. Cultivating mindfulness in your daily practice will assist you in being fully present with children, youth, and families (Didonna, 2009; Germer et al., 2013) and will enable others to develop the ability for mindfulness as well (Bruce, Manber, Shapiro, & Constantinto, as cited in Germer et al., 2013).

> Mindfulness enables you to still the mind to connect with your authentic, inner self …
> You don't fight the mind. In fact, you don't even try to change it. You just make a game
> out of relaxing in the face of its melodrama.
> —Michael Singer

TUNING INTO SELF

Tuning into self amid the distractions of everyday life is an essential aspect of practice that allows you to create this essential emotional distance. Tuning into self, or checking in with yourself as Garfat (2003b) aptly terms it, is a process of tuning into one's awareness of the experience, the thoughts involved, and the meaning this experience holds. To truly allow for oneself to tune in and check in with oneself requires space away from others (NCTSN, 2014). In this sense, checking in with self is not related to the interventive moment that Garfat (2003b) describes; rather, it is a self-less "you moment" where thinking about all other "stuff" has come to a halt. The National Child Traumatic Stress Network defines three aspects of self-care (these self-less you moments): awareness, balance, and connection (NCTSN, 2014).

Awareness requires you to slow down and focus inward to notice how you are feeling, what you are thinking, the level of stress you are experiencing, and what impact this is having on your actions. In checking in with self, practitioners provide the opportunity to determine what different dimensions of self (physical, cognitive, emotional, relational, and spiritual) require attention or, more aptly, self-care.

Exercise 28: Assessing Balance

In the space below, draw a pie chart and label each area of your life to reflect the amount of time you devote to these areas. If there is a heavier emphasis on work, this is a clear signal that you are out of balance. Acknowledging when you are out of balance (awareness) will assist you in identifying your need for rest, relaxation, and further self-care to encompass physical, emotional, relational, cognitive, and spiritual wellness practices. Table 8 will assist you in determining whether you are out of balance.

Balance in all areas of your life, including work, personal and family life, rest, and leisure, is necessary to demonstrate professional practice. Achieving and maintaining balance in your life will have positive implications in your practice. Consider how much time you devote to these different areas of your life.

Connection involves accessing support through healthy relationships with your colleagues, friends, family, and the community. Social connections are reported to be one of the most powerful influences in reducing stress (NCTSN, 2014).

I'll make a note on connecting with your social and familial supports. It is important to distinguish between venting about work and *connecting* with your supports. Connecting as a means of self-care requires stepping away from your professional self to be your personal self, removed from the demands and stressors of the work. When you find your-self ruminating about work and your conversations with others focus on aspects of the work, this often signals a need for help in detaching from work. Recognizing this presents an opportunity to reach out to counsellors or psychotherapists to assist you.

Table 8: Self-care Inventory

The following table provides the different dimensions of physical, emotional, cognitive, relational, and spiritual wellness. Review each list and rate the dimensions using the following scale:
5 = frequently; 4 = occasionally; 3 = rarely; 2 = never; 1 = it never occurred to me

Physical Self-care	5	4	3	2	1
Maintain regular meal schedule (e.g., breakfast, lunch, and dinner)					
Eat healthy foods					
Engage in physical exercise at home/the gym					
Engage in physical exercise outside: play sports, biking, jogging, other					
Engage in physical exercise through structured activities: dancing, swimming, skating, other					
Go on walks					
Get regular medical care for prevention					
Engage in regular hygiene routines					
Attend regular medical appointments (doctor, dentist, other)					
Rest during illness					
Regular sleep routines, obtain between 6–8 hours of sleep					
Dress with care in clothes you like and feel confident in					
Other:					
Psychological/Emotional Self-care	**5**	**4**	**3**	**2**	**1**
Self-monitor stress levels and engage in healthy coping means (physical, emotional, cognitive, or spiritual care)					

Psychological/Emotional Self-care	5	4	3	2	1
Engage in use of self (awareness of feelings, thoughts, judgements, beliefs, assumptions, other)					
Express self through creative outlets: journalling, drawing, writing, painting					
Participate in activities unrelated to work (e.g., watch movies, read books)					
Seek support from others					
Say no to others (i.e., not taking on additional responsibility/overextending yourself)					
Accepting support from others					
Identify and express your feelings to others					
Give self-affirmations and praise					
Engage in regular "aww" moments (images from social media, nature, others)					
Other:					

Relational/Play Self-care	5	4	3	2	1
Engage in social activities you enjoy with friends and family					
Engage in hobbies/favourite pastimes					
Take vacations/day trips					
Establish and maintain healthy relationships with others (friends and family who are positive influences)					
Speak to family/friends regularly					
Engage in fun downtime (movies, television, spa, other)					
Attend social events (theatre, dining, other)					
Spend time with family and friends you enjoy being with					
Other:					

(continued)

Table 8: Self-care Inventory (*continued*)

Spiritual Self-care	5	4	3	2	1
Experience a sense of purpose					
Connect with a higher power through prayer, reading, or meditation					
Spend time with nature					
Find joy in non-material things					
Identify what holds meaning for you in your personal life					
Volunteer or support causes important to you					
Engage in self-reflection					
Read inspirational books, listen to podcasts or music					
Act in accordance with personal values and morals					
Other:					
Professional Self-care	**5**	**4**	**3**	**2**	**1**
Take regular breaks throughout the day					
Engage in positive conversations with co-workers					
Avoid gossip or toxic conversations					
Incorporate personal quiet time throughout the day					
Participate in projects or tasks that are exciting and rewarding					
Set limits/boundaries with others at workplace (and school)					
Attend work (or school) regularly					
Attend meetings/consultations regularly					
Other:					

Self-care[1] Defined

Self-care is the integration of the physical, psychological/emotional, relational play, and spiritual dimensions (Caroll et al., 1999) of wellness that individuals practice to prevent illness and mitigate against stressors (Fereday, 2011) in day-to-day life.

This awareness, this process of tuning into self, is a precursor to identifying the dimension of self-care that is required. Step back for a moment and consider the ease or difficulty you experience in turning down the volume, the mind chatter that has you second-guessing *what you did, how you might do better, what will happen*, and so on.

Complete the following self-care inventory to determine where you rank within each of these dimensions. This will also assist you in understanding which aspects may warrant further attention. The self-care inventory can be completed at different times throughout your academic and professional journey.

Table 8 outlines different ways to achieve self-care. While this list is by no means exhaustive, it provides you with an understanding of the different ways self-care can be achieved. Consider for a moment what your go-to self-care moments are. Check those that you currently participate in and add in your own ideas. Are there self-care items on the list that you have not considered before?

Self-care Inventory[2]

In reviewing your completed inventory above, identify the areas that warrant further care. How might you begin to incorporate ways to address these areas in your day-to-day life, beginning today? The list below provides ideas for self-care, but by no means encompasses the endless opportunities available to you. As you review the list, highlight those that you actively apply to your daily life and identify new practices of interest for yourself.

Self-care Practices: Achieving Self-care

- Practice brief relaxation techniques during the workday.
- Connect with colleagues to reflect on situations.
- Identify and express your emotions.
- Use creative outlets to express your experiences from the workday.
- Set aside 30 minutes in your day to do things you enjoy.
- List those things you enjoy.
- Engage in frequent check-ins with self throughout your day.
- Notice two things that have made you smile today.
- Notice two things in the environment that have a positive impact on you (weather, sound, images, taste, scents, etc.).
- Acknowledge the efforts behind the choices and decisions you make in your daily practice.
- Identify three strengths you actively demonstrate on a day-to-day basis.
- Identify two things you are grateful for or appreciative of.
- Give yourself permission to say no to avoid being overloaded with work demands.
- Spend time with people who are important to you.
- Listen to white noise or nature music at bedtime to support healthy sleep routines.

- Engage in self-reflection at the end of each day: what worked for you/what did not; what new insights did you learn about yourself?
- Watch comedies or social media clips that involve humour and make you laugh.
- Seek counselling to address frequent patterns of stress you experience.
- Identify and incorporate opportunities that have spiritual or philosophical meaning for you.
- Purge your worries in a journal: write big, write small. Do not worry about sentence structure.
- Ask for help or clarification when things are not making sense to you.
- Trust your judgement. When things don't make sense, it's often because they just don't make sense.
- Differentiate between feelings and actions. Are you hungry or are you sad/angry?
- If you practice religious faith or spirituality, how might aspects of this support you right now?
- Listen to music that brings you a sense of calm.
- Engage in mindfulness (see below).
- Engage in mindful breathing: breathe in through your nose for a count of two, hold for two, and release through your mouth for three.

Self-care Practices[3]

Friedman (2017) asserts that mindfulness is one of the most well-studied and effective forms of counsellor self-care. Being mindful is a precursor to reflective practice, yet it is not a simple task. It is a way of being that requires time, effort, and practice to cultivate (Kabat-Zinn & Kabat-Zinn, 1997). Practitioners need to possess the capacity to separate their "stuff" from the experiences of the other. If not, the risk of reacting to others in ways that imply blame and judgement is high.

Mindfulness enables you to notice and accept your reactions as your own experiences as opposed to blaming others. Mindfulness is a way of seeing and knowing the self and others that evolves into new experiences (Didonna, 2009; Kabat-Zinn & Kabat-Zinn, 1997; Nhat Hanh, 1987).

WHAT IS MINDFULNESS AND HOW DOES IT RELATE TO REFLECTIVE PRACTICE?

Mindfulness is the awareness that arises through paying attention on purpose in the present moment through a non-judgemental lens (Didonna, 2009; Kabat-Zinn & Kabat-Zinn, 1997). It allows for ongoing inquiry (Bellefeuille & Ricks, 2010) and exploration (Didonna, 2009) as a practice, more so than a concept or technique. Mindfulness embodies a way of being, a practice that cultivates attention, clarity, awareness, and compassion (Kabat-Zinn & Kabat-Zinn, 1997) that is essential to your effectiveness as a Child and Youth Care Practitioner. Doing so creates opportunities to get out of the way of yourself so that you are better able to remain present, open, and attuned to what arises in the moment (Kabat-Zinn & Kabat-Zinn, 1997; Schomaker & Ricard, 2015).

There are distinct parallels between mindfulness, reflection, and Child and Youth Care practice. Paying attention to self within unfolding moments with an attitude of openness, non-judgement, and acceptance, while holding the intention of realizing best practice (Johns, 2009), parallels the Child and Youth Care characteristics of presence, noticing, and curiosity. It is the ability to attune to the other's lived experience (Siegal, 2007) that enriches the therapeutic alliance[4] between the practitioner and children, youth, and families. When, then, does one quiet their mind to attune to others? To let go of the overthinking that can occur during interactions with others?

Being Still

Mindfulness is an essential aspect of reflective practice as it allows opportunities for practitioners to be present in order to experiences new ideas, feelings, and alternative responses (Wong, 2017). One needs to be present and experience stillness to engage in reflective practice. In doing so, practitioners are better able to disengage from the *should* thinking that is reflective of judgemental thinking. Mindfulness allows you to create the much-needed stillness for disengaging from judgemental thinking in order to sit in the silence without interference from personal thoughts and emotional reactions (Didonna, 2009; Germer, Siegel, & Fulton, 2013).

Engaging in mindfulness will enable you to remain focused on the needs of the others while being mindful of your own internal reactions. In being mindful of your experience of others, you will be less likely to respond from a place of judgement or reactivity. Mindful breathing can support you in slowing down your response. Doing so leaves practitioners the room to expand their ways of thinking, while considering different possibilities for action (Kabat-Zinn & Kabat-Zinn, 1997; Nhat Hanh, 1987).

Mindful Exercises

Through regular practice of exercises, you will adopt a more mindful approach to practice that will assist you in shifting from a place of *reactivity* to a place of *responsivity*.

> The quieter you become, the more you can hear.
> —Buddha

Practice in Mindful Thinking

Be mindful of your focus of attention when you interact with others, notably if your focus is on finding fault in another person, situation, or idea. These are evident in disparaging comments and expectations of others: *I cannot believe they* … ; *What an* … *!*; *They are such* … ; *They are always* … ; *Here they go again.* Stop the bus! Take a step back and acknowledge that you are engaging in judgement and ask yourself, "What purpose do these comments serve?" To make yourself feel superior, to overcompensate for your own imperfections? To deflect attention from your own dissatisfaction with self by focusing on another? Recognizing the nature and purpose of your comments allows you to be mindful—to engage in purposeful awareness of the present experience (Didonna, 2009; Germer et al., 2013).

So How Does One Do Mindfulness?

1. Develop the capacity to be self-aware. You started this process in the previous chapter through the different self-exploration and noticing exercises. Take note, however, that self-awareness will continue to be an ongoing development and involves more than simply identifying your pet peeves, strengths, and values; rather, it's an awareness of your internal reactions to experiences. Practitioners need to be committed to the lifelong practice of self-exploration throughout their career.

2. Be still, be curious, and be calm. Weiss, Johanson, and Monda (2015) highlight the importance of suspending "attachment to what we think we already know," (p. 4) to allow for new learning, new discoveries of that which one has not been made aware. Acceptance of what is occurring in the present moment is key to reflective practice. The other's experience and reactions are not about you. Additionally, your reaction is not a result of the other's behaviour, but a reaction to the meaning that you have created about their behaviour. Engaging in mindfulness requires patience, time, and regular practice.

3. Breathe through experiences as they occur. Mindful breathing interferes with the potential to react to these experiences.

Engaging in mindful breathing, with purposeful focus on the breath in and the breath out, will assist you in slowing down your desire to respond and the physical symptoms (e.g., racing heart) that can occur in response to heightened interactions. Breathing in the present moment will help you to achieve clarity and awareness in the moment.

Exercise 29: Mindful Breathing

Commit to practice mindful breathing three times a day over the course of a week: when you awake, during the afternoon, and when you are settling for bed. Refrain from engaging with your phone, television, or music during these times.

Sit quietly with your feet on the floor, in an upright position. Breathe in through your nose for a count of three, hold for two, and breathe out slowly for a count of three. Repeat this three to five times at each sitting.

What do you notice? If you begin to ruminate about thoughts from the day, return your attention to mindful breathing. This interrupts the thought process to bring you back to the present. Mindful breathing will support you in managing stress, anger, and anxiety as situations occur. The more you practice, the more easily you will be able to disengage from the thoughts.

For things to reveal themselves to us, we need to be ready to abandon our views about them.

—Thich Nhat Hanh

For mindful breathing to be effective, practitioners must be intentional in their approach, which involves disengaging from all sources of technology and other forms of distraction. This point bears repeating: scheduling regular intervals of mindful breathing three to five times a day (e.g., morning, afternoon, and evening) will support you in your practice and enable you to be more mindful. Mindful practices require the time and commitment to these practices. Engaging in mindfulness and mindful breathing requires a concerted effort to focus on the present, which can be difficult when you remain focused on the mind chatter.

Using a mantra when engaging in the mindful breathing can be helpful. For instance, as you breathe in for two, verbalize the mantra of *breathing in* and *breathing out* as you release. This can support you in focusing on in-the-moment breathing. The more you do something, the more naturally it will come.

Exercise 30: What I Need

Find a quiet spot, free from external distractions, to complete this reflection and take three mindful breaths. This will bring you to the in-the-moment awareness that is essential for reflective practice and mindfulness. Pay attention to your internal state of *being*. What is it that you are feeling? Refrain from analyzing or thinking about why you are feeling this way; just notice. Identify a colour that would best describe this state of *being* right now. Using the space below, give this feeling a shape, using the colour you have selected. This in-the-moment focus without judgement requires you to just *do*—engage in the moment without worrying about what it *should* look like. Engage in the awareness of the feeling and when you notice that you are becoming stressed or annoyed, return to mindful breathing.

When you have finished, spend a few moments contemplating what this image reveals about your current experience of self. Notice any judgements that come up and the ease or difficulty you experience in silencing the judgements. What is behind the judgements that come up, if any (e.g., a desire to be right, to be perfect, etc.)? How might such judgements influence your practice with others?

> When we are mindful, deeply in touch with the present moment, our understanding of what is going on deepens, and we begin to be filled with acceptance, joy, peace and love.
> —Thich Nhat Hanh

For some individuals, working in a quiet area can provide the focus and attention required to complete these exercises. For others, working in a busy environment can be just as effective, as some individuals possess the ability to tune out the external distractions. See which works best for you. Regardless of the setting you decide on, ensure that your immediate experience does not influence your ability to complete this exercise. If you begin to notice that you engage in judgement of others (in the environment) or yourself, this may suggest that a quieter space is warranted.

The following exercises will introduce you to different ways to live in the present moment; however, they require regular practice. They can be done at any time throughout the day and are often beneficial to help you refocus during those times when the need to focus on the present is required.

The following exercise is another mindful practice that assists the practitioner in becoming grounded to the here and now and engages all of your senses.

> Inner silence promotes clarity of mind; it makes us value the inner world; it trains us to go inside to the source of peace and inspiration when we are faced with problems and challenges.
> —Deepak Chopra

> Seeing things from a child's point of view can guide you in the choices we make and helps us to be an empathic presence to each moment.
> —Kabat-Zinn & Kabat-Zinn, 1997, p. 71

Exercise 31: 5 4 3 2 1[5]

This is a popular grounding technique that can support you in creating distance from emotional and thought processes that can influence your practice.

- Identify five things you can see; describe them in detail, including the colours and shapes.

- Identify four things you can feel or touch; describe in detail the texture: smooth, rough, hard, soft, etc.
- Identify three things you can hear; can you identify the source of the sound? A child's laughter or adults speaking? If you are unable to hear more than one sound, identify sounds that bring you joy or a sense of peace.
- Identify two things you can smell; can you identify the distinct scent? Can you describe it: floral, sweet, spicy? If you are able to only notice one smell, identify those scents that you enjoy.
- Identify one thing that brings you joy.

This present-moment exercise takes you out of the thinking mind to in-the-moment awareness.

Checking In

Where are you with the concepts and exercises on mindfulness? Focus on your internal experiences of emotions and thoughts in response to this chapter. What is the connection to Child and Youth Care reflective practice?

Exercise 32: Just Be

For the next hour, simply engage in one task. Resist the urge to busy your hands or mind with another task. Pay attention to what you begin to think about; where does your mind wander to? Do you think about what needs to be done or what should have been done? Or are you able to just be and allow the thoughts to come and go without engaging with them?

Each time you allow the thoughts to come and go without engaging in them, mindfulness and acceptance occurs (Germer, Siegel, & Fulton, 2013). Many times, individuals will determine that mindful breathing or other types of meditative practices do not work. Perhaps an alternative to "this is not working" is "this requires more practice." If you find this exercise difficult, this is simply a result of habitual patterns of doing things; you are not intended to judge or criticize yourself. Mindfulness is a process and, as indicated earlier, one that develops from practice (Didonna, 2009; Germer et al., 2013; Kabat-Zinn & Kabat-Zinn, 1997; Orsillo & Roemer, 2011).

ATTENDING TO THE MOMENT

Notice how often you ask yourself, "What is the point of this?" or engage in judgement-laden comments about class discussions, assignments, exercises, or your interactions with others.

Exercises 33: Colouring and Doodling

Any adult colouring book, or pads of paper to doodle on, offers a wealth of opportunity to engage in mindfulness. While this is not an encouraged practice during class or discussion with others, colouring and doodling do offer opportunities to disengage from the mind chatter and *just be* in the present moment. Mindful practitioners are able to return to the present moment, without engaging in the reactions that can emerge as a result of different experiences, simply by engaging in mindful breathing—purposeful, in-the-moment breathing.[6]

Use the space below to create your own image. This can include a series of lines, shapes, and doodles.

Exercise 34: Mindful Listening

This practice helps you cultivate the ability to listen to the emotional content behind the sound, the voice, the content, and/or the dialogue. In doing so, we can learn to identify the underlying meaning without assumption, bias, or judgement. This is especially important in our practice with others and in recognizing the meaning of our reactions.

The next time you are listening to music, pay attention to the emotions in the words. What does the music reveal? What does it say to you?

_____

_____

_____

Sit in a public place, a coffee shop, shopping mall, or park with your back to others. This will prevent you from making assumptions or judgements about what you hear. (Alternatively, close your eyes.) Listen to the emotional content of the interactions. What do you hear?

_____

_____

_____

Listen to the audio of a television show, podcast, or webinar you are not familiar with. Do not look at the screen. What do you hear? Notice the emotional content behind the words. Share and discuss with others.

_____

_____

_____

It is not important to evaluate your comments; rather, be aware of them. The key to engaging in mindfulness that will assist you in becoming a reflective practitioner is to not engage in the mind chatter or reactions that may occur. Many practitioners will respond to these practice exercises with hesitation and judgement and assert they don't work. It is often not the action of being mindful that doesn't work; it is the inability to let go of the need to _do_. The attachment to a particular way of thinking is a barrier to mindfulness and reflective practice.

Engage in each activity and notice your reactions from each experience, free from judgement. If you notice that your reactions convey judgement, step back and pay attention to this. What is behind the judgement? Unease, discomfort, impatience? Spend some time in that experience. Where does this come from? How far back does your discomfort in new and unfamiliar experiences go? Sit with this for a moment and simply acknowledge what you are feeling in your body, what you are thinking, and what you are feeling emotionally. Refrain from engaging in finding a solution. Just acknowledge your experience.

How much of this discomfort is related to your uncertainties of the situation and the need to do right action? When you notice these experiences come up, engage in one of the practices listed above. It is through experience and doing in the moment that mindfulness becomes more readily accessible.

> Viewing self and others from a place of non-judgment and compassion allows you to experience the moment as it is and to connect with their internal experience, regardless of how others may respond.
> —Kabat-Zinn & Kabat-Zinn, 1997

Consider the Following Scenario: Jazz

The following case scenario will provide you with opportunities to notice your internal reactions (as you have done with previous scenarios) and to practice disengaging from the thoughts or potential judgements that arise. When you notice these, stop what you are doing and engage in mindful breathing.

Jazz, a 15-year-old youth, arrived at zir third home in eight months. Zi has an extensive history with children protective services since the age of eight. Zir contact with family ended one year earlier due to different extenuating factors and zi has experienced moments of rage at different times in the last eight months. Zi was charged with assault on staff at the most recent home and is currently on probation. Ten days after being placed in this home, zi was charged again with an assault on staff. Staff struggled to understand this as they had each developed positive rapport with Jazz. As Jazz was led away in handcuffs, zi requested staff come see zir in jail. Staff did not respond and later expressed their disappointment with zir behaviour. When reminded by senior staff that it was important to visit zir in custody, each of the staff refuted this direction, expressing their disappointment and judgement of zir behaviour. One staff commented that Jazz should have known better. No one visited Jazz in jail, justifying their decision to "teach zir a lesson."

The reactions of the staff above suggests that they reacted from a place of judgement that ignored this youth's previous experiences and history as potential contributing factors of zir behaviour (note here that I am not suggesting such behaviours can be justified by any means; rather, they must be considered as a potential result of a complex history). The staff's reactions appeared to be based on their personal expectations of behaviours as opposed to considering the complex experiences of this youth. Their personal judgement interfered with their ability to respond to zir needs. In demonstrating mindful and intentional practice, what do you believe was the implication for Jazz when staff whom zi had developed a rapport with over the past 10 days neglected to visit zir in custody? Might this have caused more harm? What beliefs may have been reinforced for Jazz? Could it be argued that staff did not consider the potential for emotional harm by refusing to visit Jazz in custody? Resist the urge to respond to these questions and take a few moments to engage in mindful silence. If you notice that you are distracted by the scenario or other things from the day, engage in mindful breathing. You will notice that the more you engage in mindful breathing, the quieter the mind becomes. Sit with this for three minutes and then return to the scenario.

Staff met to debrief and process their reactions of the shift. One staff member commented, "If zi thinks I'm coming to visit zir in custody, forget it. That was unacceptable behaviour." Another member suggests they refrain from making further disparaging remarks and consider the impact of their comments. Another comments on the situation as the nature of the work and the potential for others to react based on their own histories.

Give thought to what the staff's responses to zir behaviour reveal about their conditional expectations of others. What emotions do they appear to be reacting from? What is the impact of reacting from this heightened emotional place?

Responding from mindful awareness acknowledges the risks and nature of Child and Youth Care and considers the impact of earlier experiences on others.

The above debrief reflects the staff's inability to engage in mindfulness. Mindfulness is void of blame and judgement and embraces acceptance and awareness of the present moment. There is no need to blame the other nor chastise the other for their responses; instead, engage in acceptance of what has occurred and the resulting emotional experiences. By engaging in mindfulness, you move from blame and judgement to acknowledgement and acceptance of the potential risks of the work. Is it possible to view Jazz's reactions as a result of fear and previous experiences (acceptance = new understanding) as opposed to purposeful, malicious behaviour (judgement = blame)? Please note that mindfulness does not condone behaviours of others, but instead accepts what has occurred, without engaging in blame and judgement.

Mindfulness has a positive effect on the practitioner's skills and relationships that has been well documented (Rybak, 2013; Schomaker & Richard, 2015). Similar to other skills, mindfulness requires time, effort, and a commitment to practice.

CLOSING THOUGHTS

What did you learn about yourself from the concepts discussed in this chapter?

_____

_____

_____

How will your new learning influence your practice? How will you incorporate self-care practices into your day-to-day life?

_____

_____

_____

What questions remain for you still?

_____

_____

_____

NOTES

1. Self-care is an essential component of professional practice as outlined in the core competency of Professionalism and the Code of Ethics, Responsibility to Self.
2. The self-care inventory is adapted from the Child Welfare Training Toolkit (2008); National Child Traumatic Stress Network (2014); the Counselor Self Care Instrument by Fereday (2011); and Carroll et al. (1999), "The Moral Imperative: Self-care for Women Psychotherapists."
3. The Achieving Self-care table was adapted from Child Welfare Training Toolkit (2008) and National Child Traumatic Stress Network (2014).
4. The therapeutic alliance can be understood as the co-created space described in the previous chapter and the relationship that is fundamental to Child and Youth Care. The therapeutic alliance embodies core conditions of genuineness, empathy, and unconditional positive regard (Rogers, 1946).
5. 5-4-3-2-1 is a grounding technique developed by Richard (2015) to aid practitioners in becoming more aware of their present surroundings. It has been popular in managing stress and anxiety.
6. Being mindful of the other's needs embodies professional practice. Responsibility to the child, youth, and family requires practitioners to recognize the differences in individual and family needs and respond accordingly.

CHAPTER 6

The Reflective Process

You are not your thoughts; you are aware of your thoughts. You are not your emotions; you feel your emotions.

—Michael Singer

LEARNING OBJECTIVES

In this chapter, you will:

- differentiate between reflexivity and reflection
- develop the capacity for reflective inquiry
- be introduced to Dewey's four criteria of reflection
- learn about the concepts of transference and countertransference
- develop the skills necessary for observing others as a frame for reflection
- complete observation logs
- reflect on experiences through Borton's What, So What, Now What model of reflection

The previous chapters have provided you with opportunities to explore the aspects of self and others and implications for practice as the initial steps for reflective practice. Engaging in use of self requires us to explore the underlying internal processes that can influence practice. Reflective inquiry answers the "what" and "why" of the practitioner's internal reactions, which fosters greater awareness and understanding of self and allows practitioners to consider if their reactions are related to their own needs as a practitioner or the other's needs (Bellefeuille et al., 2011; Fox, n.d.; Garfat & Newcomen, 1992).

The different exercises and scenarios you engaged with provided you with opportunities to think beyond your current ways of knowing, which provided the foundation from which to engage in reflective practice. While these concepts will continue to be referenced throughout the remainder of the book, you will now begin to focus more on the reflective processes.

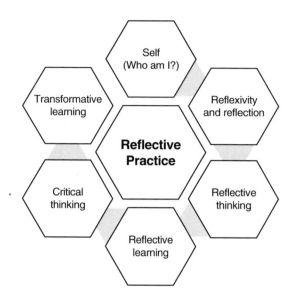

Figure 1: Reflective Practice Radial

Source: Recreated by author.

REFLEXIVITY

Reflexivity is a critical approach to practice whereby practitioners question their ways of knowing (how you know what you know) and the degree to which their knowledge is influenced by the power they hold in their position (D'Cruz et al., 2007). The connection between knowledge and power is the key focus of reflexivity and requires practitioners to explore self in determining this knowledge as it relates to their emotions and thought process (D'Cruz et al., 2007). This thinking within process (Bolton, 2009) provides practitioners with opportunities to query the basis for their knowledge and embodies an integral aspect of using self in practice (Gharabaghi, 2008a; White, 2007). How is what I am feeling in response to this other influencing my knowledge of them? This is an important question to consider; however, thinking within requires the practitioner to be aware of diverse emotions as a response to others and not as a cause of others' behaviours. This bears a clear distinction in how one's knowledge of others is generated as well as the responsibility for practitioners to own their emotional responses. Doing so, however, requires practitioners to have an awareness of their emotions.

Revisiting Kilarni, Jade, and Gavin

Recall the case scenario involved Kilarni, his co-worker Jade, and Gavin, the youth they are working with (see p. 83). Let us return to the scenario and explore Jade's comments toward Gavin from a reflexive lens. Recall that she said Gavin was rude and that this was a safe space, in response to his hiding under the table. From a reflexive lens, her comment seems to imply that *he should have acted on his best behaviour* in her presence and that there was no reason for Gavin to feel unsafe or uncomfortable. What might have contributed to her knowing here? What is the connection between knowledge (determining Gavin's behaviour was rude and safety was present) and the power embedded in her position as the support worker?

_____

_____

What emotion may have underlined Jade's response that influenced her reaction?

_____

_____

D'Cruz et al. (2007) highlight the importance for practitioners to query their ways of knowing about others and the other's perspective of them (Bolton, 2009) as essential to raising awareness of the power within their position. Achieving an awareness of how you are experienced and perceived by others is fundamental to reflexivity (Bolton, 2009). Had Jade been aware of this power dynamic embedded in her position, she may have queried, "What reaction might the family have of me, as this new person joining their team? What might Gavin be thinking as I sit across from him?" Considering the questions Jade could have asked, how might this have influenced her action toward Gavin? What might she have said to him that conveyed this awareness instead?

_____

_____

Denying the power/knowledge dynamic within your position limits your ability to see beyond your own ways of _knowing_ and _being_ with others whose experiences are different from yours (Lareau & McNamara Horvat, 1999; Ricks & Bellefeuille, 2003; White, 2007).

EMOTIONS

Emotions represent the primal aspect of one's identity and often influence one's ways of thinking, seeing, and being in the world (Dewey, 1933; Mayer, 2016; Schon, 1983), which can have significant implications for practice. Reacting from an emotional place conveys judgement and unspoken conditions for the other to comply with. The other's needs become secondary to the practitioner's need to feel okay. It then becomes all the more important for practitioners to attend to their feelings as a means for developing awareness and not as an excuse for their behaviours (Fox, n.d.; Garfat & Newcomen, 1992; Mayer, 2016).

All interactions generate feelings that require attention.
—Garfat & Newcomen, 1992

Recognizing these emotions as a common reaction to situations is a key aspect of reflexivity (Bolton, 2009). While this may seem like a seamless process for some, the idea of acknowledging feelings can be uncomfortable and unfamiliar for others. If you were raised in a family that did not openly express or talk about feelings, it is anticipated you will question the purpose or may struggle in adapting to this "touchy-feely topic," as speaking of emotions has been referred to. It could be said that Child and Youth Care practice is a touchy-feely profession since emotions and supporting others to express and manage theirs is a significant part of the work. This can provide an opportunity to explore the meaning behind the discomfort that acknowledging feelings has for you.

Exercise 35: Feelings Are …

Take a moment to consider the beliefs you may have about feelings and check off the statements that fit for you.

- Feelings are a sign of weakness
- Feelings don't change anything
- Feelings are bad
- It's a waste of time to think about feelings
- Feelings make people lose control
- Feeling angry is bad
- It's only good to feel happy
- Feelings are for the touchy-feely type
- Other people are responsible for how I feel

Where do these beliefs originate from?

_____

_____

The ability to identify emotions is an important aspect of children's development. This, however, requires that practitioners are attuned to their own emotional states. This comes easier for some than others. For practitioners who may not be tuned into their emotional states, it can be helpful to reference a chart with different emotions since emotional awareness is a distinct aspect of reflective practice (Bolton, 2009; Moon, 2004). As one of my former colleagues often said, "We can't ask others to do what we have not yet done ourselves" (Jaglowitz, 2015). This statement highlights the importance for practitioners to be aware of their own emotions before encouraging others to share theirs.

Note: Feelings are felt internal experiences. Many people confuse thoughts for feelings. It is important that these be clarified and discussed to differentiate between the two. Acknowledging the emotional feeling gives the individual more ownership for their reaction. For example, "I felt like I was going to blow" is not a feeling; this is a thought.

While this is not an uncommon expression, it risks individuals deflecting their emotional experiences if this is not addressed.

Aristotle, a Greek philosopher whose thinking contributed to the evaluation of reflective practice (Kakkori & Huttenen, 2007; Natali, 2013), believed in the importance of paying attention to one's emotions as a factor in how one perceives their situations (Kakkori & Huttenen, 2007).

Let us return to the scenario involving Jenisse from Chapter 3. If you recall, she expressed her belief that parents should be charged for spanking their children.

Consider the Following Scenario: Revisiting Jenisse

The professor requested to meet with Jenisse after class to explore her reactions and comments in class. While not to judge her for her reactions, the professor explained the benefits of exploring such reactions as a means to develop and grow as a learning professional.

Through the discussion Jenisse was asked to think about:

- The basis for her response: What emotions and knowledge influenced this strong reaction?
- How will this reaction enhance or restrict her learning as a Child and Youth Care professional?

Jenisse expressed feeling judged by the professor and commented she had a right to feel the way she did.

As discussed in previous chapters, practitioners bring their own experiences and ways of knowing that can influence their interactions with others. While this is not to suggest that practitioners forget or dismiss their earlier experiences, practitioners have a responsibility to ensure these experiences do not interfere in their ability to support children, youth, and families, or other professionals. Rather, they must be aware of them and observe the potential implications for action. When practitioners are not aware of their previous experiences nor potential impact on action, they risk responding from that experience as opposed to the present moment experience.

COUNTERTRANSFERENCE

Countertransference is a term used to describe the practitioner's conscious and unconscious emotional reactions to the other (Fox, n.d., p. 5). While it is never one's intention to allow their personal issues to interfere in their practice, the nature of this work warrants consideration of the imminent risks involved. Working with others

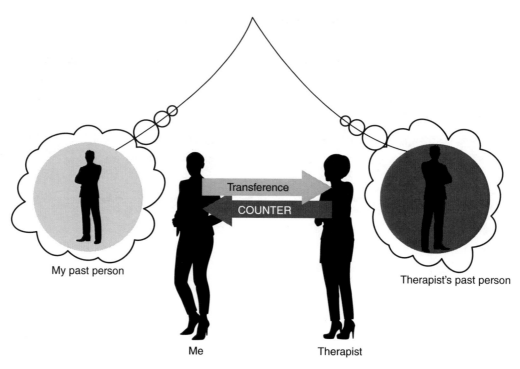

Figure 11: Countertransference
Source: 2bp.blogspot.com.

who present with complex experiences and ways of thinking, seeing, and being in the world can trigger within the practitioner their own unresolved issues from the past (Garfat & Newcomen, 1992). The emotional experiences of this past experience influences the meaning practitioners make of situations and are projected onto the other(s) (Fox, n.d.).

Consider the Following Scenario: Jenisse at Practicum

On Jenisse's first day of practicum, she accompanied a meeting with a family who requested support in managing their conflicted relationships with one another. The family spoke about the mother's boyfriend's recent re-entry into the home and the distance that was required between him and the mother's daughter and the resulting stress this was placing on the family. As Jenisse sat with the family, she experienced a sense of disgust toward the family. She realized she couldn't stand to hear them talk any longer and responded to the mother's dismay that the daughter had not forgiven her nor her boyfriend by saying, "Perhaps if you had shown your daughter the respect she deserved in the first place, none of this would be happening. It's up to you to change, not your daughter," and then left the room.

This scenario illustrates an example of countertransference and highlights the importance for practitioners to acknowledge how their ways of knowing can influence their actions. Jenisse's interactions with the family will warrant a discussion with her supervisor to explore the underlying emotions and bias toward parents to better understand her reactions. In doing so, Jenisse will want to explore the following from a reflexive lens:

- What emotions underlined my reactions?
- What influenced me to feel this way?
- What are the beliefs, values, assumptions, and personal experiences that influenced my reaction?
- What knowledge influenced my response?
- Consider the power embedded within the reaction. This "I know better than you" response to the parent's comments is reflective of the power differentials between individuals and the practitioner.
- What knowledge should have influenced me?

In recognizing the knowledge that influenced one's knowing, it is important to challenge the power differentials to consider what knowledge is necessary to influence one's knowing. Consider the knowledge you have gained in your program thus far. How will it influence your interactions with others when acknowledging their individual needs and situations?

_____

_____

The scenario presents an opportunity for Jenisse to think about her prior learning, notably that children, youth, and families bring their own experiences to situations and it is the responsibility of the practitioner to learn about these experiences through a co-constructed place of inquiry. Jenisse will be required to consider ways she can develop alternative perspectives of this family in order to support them through this conflict.

- What did I learn from this situation?

BIASES—SOMETHING TO THINK ABOUT

Biases are deeply held preferences based on an assumptive truth (Gharabaghi, 2008a, p. 193). While recognizing that everyone has biases, it is important for practitioners to develop awareness of them, to acknowledge they exist, and to ensure they do not influence one's actions in practice (Gharabaghi, 2008a). Jenisse's bias against working with parents relates to her own earlier experiences and warrants a discussion with her supervisor prior to the next meeting. Jenisse's lack of awareness of her bias influenced her reaction. How can one ensure that their biases do not influence one's actions in practice? It begins with awareness.

This scenario involving Jenisse represents one of the many challenges you will experience as a practitioner. Considering the range of individuals practitioners work with, who present with their own distinct needs and challenges, with whom might you feel challenged or hesitant to work? Who might you be more drawn to work with? This can include ages, gender, mental health challenges, behaviours, ethnicity, and other aspects. The purpose in identifying these hesitancies is not to discriminate or isolate those groups of people from your practice, but rather to support your awareness of the different biases you may hold (Gharabaghi, 2008a).

Exercise 36: Developing Awareness of Your Biases

Consider for a moment the people you are drawn to in your day-to-day interactions. This can be anyone, from your classmates and professors to individuals at your local coffee shop. Who do you prefer to engage with? For instance, when you approach the counter at your local coffee shop, who are you more inclined to engage in a discussion about their day? What is it about them, their style, their energy, their demeanour that makes this so?

Use the space below to respond to the questions above.

_____

_____

_____

Child and Youth Care Practitioners often have a bias toward those they have a preference for working with in practice (Gharabaghi, 2008a). Using the space below, identify the individuals or groups of people you may prefer to work with and those you may not. This will likely change over the course of your program as you engage in different experiences during your practice as a learning professional. For now, just focus on your preferences at this current time.

Identify if this preference is based on past experiences, current or previous knowledge, or assumptions, beliefs, or values. The intention here is not to defend your thinking but to further explore the basis for your thinking and to become more aware of the biases you hold.

_____

_____

_____

_____

_____

_____

_____

_____

_____

_____

_____

The case scenarios and exercises above provide valuable opportunities for further learning about self and the different ways of knowing that can influence your practice. By fostering greater self-awareness, you will recognize when you are not practicing from a place that aligns with professional Child and Youth Care practice and the barriers that prevent you from doing so.

Consider the Following Scenario: Dinar

Dinar is a single mom, in her first year of a Child and Youth Care Practitioner program. Her strong work ethic and family values influenced her decision to return to school and to pursue a profession that embodied helping others. During class, students were asked to think about aspects of their social locations and the potential impact on others. She acknowledged that being a mom, she would have plenty of advice to share with other moms and felt this would be a strong indicator of her CYC practice. One of her classmates challenged her by asking her to think about how that might come across to others.

Exercise 37: Conceptualizing Dinar from a Reflexive Lens

Identify the power differentials that underlie Dinar's way of knowing, based on her comment above.

_____

_____

What risks are there for Dinar in perceiving herself as an expert on motherhood?

_____

_____

How might this influence her interactions with other single moms? What expectations might she have for these moms? Consider the messages within these expectations.

_____

_____

Note any thoughts or comments that come up for you about this scenario.

_____

_____

Further Consideration

Using the space below, think of the biases you hold toward others currently, based on your day-to-day experiences. Think about those individuals you gravitate toward or are more responsive to and those you might avoid or who you might have strong opinions about (classmates, professors, supervisors, family members, community professionals, etc.). Identify their distinct characteristics to provide yourself with a reference point to explore further. For instance, if you gravitate toward individuals who are loud and boisterous and make you laugh, what is it about these traits you are drawn to? Is it the feeling you have when you are with them? Do they compensate for a lack of something in your own life? What are aspects of others you determine a dislike for upon first meeting or whose mannerisms "bother" you? Explore this thinking here. What is this dislike about? Do they remind you of someone from your past? Do they represent traits that you lack in yourself or dislike in yourself?

_____

_____

_____

_____

_____

_____

_____

_____

_____

_____

PRACTICE BEING REFLEXIVE

Reflexivity involves looking within (Bolton, 2009) and acknowledging both your emotions and the existing power dynamic that may be influencing your ways of knowing. Query these reactions to consider:

- What is this knowledge based on?
- What is the connection between how I am feeling and what I know?
- What is the connection between my knowledge and my power within my role as a learning professional?
- What is the connection between others' ways of knowing and the power within their role?

The more you attune to this awareness, the more you become aware and conscious of your ways of knowing. You will then be in a position to articulate *how you know what you know.*

In demonstrating reflexivity in your practice, you will recognize when issues of transference and countertransference occur. Countertransference, if you recall, occurs when the practitioner's conscious or unconscious emotional reactions are directed toward the other (Fox, n.d.). You must also be aware of transference, as it can also influence your ways of knowing if you are unaware.

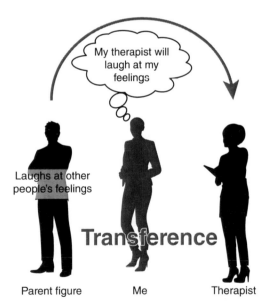

Figure 12: Transference
Source: 4bp.blogspot.com.

TRANSFERENCE

Fox (n.d.) describes transference as the individual's (child, youth, or family member) displacement of his/her/zi own feelings onto the practitioner, who possesses similar characteristics to significant people from the individual's past. When this occurs, their emotional reactions can heighten, and they respond according to their own emotions. Being aware of the potential for this to occur can help practitioners attune to their emotions while acknowledging that the other's reactions are not about them. This awareness will enable practitioners to separate their own reactions from the client's experiences.

Consider the Following Scenario: Zee

On Zee's first day at practicum at a women's shelter, she approached one of the children, Gi, to remind her about doing chores. Gi ignored Zee and, when she was reminded again, called Zee a bossy nag who was trying to control her. Zee, surprised and confused by Gi's response to her simple request, responded with another reminder about appropriate behaviour that only perpetuated Gi's silent reaction to Zee.

- What might have occurred in this response from Gi that would help us to consider this an example of transference?

    Zee would later think about the meaning of this interaction for Gi. In considering transference, Zee would wonder about who in Gi's past Zee reminded her of to have such a strong reaction toward her.

- What aspect of Zee was similar to Gi's mother's partner Tania, who was abusive and controlling?

Use the space below to note any comments or thoughts that come up for you.

_____

_____

Think of a time when you reacted toward someone in a way that may have seemed out of context to the situation. Perhaps your reaction(s) seemed extreme in the situation. Rather than focus on the details of the situation, think back to the individual you reacted to. Did they resemble someone from your past? What aspects of this interaction represented a similar experience for you from the past?

There is no need to write about this; rather, be aware of the potential trigger points you may experience in your practice. As you become more aware and embody the Child and Youth Care characteristics you learned about in the previous chapter, your inclination to react to others will lessen and you will adopt a more reflective, intentional response to others.

These situations also provide practitioners with the opportunity to reflect on these experiences afterwards, to assist them in understanding the basis for their reaction and to acknowledge the impact on the other (Fox, n.d.) and determine what next steps are required to prevent similar situations from occurring again (Garfat & Newcomen, 1992). In saying this, these experiences are not to be judged or considered a fault of the practitioner. Instead, they are another opportunity for learning more about self.

My actions are my only true belongings
—Thich Nhat Hanh

Children, youth, and family's internal and external influences of experiencing their world provide the lens from which they perceive it. Knowing this will affect your ways of doing and being in Child and Youth Care practice. This is an important reminder to consider when you are interacting with others who may not be accepting of your welcoming approach. How will you react? How might this make you feel? How do you prevent your feeling and the relative meaning you have created about this situation from influencing your reactions toward the other? Your awareness of the other's experiences necessitates a relational approach that embodies an acceptance and interest in learning more about the other's lived experiences through reflective inquiry as opposed to judging their actions. Engaging in reflective inquiry to explore the meaning of the experience for the practitioner leads to greater understanding and opportunities for further learning about self and ways to improve practice—the essence of reflective practice.

With each new experience comes opportunities for further learning. As you saw in the previous chapters, where you have engaged in different exercises, becoming reflexive in your thinking requires practice. These practices will support you in differentiating between a relational approach (that addresses the emotional, social, and spiritual growth of others) and a reactive and judgement-based perspective (that holds others responsible for your internal reactions).

REFLECTION

The definition of *reflection* has varied across the literature (Bolton, 2005, 2010; Boud, 1999; Dewey, 1933; Garfat & Fulcher, 2012; Moon, 2004; Rodgers, 2002). Much of the focus is on thinking about an experience and the impact on practice. Bellefeuille and Ricks (2010) describe reflection as a method of inquiry to establish an understanding and plan of action, whereas Schon (1983) describes it as thinking about one's own thinking and actions.

However, reflection is much more than thinking about an experience. It is a meaning-making process that moves beyond "What did I think about this?" to "What meaning have I made of this experience?" (Boud, Keogh, & Walker, 1985; Dewey, 1933; Garfat & Fulcher, 2012; Moon, 2004; Rodgers 2002) to influence action.

Reflection is considered an ongoing component of practice that takes time, awareness, and experiences (Bellefeuille & Ricks, 2010; Coulson & Harvey, 2013; Scott, 2010) and continues throughout the entirety of one's career.

John Dewey (1933) was an educator/philosopher whose contributions to the field of reflective practice are well-known across the literature (Moon, 2004; Rodgers, 2002). Fundamental to the reflective process, he believed, is the presence and meaning of experiences and the way one thinks about such experiences (Rodgers, 2002, p. 4). He also believed that one's emotions influenced context for the meaning individuals make of their experiences, which is fundamental to reflexivity. He developed four criteria of reflection that underlie the fundamental practice of reflective practice.

Dewey's criteria of reflective thought reinforces the dynamic, fluid processes involved in reflective practice and the thinking, rethinking, analyzing, and evaluating that is required when interacting with others whose experiences differ from your own.

Dewey's Four Criteria of Reflection

1. Reflection is a meaning-making process.
2. Reflection is a systematic, rigorous, disciplined way of thinking that evolves from scientific inquiry.
3. Reflection needs to happen in community, in interaction with others.
4. Reflection requires attitudes that value the personal and intellectual growth of oneself and of others.

REFLECTION IS A MEANING-MAKING PROCESS

As individuals bring their own experiences of situations, they create their own meaning of them, which explains the variance in practice and why the Code of Ethics cannot be perceived as defined solutions for complex issues. Practitioners want to focus on meaning and support others in understanding, more so than establishing an immediate solution that provides short-term change.

You have begun the initial processes for engaging in reflection. The previous exercises provided you with opportunities to think about your thinking and self and others as you explore the "whys" of your thinking and the potential "whats" of the impact on practice. In the following sections of the chapter, you will be introduced to reflective models that fit with the beginning professional's learning.

This introspective journey of the self will occur throughout your academic career and is essential to competent and ethical practice. The meaning one makes of experiences creates the impetus for further thinking. As identified above, it is the meaning of the experience that provides the focus for reflection more so than the actual event itself. When practitioners shift their meaning of situations, the situation changes.

Consider the Following Scenario: Todd and Kennedy

Todd and Kennedy are completing their second-year practicum at a community centre running groups for latency aged boys. After the evening group, both Todd and Kennedy commented that it was a great group. The meaning of "a great group" can vary between individuals, dependent upon a number of factors.

As you reflect on this, consider the meaning of their statement, *It was a great group.* Does a great group mean that there were no issues or conflict in the group? Or that Todd and Kennedy completed all requirements for the group program? What are the underlying assumptions of this great group statement?

Some practitioners believe that having no conflict can represent a great group. Let us consider the meaning within that statement, as this seems to imply that conflict is neither healthy nor conducive to a group. Whose needs is that evaluation based on?

Conflict provides opportunities for members to develop problem-solving, communication, and other skills. In saying this, would the group not benefit from experiencing conflict to develop these essential life skills? What are the potential implications for you as a practitioner and the children in this group if opportunities for conflict continue to be ignored? If they continue to experience these "great groups," whose needs is this based on? What is the experience for the group participants?

_____

_____

_____

_____

_____

_____

_____

_____

As practitioners embrace these group opportunities, they provide further learning for themselves while modelling healthy conflict resolutions skills for the group participants.

Something to Think About

- What are your perspectives about conflict?
- How do your perspectives influence your response to conflict?
- Do you appease others to avoid conflict? Do you acknowledge the conflict as an opportunity to engage in perspective-taking?
- Or do you assume a combative approach to challenge other perspectives and impose your own ways of thinking?

In thinking about your response to conflict, consider how this might influence your interactions with others and how others might perceive you.

_____

_____

_____

Identify any additional comments or questions you have.

_____

_____

Reflection is a systematic, rigorous, disciplined way of thinking.
  —Dewey, 1933

Practitioners engage in reflection with intention and purpose. As identified in the previous chapters, reflective practice is not a static, linear process, but a dynamic, methodical way of thinking about experiences and others (Moon, 2008). What you think about and the impact this has on practice requires an intentional and purposeful approach to engaging in reflection.

While these initial chapters have introduced you to the concept of reflection, you will learn about the different reflective models (Dewey, 1933; Moon, 2008; Schon, 1983) in upcoming chapters to guide you in thinking about and reflecting on practice. The common thread that links these frameworks is the intention for thinking, analyzing, and evaluating that each support.

You can do all the planning you wish; however, it is important that you create the space to be present to attend to what is occurring for the other person. If practitioners remain too focused on the outcome of their planning, their ability to be in the moment diminishes.

Reflection occurs in community and interaction with others.
  —Dewey, 1933

Child and Youth Care reflective practice does not occur in isolation from others; it requires practice experiences and relational interactions with others to occur. This being said, others, in addition to the children, youth, and families you work with, will include those professionals you interact with at different points of your practice: your supervisors, professors, peers and colleagues, and other community professionals. Regardless of your connections to others, each person you meet will influence your learning and development as a practitioner. The moment you determine that you cannot work with someone or you do not get along with someone provides an opportunity to engage in reflection.

GROUPS AND TEAMS

Child and Youth Care practice involves working with children, youth, families, colleagues, and other community professionals (Standards of Practice). Group work represents a significant part of student learning and often presents the most angst for students. Working with others with different values, ethics, and beliefs can be challenging at times; however, you do not work in isolation from others and the value of the team for reflective practice is significant. Personality dynamics, conflicts, and other factors can impede an effective working group. Taking what you have learned thus far, consider your own values and beliefs related to group work. If you value independence and leadership, there is a chance you will struggle to work effectively in groups.

Reflection requires a set of attitudes.
  —Dewey, 1933

Exercise 38: Contemplating the Group Experience

Reflect on your past experiences of groups and, in five words or less, describe your experience. Notice if you begin to engage in judgement or blaming others. Other are not responsible for what you say, do, or feel; only you are responsible. Pay attention to any assumptions that come up for you. How have others experienced you in groups? What role did you play in these past experiences?

_____

_____

_____

Reflect on your past experiences of groups to identify what you require for group experiences to be different for you. What is your role in influencing this change?

_____

_____

_____

Consider the distinct skills that relate to group work. Which of these skills are areas that you need to develop further?

_____

_____

_____

What role and responsibility do you have in influencing the group experience? Identify current potential experiences that would support this learning.

_____

_____

_____

Have you begun to implement those changes that you require? If not, what has prevented you?

_____

_____

_____

Dewey (1933) believed that reflective practice required a set of distinct attitudes that can impede or encourage one's ability to reflect open-mindedness/curiosity, wholeheartedness/presence, and responsibility/intentionality. In adopting these attitudes, practitioners are better able to consider different perspectives and new understandings, while demonstrating a commitment and awareness to their practice. This can be difficult at times as it requires students to step out of the comfort and familiarity of themselves to make room for the unknown.

To illustrate this point further, I ask that you consider the concept of *duty to report*. You will have learned that disclosures of abuse to self, disclosures of abuse from others, and potential risks of harm to self and others requires practitioners call the appropriate authorities (child welfare or the police, depending on the age of the child). What might you think about a parent who has expressed wanting to blow up their child's school? Is this a case for duty to report or is this an opportunity to reflect further on the context for her comment? How does one determine if this is a risk of threat or an expression of frustration toward a system that has failed to provide for her child's individual needs?

As discussed in the previous chapters, the Standards of Practice are guidelines for practice and are not absolutes. Responding to situations such as the one above requires practitioners to consider the issues related to cultural and human diversity[1] to determine the best course of action. This provides opportunities for practitioners to consider alternative ways of knowing, being, and doing Child and Youth Care practice.

A REFLECTIVE MOMENT

In the previous chapters, you were asked to explore and identify your values. Return to that list and reflect on the behaviours that are overt expressions of your values. How have these value-based behaviours been misinterpreted by others?

_____

_____

What assumptions have others made about you based on your ways of thinking, seeing, and being in the world?

_____

_____

How have these influenced your expectations of others? Of yourself as a learning professional?

_____

_____

These exercises have provided you with opportunities to explore aspects of self in order to develop as a reflective Child and Youth Care Practitioner and have prepared you to begin thinking about future action. Much of what you have read thus far has identified the importance of thinking about your experiences, others, and impact on practice. Reflective practice requires practitioners to further this thinking to create new experiences, new learning, and new action while ensuring your actions align with professional practice.

Consider your day-to-day experiences in class, at work, or in your personal life when you have looked back to a situation, thought about the experience, your interactions, and wished it had turned out differently. In thinking back to this situation and what you would have liked to have been different, did this lead to different action for next time? Following through on acknowledging what needs to be different is an important aspect of reflective practice. Thinking about the reasons you may not have responded differently in similar situations is the essence of reflection.

WHY REFLECT?

The function of reflection is to create meaning from experience by drawing connections and relations to previous experience, knowledge, and ideas (Dewey, 1933; Johns, 2009; Kolb, 1984; Rodgers, 2002). This process of thinking about what happened, the impacts of it, and identifying further learning aligns with Borton's reflective model of thinking, which will be introduced in the second part of this chapter.

Table 9: Benefits of Reflection

To understand why practitioners do what they do	To become aware of the emotions that influence my behaviour
To promote problem-solving skills	To explore the meaning I have attached to my experiences
To promote higher-order reasoning	To develop critical thinking skills
To take a closer look at their own ways of thinking	To view my behaviour from a distance
To test their judgements against those of others	To encourage accountability to practice
To consider different ways of thinking	To consider different perspectives
To demonstrate responsibility for their actions	To share and discuss ideas
To demonstrate competent and ethical practice	To understand self better
To demonstrate awareness of the impact of their actions on others	To empathize with others
To defend their actions and thought process with others	To identify areas to further develop or improve on

Practice in Reflection

Throughout the week, pay attention to situations you encounter that leave you feeling uncertain or wishing you had responded differently. Focus on the emotions and thoughts that come up for you. If you notice that you are blaming others for what happened, sit with this and acknowledge your own role in this situation. Use the template below to capture these experiences. Looking back on experiences will assist you in achieving greater understanding for what has occurred and, most importantly, acknowledging the role you played in these situations. You will notice through this process that your perspectives of the situation will shift; your awareness of self will develop.

Briefly describe what happened.

_____

_____

_____

Identify your emotions and thought process (i.e., what are you feeling and thinking).

_____

_____

What is your role in this? How did you contribute to this experience? (This can be based on what you did or didn't do.)

_____

_____

Briefly describe what happened.

_____

_____

_____

Identify your emotions and thought process (i.e., what are you feeling and thinking).

_____

_____

What is your role in this? How did you contribute to this experience? (This can be based on what you did or didn't do.)

_____

_____

Briefly describe what happened.

_____

_____

_____

Identify your emotions and thought process (i.e., what are you feeling and thinking).

_____

_____

What is your role in this? How did you contribute to this experience? (This can be based on what you did or didn't do.)

_____

_____

By engaging in reflection, practitioners are better able to discern the meaning they have created about situations, which can influence their interactions with others and their experiences of you (Garfat & Fulcher, 2012; Krueger, 2011). Your emotions and the meaning you have created become the focus of awareness to influence change, rather than the other's behaviours as the focus for change (Ricks, 1989). There is tremendous value in experiencing situations such as the one above, as it reminds you of the responsibility and accountability for your actions with others.

> To acquire knowledge, one must study; but to acquire wisdom, one must observe.
> —Marilyn vos Savant

CULTIVATING THE SKILL OF OBSERVATION

In Chapter 3, you were introduced to the concept of observation as a means for enhancing practice. In this chapter, you will further develop your skills by completing observation logs as a reference for your reflections. These observation logs[2] provide a framework for:

- creating meaning of others
- challenging assumptions
- enhancing understanding and knowledge
- reflecting upon experiences
- engaging in reflective inquiry
- discussing with others through collaborative reflection and reflective dialogues (see Chapter 12)
- informing future action

Remember that observing others extends beyond noticing surface behaviours. Remain open, attentive, and curious about what is unfolding before you. Observing others without engaging in the behaviour will provide you with the emotional distance and mindful practice of watching and noticing, which can lead to further understanding of others (Righton, 1983). In doing so, you will develop a greater understanding of human behaviour and the manner in which individuals influence and are influenced by their environment (Brockbank & McGill, 2007).

Revisiting Your Practice in Observing

In Chapter 3, you were introduced to different exercises to support your practice in observing others. It is important that this practice continues during your day-to-day interactions with others. If you recall, being present, noticing, and curiosity are important aspects of effective observations. Continue to observe others' body language, their facial expressions, the context for their behaviours, and the emotional tone within their comments. Be open to inquiry by asking yourself, "Does this align with what they say? What message is conveyed through their body language and facial expressions?" This is important to consider before engaging in the formal process of observing others.

ATTENTION TO EMOTIONS

In Chapter 3, you were introduced to the concept of the co-constructed space, the in-between space of interactions (Bellefeuille & Jamieson, 2008; Fewster, 1990b; Garfat, 2003b; Garfat & Fulcher, 2012; Mann-Feder, 1999). When first meeting someone, you will develop your own impression that can be influenced by previous experiences, knowledge, assumptions, and emotions. Can you identify times when you have had a gut response to someone? Recall how your initial impression influenced your ways of thinking and actions toward them.

This is important to consider when you are preparing to observe others, as your initial impression may influence your observations. Acknowledge the feeling you may be experiencing and explore the meaning through self-inquiry. Ask yourself what you are reacting to (the other person's tone, their comment, body language, whom they might represent, etc.). These are powerful indicators in understanding what influences your emotions. The key to effective observations is to not allow oneself to be influenced by assumptions or emotions (Brookfield, 1987).

THE OBSERVATION

Gannon (2002) urges practitioners to pay attention to the emotion underlying the behaviour and to distinguish between what signals concern and what is just a behaviour. For instance, some children who struggle with emotional dysregulation will express wanting

---

Observation Log

Name of the individual completing the form: **Date:**

What happened? What did you see? (Describe specific behaviours.) What did the other do? What is the evidence to support what you saw?

Who was involved? Adults, children? What was the nature of the interactions?

Where did this observation take place?

When did this observation take place?

How (if so) did you come to observe this situation? What is your understanding of what you observed (based on fact, not on your opinions)?

Reflection of the experience to include any of the following prompts as it relates to your experience: I think ... I want ... I realized ... I know ... I found out ... I thought I knew ... I was unaware ... I knew ... I felt ... I was overwhelmed by ... I went blank ... I wanted ... I am feeling ... I am wondering about.

Remaining questions/Next steps:

Signature

Figure 13: Observation Log Template
Source: Created by author.

Consider the Following Scenario: Bill

Bill, a second-year practicum student, was asked to observe a 10-year-old boy, Bruce, during art class as a part of his orientation for practicum. He was made aware that the child had struggled with overt behaviours over the past three weeks, and none of the interventions that had been tried had been successful in deterring his behaviours. Bruce, he was told, often arrived late to class and engaged in challenging behaviours. His supervisor recommended that Bill just observe Bruce over a week to identify any patterns or triggers in his behaviours. When Bill asked for further information about Bruce, his supervisor told him she did not want to risk influencing his observations and did not share any further information. The observation log in Figure 14 was completed after the third time observing Bruce. As you review this, pay attention to the emotional tone of this observation log and identify any areas of uncertainty for you.

to die in response to a challenging task. These comments, while concerning to hear, often represent their frustration and inability to express emotion. Through observations, you will distinguish between an intent to harm self (concern) and an expression of frustration (behaviour). It will be important to track their behaviours to develop a sense of the existing context that may be influencing their comments and behaviours. Context, as you recall, involves the circumstances that influence behaviours. These can be internal (emotions, temperament, ways of thinking, self-concept, and other underlying issues that can influence behaviours) and external factors (environmental, relational dynamics, weather, safety risks). It is recommended that you observe others in different environments to better establish the role that context contributes to the behaviours.

The template in Figure 13 provides you with an overview of what to observe, which can assist you in further clarifying your reflections as you look back to consider the details of events.

In reviewing these observation logs after a week, you may have identified patterns or themes that will provide you with an opportunity to further explore. This may not occur all the time; however, considering where there are issues or questions you have about what you have observed can support you in engaging in reflective inquiry. What are you most curious about? What uncertainties arise for you? What new information have you established about the other from these observations? These questions are reflective in nature and are intended to assist you in expanding your ways of knowing about others that will inform your actions. Completed observation logs can be used as a focus for written reflections and reflective dialogues (Stevens & Cooper, 2009), which will assist you in developing as reflective practitioners.

Brockbank and McGill (2007) have identified the following prompts as beneficial to include in the reflective portion of the observation log: *I think ... I want ... I realized ... I know ... I found out ... I thought I knew ... I was unaware ... I knew ... I felt ... I was overwhelmed by ... I went blank ... I wanted ... I am feeling ... I am wondering about.*

Unless we are in touch with the child who speaks, the child to whom we should listen, we can know nothing about what it is that the worker needs to do and needs to be.
—Peter Righton, 2006

Observation Log

Name of the individual completing the form: *Bill C*   **Date:** *Nov. 10, xxxx*

What happened? What did you see? (Describe specific behaviours.) What did the other do? What is the evidence to support what you saw?

I observed Bruce arrive to class half an hour late. He threw his bag down and joined a group of children who were working on their art project. He seemed angry that the group had started without him, as he approached them with an angry expression and asked why they didn't wait for him, and when they ignored him, he banged his hand on the table. When one of the other children said to stop, Bruce mimicked him and grabbed his pencil out of his hand and threw it across the table. He said loudly, "That's what you get for ignoring me." The teacher called out to Bruce to leave the group and sit at the back table by himself. Bruce ignored the teacher and tried to talk to the other children in this group about what they were doing. When they ignored him, he kicked the table and yelled, "Stop ignoring me." The teacher called out again to Bruce and said, "When you disrupt the group, Bruce, no one will listen to you." This seemed to anger Bruce further as he banged his hand on the table again and grabbed another child's pencil and threw it across the room. The teacher told him to leave the class to go to the principal's office. As he grabbed his bag, he kicked another child's chair and knocked the pens off the table and left the room.

Who was involved? Adults, children? What was the nature of the interactions?

The art teacher tried to redirect Bruce, but this seemed to anger him. The children in Bruce's art group (4 children) ignored Bruce, even when he tried to get their attention.

Where did this observation take place? *This observation occurred in the art room, during art class after lunch.*

When did this observation take place? *This observation occurred after lunch.*

How (if so) did you come to observe this situation? What is your understanding of what you observed (based on fact, not on your opinions)?

I was asked to observe Bruce to identify any triggers or patterns for his behaviours. Bruce seemed to try to participate with his group, but they ignored him. This seemed to bother him a lot, based on his reactions and attempts to get their attention. The teacher did not seem to be aware that he was getting angry because they were ignoring him. She didn't seem to hear what he said to the other kids about not ignoring him.

Reflection of the experience to include any of the following prompts as it relates to your experience: I think … I want … I realized … I know … I found out … I thought I knew … I was unaware … I knew … I felt … I was overwhelmed by … I went blank … I wanted … I am feeling … I am wondering about.

I think that lunchtime might be an issue for Bruce, as he is always late and seems angry when he arrives. Maybe he doesn't eat lunch or maybe he is doing something that upsets him. I think that he tried hard to get involved with his group, but their ignoring him really bothered him and could be a trigger that sets off his behaviours. I wanted to point out to the group that he is trying to involve himself and that their ignoring wasn't helping. I also think Bruce might feel angry because the teacher is not trying to help him get involved in his group. This was frustrating for me to watch because I think he may not have reacted like he did if the other kids had responded to him or if the teacher had come over and helped him get started.

Remaining questions/Next steps:

How will Bruce experience success with his peers if they ignore him? Can I work with him to develop the skills for working with others?

Figure 14: Bill's Sample Observation Log

Source: Created by author.

As discussed above, observation logs can assist practitioners in recommending or discussing a course of action with others to best meet their developmental, emotional, social, and spiritual needs. This process of thinking about what happened, the impact on, and identifying further learning opportunities aligns with Borton's reflective model of thinking.

Figure 15: Borton's (1970) What, So What, Now What model
Source: Adapted from Borton (1970).

Borton's reflective model (1970) represents more of a linear process that is beneficial for practitioners to adopt in the early stages of their learning. This model provides a framework to engage in reflective thought, which is useful in identifying further learning as a means to grow and develop in practice. Reflection, as you recall, involves more than just thinking about a past experience; it involves thinking about the meaning you created of the situation and your response to this meaning. Through reflection, practitioners will discover that the meaning they have created of the situation may not always reflect an accurate depiction of the situation. The beauty of reflection is that it allows time for practitioners to look back on the event and unpack their thinking about it. New discoveries and personal insights are often established when practitioners reflect on their experiences.

The *What* involves a description of the situation (the event, who was involved, the context).

The *So What* involves identifying your interpretations (creating meaning) and response to the situation (your thoughts, emotions, the meaning you established, and your actions).

The *Now What* involves deciding what you will do as a result (your plan of action).

Consider the Following Scenario: Shannon

Shannon, a second-year practicum student, was preparing for the weekly girls' group. She often dreaded this group, as she found teen girls to be too much into their drama. It made her cringe; their comments and attempts to show each other up was too much at times. On this particular night, one of the girls, Ruby, arrived early to assist her in setting up. It had only been two weeks, but Shannon noticed Ruby was always making an effort to help the other girls and Shannon. Shannon enjoyed this pre-group time alone and groaned when Ruby walked in. Shannon did not have the energy for talking and realized this was due to the late night before. She said hi to Ruby as she walked in and kept busy with other tasks as a means to deter Ruby from engaging with her. When Ruby approached her, Shannon pretended not to hear, hoping Ruby would leave until group was ready to start. Ruby left shortly after and did not return to the group. When Shannon later asked the other group members about Ruby's whereabouts, one shrugged and explained that Ruby had left upset earlier. When Shannon left group that night, she experienced a pang of guilt and wondered if she was responsible for Ruby leaving. She reflected on this after the group.

Review Borton's framework to follow Shannon's thinking about the night and add in your own thoughts or questions.

What

As I set up for girls' group, I remembered thinking I was not in the mood to talk to anyone. When Ruby, one of the girls from the group, arrived to help, I distracted myself with set up, hoping she would busy herself with other tasks. She left without saying goodbye.

So What

Ruby likes to talk about her day and ask for advice about peer issues (assumption), and I was not in the mood for this. She can be so needy (creating meaning) and it's exhausting. I realized I had nothing to give to her tonight and hoped by ignoring her (response) she would figure it out herself.

Now What

I realized I let my own feelings of fatigue interfere with being present for Ruby. I assumed she wanted advice again about her relationship and ignored her. I find it frustrating when I give her advice she is asking for, since she ignores it and brings up the same issue time and again. I did not have the energy for her tonight. How do I let her know this without offending her? Maybe I just follow up with her and acknowledge she may have wanted to talk, and I didn't create the space for her to do this. I also realize staying up late the night before practicum is not beneficial. Perhaps I could have listened to her and then encouraged her to think of what she could do instead of always responding with ideas (further learning). I'll need to follow up with her next week before group to apologize for being so rude (further learning).

Shannon's reflection revealed her frustration with Ruby and the impact her frustration seemed to have on her ability to be available for Ruby. She also recognized a pattern in Ruby's behaviours that will warrant exploring with Ruby. Shannon is beginning to identify that providing advice is not beneficial and wonders about how to share this with Ruby. How might she continue to support Ruby's need for guidance without telling her what to do?

Use the space provided to identify any comments or questions you have about Shannon's reflection. Would you have identified a different approach in following up with Ruby?

_____

_____

_____

_____

_____

_____

_____

_____

_____

_____

_____

_____

_____

_____

The following scenario provides you with another opportunity to reflect on an experience utilizing Borton's model. As you review the following case scenario, imagine that you are the practitioner in the scenario. Pay attention to emotions or thoughts that come up for you and questions you may have about this scenario. Complete the reflective template below based on your experience. It is important that you complete this individually, as this is based on your experience of the scenario and not based on _right action_ or the _right responses_. Pay attention to your emotions and thought process and the interpretations you make based on this scenario, and let this guide your reflection. This exercise provides you with an opportunity to explore your own ways of thinking.

Consider the Following Scenario: Luca

Luca is a 15-year-old youth who was recently admitted to open custody for three months. He was charged for obstruction to property. His therapist, who had been working with Luca for the past year, submitted a report to the custody house outlining his strengths, challenges, and recommendations for supporting him. As the Child and Youth Care Practitioner, you declined to read the report, believing it would influence your perspectives of Luca and decided it was more important to learn about him through your interactions. That very night, Luca and his peers were caught with alcohol in the rec room and were subsequently placed on restricted community access as a result. You approach Luca and let him know of the consequences and ask him why he would do such a thing after having just been placed in custody. You then remind him that there will be more serious consequences if he continues this again. He tells you to stop being fake about caring for him and tells you to get lost. The following day, the therapist calls you to point out this could have been avoided if you had read the report. Your supervisor wants to meet with you to discuss this.

Exercise 39: Practicing with Borton's What, So What, Now What Model

What: Briefly describe what occurred, and who was involved.

_____

_____

_____

_____

So What: How do you understand Luca's behaviours with his peers? His reaction toward you? Identify any emotions and thoughts that come up for you. How might you respond to the therapist who challenged your decision to avoid reading the report? Give thought to the consequences and your decision to avoid reading the report.

_____

_____

_____

_____

Now What: What will do you? Consider any follow-up that is necessary with Luca, the therapist, or others. How might similar situations be avoided in the future?

_____

_____

_____

_____

Use the space below to identify any further questions or comments that you have.

_____

_____

_____

_____

The problem is not the problem. The problem is your attitude about the problem.
 —Captain Jack Sparrow, *Pirates of the Caribbean*

The above quote presents a strong reminder that one's ways of knowing are influenced by personal beliefs, values, and assumptions. In assuming a reflexive lens, it is important to consider the implicit message in declining to read a youth's report. This case scenario provides you an opportunity to think about how reading reports will influence your perspectives about others. The scenario illustrates the risks in not reading the report and the implicit power that underlies this way of thinking. Consider the purpose of reports and the benefits this can have for the children, youth, and families you work with. How might not reading reports impact your interactions with others? What information do reports offer that would enhance a child's care? Use the space below to respond to the questions above and discuss with a partner.

When we abandon curiosity for judgment, we lose a little of our CYC selves.
 —Donicka Budd, 2017

Authors of reports provide a perspective based on their own experience of others. Each experience you encounter need not be defined by others' experiences. Considering other community professional perspectives is another aspect of reflective practice.

RETURNING TO LUCA

Imagine that you have gone back into Luca's file to read his therapist's report. The therapist described Luca's history of child abuse that resulted in a traumatic brain injury that has impaired his decision-making skills. As a result, Luca's potential to engage in high-risk behaviours with peers is significant, and he requires close supervision when with others.

Practice Reflection—Borton's Reflective Model

As discussed in the previous chapter, reflective practice requires that practitioners objectively evaluate their approach and identify key areas for further learning in order to improve in practice (Finlay, 2008; Kruger, 2011), while embracing moments of uncertainty. Evaluating your practice takes practice, and it is recommended you continue to complete the tasks included in each chapter. For the next few days, pay attention to situations you encounter that challenge you and capture these using Borton's template.

Practice Reflection

What: Briefly describe what occurred, and who was involved.

_____

_____

_____

_____

_____

So What: Describe your interpretation of the situation, including your thoughts and emotions.

_____

_____

_____

_____

_____

Now What: Describe what it is that you will do, based on your current knowledge and skills as a developing Child and Youth Care Practitioner.

_____

_____

_____

_____

_____

Use the space below to identify any further questions or comments that you have.

_____

_____

_____

_____

Checking In

Where are you at with the concepts and exercises you have learned so far? What is making sense? What is not? What questions do you have that warrant further exploration to support your thinking? Take pause to think about your learning and respond to the questions above.

_____

_____

_____

Reflective practice also involves considering the perspectives of others and how others may perceive you. In thinking about what you have learned up to this point, how might you respond to the situation below from a reflexive, reflective lens?

Consider the Following Scenario: Krista

Krista started her practicum at an elementary school, supporting children in the classroom. When one of the children threw his math sheet after marking it with a big X, Krista approached him and acknowledged his frustration with the work. After coaching him to take in a few mindful breaths, she sat with him to support him in completing the work. After class, the teacher approached Krista and commented about her "buying into his manipulation." "You know," the teacher said, "he does this for attention."

Reflect on the meaning that this teacher's comments might have for you (focus on the emotions, thought process, and assumptions).

_____

_____

_____

How might this meaning influence your perspectives toward the teacher?

_____

_____

_____

What perspectives might this teacher have of the child and Krista's approach? Pay attention to any judgement you might have toward the teacher.

_____

_____

_____

In considering further action that is required, how might you approach the teacher? How might your awareness of her perspectives influence your approach toward the teacher? Include any additional comments or questions you have about this scenario.

_____

_____

_____

Share and discuss with a partner.

REFLECTIVE MOMENT

What is your understanding of other professionals who will or have questioned your approach as a Child and Youth Care Practitioner? Use the space below to explore your thinking around this.

_____

_____

_____

> If we are too attached to ideas and practices, we do not have the freedom to love others.
> —Balmer, 2018

The following chapters will focus on the more complex processes of reflective thinking and critical thinking. While the previous chapters have introduced you to the initial processes involved in reflective practice and reflection, the more complex concepts of reflective practice will shift you away from merely thinking about your ways of knowing to analyzing and evaluating your actions and the impact they have on your practice. Engaging in reflective and critical thinking will require those _real-life_ experiences that your practicum will provide. As you begin practicing as a Child and Youth Care Practitioner, you will apply your learning to your day-to-day experiences, which will provide you with opportunities to engage in reflective practice. Your reflections will also begin to include other students to further enhance the importance of considering alternative perspectives that will influence your learning.

CLOSING THOUGHTS

What did you learn about yourself from the concepts discussed in this chapter?

_____

_____

_____

What is the connection between observing others and reflective practice?

_____

_____

_____

How will your new learning influence your interactions with others?

_____

_____

_____

What questions remain for you still?

_____

_____

_____

NOTES

1. Acknowledging your bias in practice relates to the core competency of Professionalism and the Code of Ethics, responsibility to the child, youth, and family (Code of Ethics; CYCCB, 2018).
2. Templates of the observation logs are located in Appendix VIII at the back of the book.

CHAPTER 7

Reflective Thinking

Reflective thinking turns experience into insight.

—John C. Maxwell

LEARNING OBJECTIVES

In this chapter, you will:

- be introduced to and define reflective thinking
- explore the concept of uncertainties in practice
- revisit reflective inquiry as an aspect of reflective thinking
- apply the reflective thinking model to current events and case scenarios
- be introduced to and apply the Reflective Process Model to case scenarios and your practice
- be introduced to and apply Schon's reflective models to case scenarios and your practice
- differentiate between Schon's Reflection on Action and Reflection in Action reflective models
- identify further learning from experiences
- explore the concept of relationship repair as it relates to identifying further action

In the previous chapter, you were introduced to the concepts of reflexivity and reflection. Reflexivity, as you recall, is a thinking *within* process (Bolton, 2009) that involves the awareness of one's personal internal process (values, assumptions, thoughts, emotions) in relation to others (D'Cruz, 2007; Moon, 2004), whereas reflection is thinking *beyond* one's internal experience to consider the minute details of the event (Bolton, 2009: Johns, 2009): the *what happened* to *what I did and the impact on others.*

You will notice that there is less structure for the case scenario questions as you begin to apply your learning from previous chapters to the case scenarios and your day-to-day

Figure 1: Reflective Practice Radial

Source: Recreated by author.

experiences as a practitioner. This will assist you in thinking about your interactions during practice and to prepare you for the more advanced processes of critical thinking and collaborative reflection, which will support you in developing further awareness about the process of your work (Garfat & Ricks, 1995) with others and your intentions for practice.

REFLECTIVE THINKING

Dewey (1971) described thinking as a process of questioning, analyzing, turning over, probing, or delving into in order to find something new or to be perceived in a different way. Suspending judgement gives rise to doubt, which is essential during this process of inquiry and reflective thinking (Bellefeuille & Ricks, 2010; Dewey, 1971; Garfat & Fulcher, 2012; Krueger, 2005). In order to effectively engage in reflective thinking, practitioners are required to have a firm sense of self (Brockbank & McGill, 2007); an awareness of their values, beliefs, and social location will better enable them to challenge their assumptions and to consider alternative perspectives to analyze and evaluate their decisions to take informed action (Brockbank & McGill, 2007; Dewey, 1971; Moon, 2008). Through this process of analysis, practitioners query their current knowledge related to Child and Youth Care practice (what do I know), identify what they do not know and what there is to know to determine a more holistic understanding of the situation, in the sense that they are considering other perspectives through a process of reflective inquiry. This will be a result of their observations and interactions with others and their indirect experiences relating to written reports and news events, all of which provide diverse learning experiences to reflect upon.

> Reflection is a systematic, rigorous, disciplined way of thinking that evolves from scientific inquiry.
> —Dewey, 1933

Revisiting Reflective Inquiry

Thinking is questioning (Dewey, 1971) that assists practitioners in connecting their knowledge and ways of knowing to better understand other perspectives (Lyons, 2010). By engaging in reflective inquiry, practitioners demonstrate an openness, a curiosity to consider the diverse perspectives of others. As discussed in previous chapters, engaging in reflective inquiry requires practitioners to be intentional in their questions (Garfat & Fulcher, 2012) by ensuring they bring further understanding about others' experiences (Lyons, 2010; Ricks, 1997) that will assist practitioners in expanding their ways of knowing (Dewey, 1933; White, 2007) to influence new ways of doing.

In being intentional, practitioners narrow their focus to thinking about issues unique to the individual as opposed to the superficial, general questions that limit the potential for learning. Dewey (1933) believed that engaging in active inquiry requires careful deliberation of issues that underlie reflective thinking. These questions will provide you with context from which further questions evolve. Superficial questions lack depth and do not generate knowledge or further learning.

Revisiting Kelly

Kelly, the 15-year-old youth who was moved 13 times in two years, was first introduced to you in Chapter 4 to reinforce the concept of context and meaning-making. What information will assist you in better understanding Kelly and her individual needs in order to provide a different experience at her new residential home? As you think about your questions through reflective inquiry, ensure that they do not imply judgement. Consider the intent behind the questions (to seek understanding, to provide her a different experience).

Review the questions below, and pay attention to implicit messages embedded in each.

1. Why was she moved 13 times? What did she do to be moved 13 times?
    Both of these questions imply judgement and are superficial in nature. These questions are implicit in holding Kelly solely responsible for these moves and do not consider the greater context in which these moves occurred. What have we learned to support our understanding of Kelly and what she requires for a new experience to occur?
2. What was missing from her experiences at these previous homes? What did she require to experience a sense of security at these homes?
    These questions are intended to establish an understanding of her experiences. They are investigation-oriented questions that query the context for these moves.

Everything Child and Youth Care practitioners do is intentional and purposeful.
—Garfat & Fulcher, 2012

In Chapter 3, you were introduced to the concept of intentionality as a key characteristic of Child and Youth Care practice. Each decision you make, each interaction you approach requires you to be intentional in your actions and always acting in the best interest of others. Recall your reasons for pursuing the field of Child and Youth Care practice.

Many learning professionals will and have attested that becoming a practitioner has provided them with opportunities to offer a different experience to children and youth who have similar histories as they themselves have, while others will attest that becoming a practitioner has and will enable them to change the system they were once part of. Still others will acknowledge their love for children and youth, working with others, and pride themselves on being a strong mentor and "advisor" to friends and family. It simply isn't enough to acknowledge your intention to want to help others or change the systems in place to support children and youth. One must be committed to a process of conscious inquiry that is free of judgement and open to considering all ideas that confirm or deny the validity of the intentions behind one's actions.

Consider the idea of wanting to change the different systems in place to support children and youth. The idea is often based on wanting to do better and often begins with what is wrong with certain systems. Focusing on what is "wrong" implies judgement and leaves little room for doubt, which is pivotal to reflective thinking (Dewey, 1933). If you are thinking about changing an entire system without breaking that system down into parts that enable you to understand the larger system more clearly, you will be overwhelmed. This same concept applies to when you are approaching a child presenting with behaviours. Responding without considering the context risks perpetuating this behaviour and a reactive response from the practitioner will lead to little or no change in this behaviour. Where, then, do you start?

Let us explore the diverse elements of the reflective thinking model.

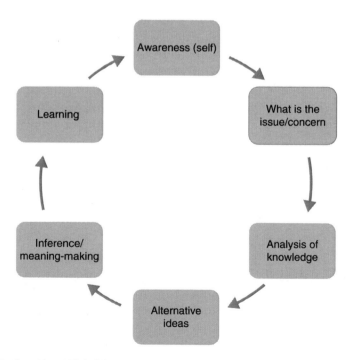

Figure 16: Reflective Thinking Model

Source: Adapted from Gibbs (1988), Dewey (1933).

The Reflective Thinking Model[1]

The reflective thinking model provides a framework for exploring complex situations that do not have an easy solution, despite best intentions. Thinking about complex situations can result in complex approaches that will only confuse and overwhelm practitioners. Adopting an intentional approach to complex situations will support practitioners to slow down their thinking and avoid unnecessary, superficial, or heightened responses that will only further complicate these complex situations. Where to start?

Start from where you are at:

1. **Awareness**

   Check in with self. How are you feeling and thinking about this issue?

2. **Define the issue**

   What specific change is warranted? What do you know about the system in question for such changes to occur? What is there to know that will provide you with a more balanced perspective (judgement-free) of the system and potential for changes you are seeking to make?

3. **Analysis of knowledge**

   Dewey's (1933) second criterion of reflective thinking speaks to the systematic, rigorous, disciplined way of thinking that underlines the analysis aspect of the reflective thinking model. The manner in which practitioners analyze their current knowledge and the knowledge that they require to inform their understanding relates to the systematic process for thinking about experiences.

   • What do you know?

   Consider the knowledge you have acquired about Child and Youth Care practice and reflective practice. How has this learning connected to the different case scenarios you have been introduced to? How has this knowledge influenced your interactions with others in your practice?

   In previous chapters, you were introduced to Bronfenbrenner's ecological systems theory, social location, and worldviews as ways to understand the internal and external contexts that influence others. These different concepts provide you with a point of reference for which to explore and consider alternative perspectives that enable practitioners to develop new ways of thinking about others, their experiences, and their approach to practice.

   • What is there still to know?

   Consider the ways you have generated knowledge about others. Through inquiry you have challenged your ways of knowing to determine that there is still more to know. What questions remain for you about these others? Their experiences? Their perspectives? How will this lack of information influence your interactions with them?

4. **Alternative ideas**

   How, if at all, has your inquiry above shifted your thinking about this issue? What additional ideas have you considered that may explain or lead to further action required for this situation?

5. **Establishing inference/meaning-making**

   How do you understand this issue, based on your analysis? Based on what you know and what you identify as still needing to know, what is your understanding of this issue?

6. **Learning**

   What have you learned that you can transfer to your practice? How might this new learning influence your approach with youth in care? What aspects of theory do you need to consider in this situation? What further action is required to prevent future similar situations?

Exercise 40: Kelly: A Case for Reflective Thinking

Utilizing the reflective thinking model will support you in querying the greater sociocultural context that influenced Kelly's multiple moves.

1. Awareness

What was your initial reaction to the scenario involving 15-year-old Kelly and her multiple moves? Notice the emotions and the initial thoughts that arose and list them below.

_____

_____

_____

_____

2. Define the issue

What is the presenting concern? Thirteen moves in two years of Kelly being in care. Before determining if this is typical of system care, consider the impact these multiple moves have had on her emotional and spiritual development.

_____

_____

_____

_____

3. Analysis of knowledge

What do you know about Child and Youth Care practice that relates to this situation? All behaviours serve a purpose (Garfat, 1992). Exploring the context that surrounds this scenario requires you to establish what there is to know about system care and the nature of relational practice.

Assume the role of the investigator to access the necessary information to include here. Include your current learning about relational practice as well.

_____

_____

_____

_____

What else is there to know? This is an opportunity to engage in reflective inquiry. Which questions will you consider to support your understanding of Kelly's experience? You may wish to refer to the template in Appendix V. List your questions in the space below. If you choose to create your own, ensure you are differentiating between superficial, general questions and intentional, deliberate questions that will lead to further learning. It is important to keep with the line of questioning, rather than jump ahead to the solutions. Inferences (or creating meaning), however, are ideas that result from the answers to the questions. The questions you ask will change with each situation or issue that is presented to you; however, the process for analyzing, inferring, and learning will remain consistent.

_____

_____

_____

_____

_____

4. Alternative ideas

How has your inquiry above shifted your thinking about this issue? What ideas have you identified that may be worth considering, as a result of the questions you addressed?

_____

_____

_____

_____

5. Inference/meaning-making

How do you understand this issue, based on your analysis? Can you establish a hypothesis about what has happened, based on your inquiry? Establishing a hypothesis refutes the potential for doubt and judgement and is not to be perceived as fact. At times, working from a hypothesis provides a chance to test out your ways of thinking. Monitor your thinking to ensure you are not querying diagnostic labels. This is beyond your scope as Child and Youth Care Practitioners. Consider Kelly's unique needs that may not have been adequately met in a home with rotating staff and five to seven other youth.

_____

_____

_____

_____

6. Learning

What have you learned that you can transfer to your practice? How might this new learning influence your approach with youth in care? What aspects of theory do you need to consider in this situation? What further action is required to prevent future similar situations?

_____

_____

_____

_____

The value you receive from reflective thinking will depend on the kinds of questions you ask yourself.
—John C. Maxwell

It is important to stay with inquiry, rather than jump ahead to solutions (Bellefeuille & Ricks, 2010; Ricks, 1997). The inferences (or meaning) you establish are based on your inquiry and will change depending on the situations or issue you are exploring. Possessing an understanding of the distinct theoretical models can assist practitioners in enhancing their understanding of others. While it is not the intention of this book to differentiate and explore the diverse theoretical frameworks that underlie Child and Youth Care practice (with the exception of Bronfenbrenner's ecological theory, which was introduced previously and is referenced throughout this book), these do provide a reference to assist you in understanding or defending the rationale for your practice.

Table 10: Theoretical Frameworks

Theoretical framework	Overview
Maslow's Hierarchy of Needs	Hierarchy of five levels of basic needs: physiological, safety, needs of love, affection, and belonging; need for esteem; need for self-actualization.
Circle of Courage	A model of positive youth development that assumes a holistic approach for child-rearing and child development based on Indigenous philosophies, education, youth work, and resilience research (Brendtro, Brokenleg, & Van Bockern, 2002). The model is based on four universal growth needs of all children: belonging, mastery, independence, and generosity (Brendtro et al., 2009).
Bronfenbrenner's Ecological Systems	Environmental elements of an individual's life affect their development (microsystem, macrosystem, mesosystem, chronosystem) and impact an individual's function.
Relational Practice	The fundamental agent of change in Child and Youth Care Practice is the relationship between practitioner and individual.
Attachment Theory	The presence or absence of key individuals in a child's life can impede or encourage their development.
Erikson's Developmental Theory	As children grow, they transition through distinct developmental stages that foster or inhibit their social, emotional, and physical growth.
Family Systems Theory	A systems approach to creating change. Difficulties are not isolated to the individual child; they are created and maintained by the interactions within the family. Changes in one aspect of the system create changes in other aspects of the system.
Trauma-informed Theory	Many individuals you will work with have experienced one sense of trauma or another that will impact their social, emotional, and developmental growth and require trauma-informed approaches to aid their development. Using behavioural approaches are not effective in supporting an individual to reconcile their previous trauma.

The models listed here are meant to provide an overview and are not a detailed summary of each theory. For more information, refer to course material and corresponding texts from your program.

There will be times when your approach is called into question and with time, knowledge, skill, and experiences you will be able to discern the distinct theoretical frameworks that underlie your approach to practice, which provide an understanding for why you do what you do (Garfat & Fulcher, 2012). Similarly, as you engage with the reflective journals and reflective dialogues in the following chapter, you may begin to notice which theoretical model influences your approach most.

Continue to pay attention to your internal reactions, notably the urge to respond with judgement or with routine-oriented replies. Take a step back to determine how these responses serve others and you. "It is not all about you" can be a helpful reminder to keep things in perspective. Returning to the place of empathy, one of the core conditions in Child and Youth Care practice, and embodying presence and curiosity can support you in considering alternative ways of knowing, being, and doing.

CONSIDERING ALTERNATIVE PERSPECTIVES

The benefits of engaging in *what-if* questions to consider alternative perspectives is outlined in the literature (Garfat & Ricks, 1995). What-if questions shift the focus from a lens of knowing to a lens of inquiry that allows for new ways of knowing, which can shed valuable insight into how these experiences may influence other worldviews. Review the questions below and notice your internal reactions.

- What if you were blamed for you and your sibling's apprehension into care?
- What if you were told how *bad* you are every day as an eight-year-old child?
- What if this was the fifth time your parents didn't show up for a supervised access visit?
- What if you were responsible for taking children away from their family each and every day? How might this influence your interactions with families?
- What if you did not value relationship as essential to change? How might this influence your approach with others?
- What if you were a 15-year-old youth who had moved 13 times in the past two years? What might you think about adults, caregivers, and the system?
- What if you believed that no good could ever come from anything? How might you think about the future?

- What if you were told that you could never see your family again and then were expected to call your foster parents "Mom" and "Dad"?
- What if your teacher wrote in your agenda about all of the bad things you did each day?
- What if the only way a child knew how to express his hurt was through swearing?
- What if you are the fourth CYC for a 10-year-old child? How willing would she be to trust you?
- What if adolescents in care had five different workers in the past two years?

Use the space below to add in your own what-if questions.

_____

_____

_____

Exercise 41: What If?

Select two to three what-if scenarios from the above list as a frame of reference to explore alternative perspectives. List the scenario in the respective spaces and fill in the columns. The first one has been completed as an example.

As you consider the diverse perspectives from the scenarios, consider what other questions might inform your inquiry. List these in the final column. Ensure your focus of inquiry is intentional in assisting you to understand this individual.

This exercise will assist you in seeking to understand another's experiences, which will influence your interactions with them. Within this lies the opportunity to seek further knowledge about their circumstances from a sociocultural perspective. For instance, in the example, what further questions might this lead you to ask: what larger organizational structures are in place for a child's care? What about the child's experiences? How might these contextual factors influence the worldviews and further experiences of the children in the what-if scenarios? Using the space below the table, list any questions or comments you have.

What-if scenario	What emotions might they have? Try to go beneath the presenting anger you might expect.	Thinking: What meaning might they have created from these experiences?	How might their emotions and ways of thinking influence their behaviours?	What additional questions might you have to assist your understanding of others?
Example: What if adolescents in care had five different workers in the past two years?	Uncertain, confused, numb, empty.	Why do workers leave? Is it because of me? I must have done something for them to leave. Can't trust adults to stick around. Can't rely on adults.	Distant; would not open up to others. Wanting to do things for self.	How did these relationships end? Was there a process involved for these relationship endings? Were they made aware in advance of the workers leaving? Did they have a choice in who their workers were?

The following case scenario will provide a frame of reference to learn about the remaining concepts of reflective practice and to support your understanding of both Xandu and Challah's experiences. Apply the reflective thinking model to this scenario and respond to the questions that follow. List any additional questions or comments that you have about this case.

Exercise 42: Applying the Reflective Thinking Model to Xandu and Challah

Challah is a 15-year-old youth who has been in the care of Child Welfare for the past six years. She is a new resident at Dee's Home for Youth, having moved in this very night. She previously lived in a foster home for four years and has been in residential home care for the past two years. Challah previously had a close relationship with her foster parents; however, they decided to retire and would no longer be caring for Challah. She moved to another foster home at that time and was removed within a month as a result of her aggressive, non-compliant behaviours. Since then, she has moved between three residential homes within the past two years. She was discharged from her most recent residential home as a result of her non-compliant behaviours. It was recommended that she be placed in a foster home as the smaller setting may be more fitting for her needs; however, Challah declined and agreed to another residential home instead.

Dee's Home for Youth is a co-ed residential home for adolescents. Xandu is one of the Child and Youth Care Practitioners and has worked at the home for 15 years and prides zirself as an authority figure, which has often led to several power struggles with the youth and staff. Zi often enforces strict rules about how the program runs, which has led to staff referring to zir as a "sergeant on duty." The night before Challah arrived, the supervisor made Xandu and the other practitioners aware of the new intake, adding a summary report would be available for them to review. Xandu declined to read the report as zi did not want to risk being influenced by another's perspective. Based on the information provided, apply the reflective thinking model to this case. Remember that reflective thinking is not about reaching a solution, but is designed to enhance your understanding and learning about the diverse experiences and perspectives of others.

1. Awareness

What are your initial assumptions of this case scenario? What did you feel or think about what you have read? How will you challenge your assumptions and ensure that your emotions and thoughts do not influence your perspectives of this case scenario?

_____

_____

_____

2. Define the Issue

What is the presenting concern?

_____

_____

_____

3. Analysis of Knowledge

What do you know about this situation/individual (based on the information presented to you)? How does this issue connect to Child and Youth Care practice, knowing what you know?

_____

_____

_____

What Else Is There to Know (Inquiry)?

What information is important for you to establish an understanding of this youth and her experiences? List the questions that form your inquiry.

_____

_____

_____

4. Inference/Meaning-making

How do you understand this issue, based on your analysis?

_____

_____

_____

What other inferences/meanings have you made based on your inquiry? What is your hypothesis?

_____

_____

_____

5. Alternative Ideas

How has your inference above shifted your thinking about this youth/practitioner/situation? What ideas have you identified that may be worth considering, as a result of the questions you addressed?

_____

_____

_____

6. Learning

What have you learned from this scenario that you can transfer to your practice? How might this new learning influence your approach with youth in care? What aspects of theory are important to consider in this situation?

_____

_____

_____

Include any additional comments or questions you have.

_____

_____

_____

Share and discuss your responses with two other students.

Engaging in reflective thinking can also support practitioners with considering the rationale of other approaches to practice, which is important and necessary to avoid the risk of judgement and assumptions when working with others whose approach differs from your own. In the following section of this chapter, you will be introduced to two reflective models that will support your understanding of Xandu's approach.

Exercise 43: In the News

As a group, select an article or case study related to the field of Child and Youth Care that has been featured in the news within the past three years. Apply the Reflective Thinking Model Framework to guide your analysis. Refer to the steps listed in the earlier part of this chapter as a reference.

1. Awareness

_____

_____

_____

_____

2. Define the issue

_____

_____

_____

_____

3a. Analysis of knowledge

_____

_____

_____

_____

3b. Current/future-oriented knowledge

_____

_____

_____

_____

4. Inference/meaning-making

_____

_____

_____

5. Alternative ideas

_____

_____

_____

6. Learning
Consider the relevant theory that may influence your thinking.

_____

_____

_____

As you engage in the reflective inquiry, identify further questions that may arise for you to consider.

_____

_____

_____

_____

Something to Think About

As you engage in reflective inquiry throughout your practice, consider if there is a pattern or theme within your reflective inquiry. Do your inquiries remain the same from situation to situation? Do you adapt the questions to reflect the presenting issue?

Exercise 44: Thinking about Practice

Consider a recent issue or situation from your practice that has left you feeling uncertain or that you require more clarity about. Apply the reflective thinking model from earlier in the chapter to this situation. Follow the framework below.

1. Awareness

_____

_____

_____

2. Define the issue

_____

_____

_____

3. Analysis of knowledge

_____

_____

_____

Questions from your inquiry

_____

_____

_____

4. Inference/meaning-making

_____

_____

_____

5. Alternative ideas

_____

_____

_____

6. Learning

_____

_____

_____

What further action is required?

_____

_____

Discuss and share with a partner.

The first part of this chapter offered opportunities to engage in reflective inquiry as a means to enhance your understanding of other perspectives. The reflective thinking model introduced in the earlier part of this chapter provided you with the tools to analyze and identify further learning opportunities in each of the distinct case scenarios. The reflective thinking model represents a precursor to the reflective models you will learn about in this section of the chapter. You will revisit the scenario about Xandu and Challah, utilizing the reflective models below. You are encouraged to begin using the reflective models as a frame of reference for thinking about your practice, while identifying ways to improve your practice.

REFLECTIVE MODELS

There are two models of reflection that can assist you in thinking about your practice with others: the Reflective Process Model and Schon's Reflective Models, Reflection in Action and Reflection on Action. The cyclic process of this model reveals points where shifts can occur that will influence the outcome (Tripp & Pollard, as cited in Basol & Gencel, 2013). This is a pivotal learning point for practitioners. When you realize how much of your thinking influences your actions and experiences of the other, you will develop the skills to question your own thinking, which impacts your practice and others' experiences of you.

The Reflective Process Model is a process-oriented framework that assists you in evaluating your actions in order to identify further learning and opportunities to assist you in achieving a desired result (Mann et al., 2009). Schon's reflective models embody thinking and rethinking about experiences to create new meaning and ideas for current and future action. The focus of both models is to query the efficacy of your action on others, which pulls from previous and current knowledge and encourages you to consider how to determine that your approach was for the other's best interest and not based on your own needs.

The Reflective Process Model

The model below provides practitioners with a succinct way to understand their actions in response to issues of concern by analyzing their interpretations and actions in a more comprehensive manner. This model presents a visual way for practitioners to understand the process from which they make sense of their experiences, and reflect upon and act upon their understanding. In addition, this process enables practitioners to identify the point in the reflective process from which shifts can occur that ultimately alters one's understanding of events and influences their actions. It does so by encouraging practitioners to explore the experience (what happened, who was involved, their assumptions); their understanding of the situation (interpretations based on personal reaction, e.g., emotions, beliefs); and how that informs their hypothesis (conclusion) to act. The reflective process model can assist practitioners in thinking about their actions after the experience or in the midst of the experience.

In previous chapters, you learned about the influential nature of your thinking on practice. Creating the space to expand on this way of thinking through reflective inquiry enhances your understanding of situations and diminishes the opportunity for judgement to remain (Brockbank & McGill, 2007).

> Every opportunity for reflection begins with acknowledgement of a challenging experience.
> —Brockbank & McGill, 2007

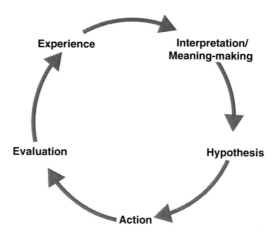

Figure 17: Reflective Process Model[2]
Source: Adapted from Borton (1970), Dewey (1933), Kolb (1984), Kember et al. (2000).

1. **Experience**
   Involves the details surrounding an experience; your internal reactions; what happened; who was involved. Experiences are subjective and will vary from person to person.

2. **Interpretation/Meaning-making**

    The manner in which one makes sense of their experiences is often based on their values, beliefs, assumptions, social location, and personal experiences. The interpretations and meaning you make of experiences are the keys to guiding your inquiry (Garfat, 2002; Garfat & Charles, 2012; O'Connell & Dyment, 2013; Wosket, 2002). Remember that interpretations and meaning-making are subjective experiences and are unique to each person. It is important to acknowledge the meaning you have created about the situation and the ways this influences the outcome and your actions. The other's reactions can reinforce your interpretations of this situation. What has been the impact of the meaning you have created on your interactions? The other? Do you have enough information to proceed? Are you basing your decision to act on use of self or in response to what you believe to be occurring with the other person?

3. **Hypothesis**

    Your hypothesis of the situation is based on the interpretation/meaning you created about the situation, which will influence your response/action.

4. **Action**

    The hypothesis informed your actions. Responding to others based on your hypothesis (what you think should occur) provides an opportunity to evaluate the outcome. What did you do and what was the result?

5. **Evaluation**

    Evaluating the potential outcome of your actions based on your hypothesis of the situation. How did your action address the emotional, developmental, and spiritual needs of children, youth, and families? How did it not? What learning occurred?

Where attention goes, energy flows; where intention goes, energy flows!
—James Redfield

Reflecting on your actions enables you to identify areas where you require further development or areas to revisit (how one makes meaning of a situation can alter your hypothesis and action). It is important to focus your energy on creating *new meaning* of your interpretations. Dewey (1933) believed that the meaning one makes of situations does not always represent a complete, accurate picture of the situation. Interpretations evolve from past experiences that can influence the meaning you make of experiences.

The concept of meaning-making has been discussed throughout the text and bears repeating as it has significant implications for practice. The meaning you make of your experiences will influence your thinking and your actions in practice. It is therefore essential to slow your thinking down to reflect upon the meaning you have created based on this situation, as opposed to responding with routine-oriented or "quick-fix" solutions. Jumping to solutions, as you have learned from previous chapters, negates the importance of context, which is present in every situation. When you find yourself jumping ahead to reciting the consequences for behaviours, this is a cue for you to pause and take a step back.

Routine-oriented responses often relate to the practitioner's need for control and to provide them with a sense of *doing something*. Some practitioners believe that *doing something* is better than *doing nothing*; however, this does not consider the potential implications for practice. Routine-oriented responses limit one's own learning and the experiences of others (Dewey, 1933; Rodgers, 2002; Schon, 1983). Consider the impact that these routine-oriented responses can have on others. How might these influence other perspectives of you? From a reflexive lens, consider the power and privilege embedded in your response here. Use the space below to respond to the question and to identify any questions or comments you may have.

Consider the Following Scenario

Imagine it is your first week of practice and you are accompanying the other practitioner to pick up a 10-year-old child from her therapy appointment. As you greet her, she tells you to shut up, pushes past you, and slams the car door. Rattled, you respond about the rudeness (routine-oriented response) of her comment, which only elicits further comments from the child. You attempt to warn her about a consequence (routine-oriented response), when your colleague shakes her head "no." You stop and remain quiet through the rest of the drive home.

The intention of your response was perhaps to deter further comments or perhaps to teach the child a more "appropriate" way for responding; however, this young girl, who just finished her session with her therapist (consider the context in addressing emotionally laden issues in therapy), may have perceived you as insensitive and uncaring. From a reflexive lens, is it the child's responsibility to make you feel okay? These routine-oriented responses seldom lead to long-lasting change, if any at all, as they do not consider context as the root of the behaviours (Steele & Malchiodi, 2012). As all behaviour serves a purpose (Garfat, 1992), it becomes the practitioner's responsibility to engage in inquiry to learn more about the seemingly unmet need that many behaviours represent (Steele & Malchiodi, 2012).

Exercise 45: Emotions Influence Actions

Think back to a recent challenging situation where you reacted from a place of heightened emotions. How might this have influenced your actions? Use the Reflective Process Model to deconstruct this experience.

1. Experience (briefly describe what happened; your internal reactions, the situation, and who was involved)

_____

_____

_____

2. Interpretation/Meaning-making (briefly describe the meaning/interpretation you made of this situation)

_____

_____

_____

3. Hypothesis (what did you determine needed to occur, based on your interpretation/meaning of situation?)

_____

_____

_____

4. Action (briefly describe what you did based on your hypothesis)

_____

_____

_____

5. Evaluation (what was the result? How did your action address the emotional, developmental, and spiritual needs of children, youth, and families? How did it not? What learning occurred?)

_____

_____

_____

Identify any additional questions or comments that emerged from this exercise.

_____

_____

Checking In

Where are you with understanding the concepts and exercises in this chapter thus far? How do they connect to your understanding of reflective practice and the previous chapters' concepts? How do they not? What areas require further exploration to support your thinking about this chapter?

When you have finished Exercise 45, return to the experience and your interpretation to engage in reflective inquiry. What questions might you consider that may shift your interpretation/meaning of the situation? Refer to the template in Appendix V to guide your inquiry. Think about the interpretation/meaning you created. How similar is this to your other experiences? Considering this may highlight the pattern you engage in when creating meaning of your experiences. Use the space below to list the questions from your inquiry.

_____

_____

_____

In the proceeding part of this chapter, you were introduced to Xandu and Challah. The following scenario illustrates the interactions between Xandu and Challah when she arrived at the home the next day.

Challah arrived at the residential home with her worker, after having been discharged from her previous residential home for "non-compliant" behaviours. She was introduced to Xandu as her primary worker. Xandu explained the rules of the home and gave Challah space to familiarize herself with the surroundings. She kept to herself for the majority of the shift, spending time between her room and the living room. When reminders about chores were provided, Challah remained in the living room, ignoring the other staff. Xandu approached Challah to remind her that completing chores was an expectation of the program. When zi returned again, Challah had not moved. Zi pointed out that this was not a hotel where she was vacationing from her last home. Challah told Xandu to get out of her face, flipped zir the finger, and knocked a vase over before leaving the room. Xandu called out about the consequence for incomplete chores and damage to property. Xandu's shift partner, Lauren, approached Xandu and commented that zir reaction was a bit harsh and asked Xandu to think about why zi makes situations bigger than they need to be. Challah remained in her room for the remainder of the night.

Exercise 46: Xandu's Reflection

Following the Reflective Process Model as a framework to guide your thinking, reflect on Xandu's reactions toward Challah. This exercise will support you in considering Xandu's perspective.

1. Experience

_____

_____

2. Interpretation/Meaning-making

_____

_____

3. Hypothesis

_____

_____

4. Action

_____

_____

5. Evaluation

_____

_____

   After you have completed this exercise, review which points in this process necessitated a shift in Xandu's thinking to influence a different action. What was necessary for this to occur? Note this on the template above. For Xandu to engage in inquiry, which questions are important for zir to consider in order to achieve a different understanding of Challah?

_____

_____

_____

In order to create a new meaning of Challah's behaviours, Xandu will need to engage in reflective inquiry to shift zir way of knowing. Through this reflective lens, Xandu's need to assert control will give way to curiosity about Challah's lived experiences. What is there to learn about Challah that zi is not aware of yet is important to know? It is this meaning-making stage that invites opportunities to consider alternative perspectives, which in turn will foster a new way of responding.

From a reflexive lens, how might Xandu's initial interpretations connect to issues of power and privilege?

_____

_____

_____

> By doubting we are led to question; by questioning, we arrive at the truth.
> —Peter Abelard

The meaning and interpretations you create develop from your worldviews, which leads you back to the very meaning you create of situations that inform your actions (Rodgers, 2002, p. 802). Worldviews, if you recall from Chapter 4, reflect internal representations of an individual's sense of self that drives behaviours subconsciously (Whitehead, as cited in de la Sienra, Smith, & Mitchell, 2017). The lens from which individuals view the world is based on their values, beliefs, past experiences, and meanings they make of experiences (de la Sienra et al., 2017).

Return to Xandu's reflective process. What further action is required of zir? (Give thought to the impact of zir actions on Challah, who just arrived at Dee's Home for Youth.)

_____

_____

We will return to this scenario later in the chapter, when you are introduced to Schon's reflective models.

Pause to Reflect

When practitioners do not pause to self-monitor their internal reactions during challenging situations, such as Xandu and Challah's case scenario, the potential for reacting to others is notably higher (Brockbank & McGill, 2007). Reflective thinkers shift deliberately from the *content* of the experience (observable behaviours) to formulating a hypothesis that influences action (Dewey, as cited in Rodgers, 2002) that considers context and the unique needs of the individual.

Practice

Over the next few weeks, continue to pay attention to situations that emerge during your practice or in your day-to-day life and engage in the Reflective Process Model to develop your understanding of your experiences. You may wish to follow the prompts below or copy the Reflective Process Model image to include your points in the respective areas.

The Reflective Process Model

Experience:

_____

_____

_____

Your interpretation/meaning-making of the situation:

_____

_____

_____

Your hypothesis based on your interpretation:

_____

_____

_____

Your action influenced by your hypothesis:

_____

_____

_____

Your evaluation of your action and new learning identified:

_____

_____

_____

Donald Schon (1983) was an educational theorist whose contributions influenced reflective practice as a core element of professional disciplines and whose ideologies have influenced the practice of Child and Youth Care, notably Reflection in Action and Reflection on Action. He defined reflection as a constant, interconnected process of thinking and doing (Schon, 1983).

He strongly believed that, while theoretical frameworks played an important role in professional disciplines, listening to one's intuition, that *gut instinct* feeling everyone has the potential to experience, played a valuable role in practice as well. This gut instinct is similar to Aristotle's practical wisdom, which defines Child and Youth Care practice (Kakkori & Huttenen, 2007; Smith, 2008; White, 2007). Schon (1983) points out that individuals' lives range in complexity and needs and that there is not a textbook solution for every complex situation that individuals experience in their lives. Schon (1983) believed that practitioners risk becoming too routine-focused when faced with situations that require more consideration given the context and circumstances of others and believed in the importance of thinking about the implications for every decision a practitioner makes (Schon, 1983).

SCHON'S REFLECTION ON ACTION

Reflection on Action involves thinking about your actions after the experience to determine what happened, to evaluate your actions and their impact on practice, and to identify an alternative action and further learning to assist you in future similar situations (Schon, 1983). The need to reflect on action will present itself when situations have been experienced as challenging, when there is a lack of resolution between the individuals involved in the situation, when practitioners experience a gut reaction that tells them they are not satisfied with how the situation ended, or when others provide feedback about your approach in a situation. Reflection on Action provides a way for you to assess the efficacy of your approach with others (Mezirow, 1991): what you did, the rationale for your approach, the impact on others, and what can be different next time.

Reflection on action requires a deliberate and intentional consideration of evaluating your actions and determining alternative action for next time. This can be difficult for some to do when assuming responsibility is difficult. That alone presents an opportunity to reflect on the meaning of responsibility for you. The central idea of Reflection on Action is that within each challenging experience is a learning opportunity. It is important for practitioners to consider what further action may be required to repair or revisit the situation with others.

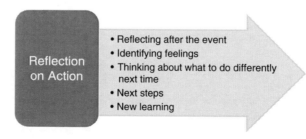

Figure 18: Reflection on Action

Source: Created by author, adapted from Schon (1987).

Exercise 47: Doing Reflection on Action

Think back to a recent event that did not result in the changes you had hoped for. As you think about this event, you might feel upset with yourself and the situation. Sit with this for a moment and allow yourself to experience *being comfortable being uncomfortable*. Briefly describe what happened and the emotions that arise for you now.

_____

_____

What assumptions underlined your actions in response to what occurred? What did you think would happen based on your actions?

_____

_____

What was the impact of your actions? For you? On others? The situation?

_____

_____

When you think about the impact on others, what might their perspectives be of you?

_____

_____

Consider the context involved in this situation. If this situation involved another person, what was the context for their behaviours that you hadn't considered? What context influenced your decision to act?

_____

_____

What would you do differently next time? What new learning occurred as a result?

_____

_____

What further action is required to address or remedy this situation? What might prevent you from doing this?

_____

_____

This concept of *being comfortable being uncomfortable* is an essential aspect of reflective practice. Many individuals struggle to sit with discomfort and may often try to avoid it through distraction or denial. While this can be considered as a means to cope with difficult experiences, it has significant risk for practice. New ways of knowing and doing are limited and change does not occur.

It is often at these times of looking back that practitioners tend to ruminate about the situation and identify what they *should* have done. In order to prevent further judgement, which impedes the learning potential in these situations, it is beneficial for practitioners to consider the context for their actions and to engage in reflective inquiry. For instance, you might ask yourself, "What outcome did I expect to achieve? What was the result? What other options were available to me that might influence a more desirable outcome? What did I learn from this experience?" When practitioners can slow their thinking down and reflect on their actions, they are less likely to engage in the self-judgement that often leaves little room for learning.

> Let go of what can't be changed and be open to further, new learning ahead.
> —Donicka Budd

When you reflect on your actions, you can achieve further clarity about:
- Your actions—were they based on assumptions, your beliefs, or values; were they based on a need to control?
- The situation—what may have been the context for the behaviour?
- The impact on others—what message might have been conveyed through your actions?
- Their perspectives—what might they be thinking?
- The other's needs.
- Achieving new meaning and understanding of the situation.
- Further learning that influences new action for the future.

The scenarios in this book are intended to introduce to you the content for what to reflect on and the process involved. Return to the case scenario from Chapter 3 involving Kilarni, Jade, and Gavin as a frame of reference for reflecting on Jade's experience using Schon's Reflection in Action model.

If you recall, Jade responded to Gavin hiding under the table by commenting on how rude he was being when she was introduced to the family. Imagine that Kilarni approached her after the meeting to question her reaction to Gavin. Jade took the time to think about her actions and reflected on the following:

Jade acknowledged her feelings of embarrassment and surprise (internal reaction—feelings) when Gavin hid under the table upon her introduction to the family. She remembered thinking about what Gavin's mother must have thought about her for her son to hide under the table. Jade felt so humiliated. She assumed he was being a little brat (assumption) who had no manners and wanted to show them he was in control and thought her comment would change his behaviour (creating meaning). "I mean who does this … hides under the table at first meeting someone?" As she thought this, she paused to realize that children who are feeling scared and uncertain about what is happening will demonstrate just this (context). "Oh my gosh," she thought, "how did I miss this!" (reflexivity). Still, she wondered why she had such a harsh reaction to Gavin's behaviour. Her comment could not have gone over well with his mother. "What must Gavin have thought about me?" She determined that his initial reaction to her as an unsafe person was reinforced by her comment toward him (impact of her behaviour). He likely decided that he did not like her, that she was mean, and that he did not want to see her again (Gavin's perspective of Jade). As she considered this, she realized her reaction was more about her discomfort with uncertainty and not knowing what to do or say in situations like this (new meaning). She realized her go-to response was the reactive comment: "So not helpful," she realized, "but I continue to do this." She should have just ignored the behaviour if she wasn't certain what to say and engaged the mother instead (alternative action). In reflecting on this, Jade realized that she needed to not react so quickly and step back when behaviours like this occur (what needs to be different for next time). She also realized that she needed to follow up with the family and to acknowledge Gavin's discomfort in meeting new people (further action).

Add in your own ideas for Jade to follow up on. Add in any questions or additional thoughts you may have about this process. Is there anything different you would suggest for further action?

_____

_____

_____

_____

_____

As you will notice, Schon's reflective model has less of a structure than the Reflective Process Model does; however, there are key points to capture within your reflection. The reflective journals in Chapter 11 will provide you with the structure for capturing your reflections. Writing about your reflections is significant for your learning when beginning to reflect on your experiences (Moon, 2004; Stevens & Cooper, 2009):

- A difficult situation or experience
- The awareness of initial feelings, thoughts, and assumptions

- Awareness of the practitioner's behaviours, impact on the others, and the other's perspectives of the practitioner
- The context that influenced behaviours/responses
- New learning
- Alternative behaviour(s)
- Identified action to follow up on

As you reflect on your experiences, you will notice that other thoughts or insights will emerge. You may realize that certain situations have triggered earlier experiences that are similar in nature to the situation you are reflecting on. This is common and does not need to be about how to undo or resolve earlier experiences; rather, be aware of them and acknowledge that this is what has happened (Moon, 2008). For some practitioners, acknowledging these previous experiences is sufficient to inform alternative future action; for others, seeking out counselling support can assist in further making sense of these earlier experiences.

REVISITING XANDU AND CHALLAH

In the earlier part of this chapter, you were introduced to the case scenario involving Xandu and Challah and engaged with the reflective process model to better understand Xandu's experiences and approach with Challah. We will apply Schon's Reflection on Action model to this case scenario as a means to provide you a different method for reflecting about an experience. Review Xandu's reflection and add in your own thoughts and ideas that may enhance the reflection process. Be prepared to defend your thinking.

Exercise 48: Reflection on Action: Xandu and Challah Scenario

Xandu initially felt offended that zir shift partner called zi out on zir interaction with Challah. Zi struggled when other staff did this; zi always felt so embarrassed. Even after all this time, zi struggled with hearing feedback from zir shift partners (an area that warrants further reflection). Zi thought about the night and realized zi needn't have been so hard on Challah.

Why did Xandu always need to engage in power struggles with the youth? (Consider the feelings, thinking, and assumptions zi may have experienced as a result of Challah's response toward Xandu and the chores.)

_____

_____

_____

What meaning did Xandu make of Challah's behaviours?

_____

_____

_____

Xandu realized that zir own need for control influenced zir actions toward Challah. When the youth defied Xandu, zi always felt stupid and that zi needed to gain back control—hence zir reactive comments. Zi thought about the impact of zir comments on Challah. Identify these below.

_____

_____

_____

_____

Zi realized that context played a significant role in Challah's behaviours. From what you know about Challah from the case scenario, what connections do you make between her behaviours and worldviews? Identify these below.

_____

_____

Instead of reacting to her behaviours, Xandu realized zi should have … (identify the preferred alternative behaviour). (Consider whether reading the report before Challah arrived may have influenced zi to act differently toward her.) The summary report was purposely omitted from this scenario to avoid the potential for bias toward Xandu. As has been addressed earlier in the text, there will be times that you will not have access to summary or intake reports. There are risks to this of course, in that practitioners are not made aware of recommendations to inform their practice. However, there are benefits to this as well if practitioners can attune to the other through astute observation and meaning-making skills.

_____

_____

Xandu realized that for future intakes, zi will … (identify the new learning for future action).

_____

_____

Xandu realized that further action is required to establish some sense of repair in the relationship with Challah and is considering … (identify what may be important for Xandu to do to follow up with Challah). Think beyond an apology; consider what other actions Xandu could take.

_____

_____

When considering context for others' behaviours, it can be helpful to explore their worldviews. Based on the limited information you have about Challah from the case scenario, how might her worldviews influence her behaviours? How might her worldviews be connected to the challenges she experiences with others?

_____

_____

_____

Exercise 49: Challah's Worldviews

In the space below, draw the image of an iceberg similar to the template from Chapter 4 (see p. 117). List the behaviours that Challah presents at the top of the iceberg and what you believe are Challah's values and beliefs and significant past experiences based on what you have read about her from the case scenario. Many times, you will have limited information on others and your hypothesis of their worldviews may be just that: a hypothesis based on your observations and understanding from any written reports you may have access to. Your hypothesis will inform your approach with the other and your approach can be considered a test of your hypothesis.

What might you hypothesize about Challah based on her worldviews?

_____

_____

Practice: Reflection on Action

Identify a challenging or confusing situation during your practice as the basis of this reflection and consider the following:

- Awareness of the initial feelings, thoughts, and assumptions
- Awareness of the practitioner's behaviours, impact on others, and others' perspectives of the practitioner
- The context that influenced behaviours/responses
- New learning
- Alternative behaviour
- Identified action to follow up on

How you think about and understand yours and others' experiences is fundamental to becoming a reflective practitioner.
  —Schon, 1983

Establishing Further Action: A Cause for Relational Repair[3]

Further action, as identified in the Reflective Process Model and Schon's Reflection on Action model, is an important aspect of reflection that highlights the practitioner's responsibility to ensure the other's best interests and individual needs are always at the focus of their actions. It is important that practitioners remain mindful of their accountability to others for their actions. As addressed earlier in the book, responding to others from your own ways of knowing risks negating their unique lived experiences (Bellefeuille & Ricks, 2010; Dewey, 1933; White, 2007), which can lead to misunderstandings and conflict. Interactions with others allow for opportunities to reconsider one's way of doing things that may require stepping outside the realm of familiar behaviour. Consider the ease or difficulty you experience in taking responsibility for your actions as a practitioner. Do you try to forget about the situation and carry on as if nothing happened? Do you avoid the other person until the conflict has blown over? Consider what you might do in situations that involve children, youth, and families where further action is required to repair the relationship. Boulton and Mirsky (2006) highlight the benefits of assuming a restorative practice focus on repairing the harm to relationships (p. 1). For the context of this book, this process is initiated by the practitioner taking responsibility for their role in a situation with the other. These typically involve situations where the practitioner responded without considering the different contexts influencing behaviours.

Simply apologizing is not sufficient for many reasons. Apologizing with a one-word response—sorry—conveys little to no regard for the other's experiences and does not account for ownership of poor judgement. "Sorry," for many, is meaningless, when you consider the experiences of many children, youth, and families who may have been told this over and over again, with little change occurring as a result.

Determining the action required will often involve some form of remedial action involving others and is vital to your role as a practitioner. When you consider the previous experiences of children, youth, and families, facilitating restorative practices (aka, relationship repair) can represent a critical learning experience for their development (Boulton & Mirsky, 2006). Relational repair, or remedial experiences, provides a way to challenge the assumptions others have about relationships that conveys accountability, respect, empathy, and acknowledgement for the other. Children, youth, and families have a different experience of relationship and others taking responsibility for their behaviours.

Relational Repair

The practitioner assumes accountability for behaviour during the interaction and demonstrates respect for the other by acknowledging the impact of that behaviour on the other. The practitioner empathizes with the other by identifying the perceived emotional experience of the other. Relational repair conveys to the other, "I see you and you deserve to be treated with respect and to feel upset when situations like this occur."

Consider the Following Scenario: Xandu and Challah

Xandu has established that it is the home's responsibility for creating a different experience for Challah, and zi has acknowledged that this begins with a follow-up from the previous night.

Having learned from her file that Challah enjoys cooking, Xandu approaches Challah about her interest in cooking that evening. Her face beams momentarily, then gives way to indifference, and she responds with "I don't care." Zi comments that the house would appreciate someone who knows how to cook, admitting that it is not zir forte. As they prep the items for cooking, Xandu comments, "So I was an a** to you last night." Challah shrugs, and Xandu continues with saying sometimes zi forgets what it's like to be a youth in care, having decisions made for them, being moved from here to there. When Challah shrugs again, responding, "I'm used to it, it doesn't matter," zi says, "You matter" and asks how they can make a go of it here. "I'm guessing you need people to give you some slack now and then. What do you need for this to be a different experience for you?"

Something to Think About

Relational repair requires a strong awareness of self and the ability to assume responsibility for one's actions. What may impede this process? What may make this a difficult or challenging process for you or others? From a reflexive lens, what value does facilitating relational repair offer your and others?

If you have not engaged in this before and prefer to ignore the situation until things blow over, reflect on the impact this has had for you and others.

Explore the assumptions and beliefs that underlie your discomfort in engaging in relational repair. Use the space below to note any additional thoughts or questions you might have.

_____

_____

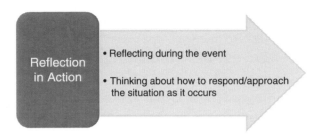

Figure 19: Reflection in Action

Source: Created by author, adapted from Schon (1987).

A relationship is like a house. When a lightbulb burns out, you don't go and buy a new house, you fix the lightbulb.

—Anonymous

Reflection in Action

Schon (1983) defined Reflection in Action as the rethinking of some part of one's knowing-in-action that leads to on-the-spot experiment and further thinking that affects what one does—in the immediate situation (p. 2). Reflecting on an immediate experience as it occurs to prompt a different action is the basis for Reflection in Action. Reflection in Action requires the practitioner to consider the context for the behaviours and the use of self to influence their response in the immediate moment. This will require you to pause in your habitual way of responding and create the space necessary for monitoring your own internal reactions: what you are noticing in self, others, the context, and alternative ways for responding.

It is at the meaning-making point that reframing and challenging of assumptions (as outlined in Chapter 3) must occur. Reframing the meaning that you have made allows you to respond in a way that considers the unique lived experiences of others and which Schon's (1983) Reflection in Action needs to occur in order to shift the practitioner's experience (Dewey, as cited in Rodgers 2002) and habitual response.

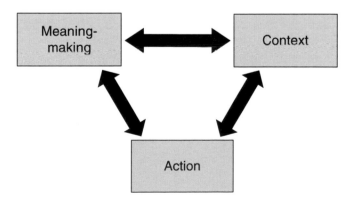

Figure 20: Reframe in Action

Source: Adapted from https://technovice.coetail.com/2016/05/05/play-is-the-highest-form-of-research-albert-einstein/ under CC BY.

In the midst of a situation, something happens. You monitor your internal reaction, consider the context for the situation, and determine the best response for the situation and respond at that moment. It is helpful to consider the potential impact of your actions on the other if you continue in this approach. What purpose does your response and approach serve for self, others, and the situation? This reflecting in action provides you the opportunity to shift your response according to the situation.

Let us return to the scenario involving the student's first week at practicum and the child, who upon leaving therapy, told the student to shut it. In reflecting in action, the process occurs as follows:

Imagine that when the child tells you to shut it (situation), you monitor your reactions (surprise, confusion), consider context for her behaviours (the child may be upset from her therapy appointment), and consider the meaning based on context (she's projecting her upset from therapy onto me; her comments reflect her difficulty in expressing herself). How do you respond? Do you ignore her comment? Do you reply, "I'm glad to see you too"? Do you say, "tough session, huh"? What do you envision as the best way to respond in this situation, given the context for her behaviours?

Some practitioners might comment about the rudeness or inappropriateness of the behaviour or believe that ignoring the comment excuses the behaviour. Remember the importance of the co-constructed space and examining context during interactions with others (see Chapter 3). When labelling such behaviours as rude or inappropriate, consider the judgement and assumptions that underlie this way of thinking. Identifying such messages as disrespectful or inappropriate signals to you that you have personalized the comment and can be a reminder to take a mindful step back from this way of thinking to consider the context for the child's comment:

- The child's developmental age.
- The child's capacity to regulate their emotions.
- The relationship—has safety been established to express themselves with you?
- The environment—the therapy session. Therapy can bring up a range of emotions and memories that can be painful reminders of past experiences. This can be difficult for a child to process.

By considering context, you are better able to understand their responses are context-dependent and not a direct insult toward you. Is this an area to focus on as a goal? Yes, but not at that moment.

The scenario above reminds us of the importance for considering context—the circumstances surrounding the behaviours. Schon (1983) and Dewey (1916/1944) believed that practitioners risk becoming too routine-focused when faced with situations that require more consideration given the context and circumstances of others. We must always be thinking about the implications for every decision we make (Dewey, 1933; Rodgers, 2002; Schon, 1983).

Reexamining Context

The child has just left her therapy appointment. Consider the child's emotions and experiences during the therapy session that may have left her feeling angry. Consider also who you are to this child: you are an unfamiliar person and unfamiliarity can create anxiety and discomfort for many individuals. Given this context, we can appreciate that her comment was about her internal experiences as opposed to you as a person. Knowing this will shift your perspective of the child and your response. What response might be more honouring of her experiences? Would you ignore the comment? Would you acknowledge her discomfort in meeting someone new? Knowing what you would say will depend on what is occurring in that present moment. Give some thought to this. This scenario reinforces the importance for reflecting in action.

_____

_____

_____

If you realize that you are adamant about this comment being disrespectful, this is an opportunity for you to explore the meaning for you and where this originates from. I then challenge you to think more about the power imbalance the idea of "disrespect" might imply. Is it the child's responsibility to make you feel accepted and confident in your role? Is there an alternative to thinking that others' comments are about you? Or is this an opportunity to challenge your thinking and bring use of self (exploring those beliefs, values, experiences, and social location) to this present experience? Use the space below to respond to these questions. What are the implications of this thinking in your current and future interactions with others?

_____

_____

_____

Situations such as these remind us that there is no single way of responding to others (Gharabaghi, 2008b), since behaviours are context-dependent. Context influences behaviours, behaviours influence context (Garfat & Fulcher, 2012). This process of contemplation and reflection takes precedence over the techniques and strategies for working with others (Krueger, 2004). Knowing this signals to you that, while having a knowledge base is beneficial, you cannot prepare for every situation.

Let us return to Xandu and Challah's case scenario to support your learning of Schon's Reflection in Action (1983).

Revisiting Xandu and Challah

In the midst of Xandu's interaction with Challah, zi acknowledges the need to consider the context for Challah's behaviours in order to shift zir perspective when responding to her. Challah's lack of response provided Xandu with the necessary feedback to step back and shift zir approach to consider the context for Challah's behaviours through inquiry:

- How has she understood another discharge from a residential home? How might this influence her sense of self? Her current behaviours?
- What might her current behaviours (ignoring staff) be communicating?

Xandu considers the context for Challah's behaviours (change, transition, sense of self, need for control) and may determine that acknowledging this takes precedence over zir need for control and chores being completed. Zi might comment, "You're letting me know you need your space tonight to adjust to the new place. Let's check in tomorrow." In reflecting in action to consider the need for a different response, how might this impact Challah's perspectives?

_____

_____

_____

Use the space below to share your thoughts or questions you may have in response to this scenario and the points above.

_____

_____

_____

> There is always truth behind just kidding, A little emotion behind I don't care, A little pain behind it's ok, A little I need you behind leave me alone, And a lot of words behind the silence.
>
> —Author Unknown

Recall Chapter 3, when you were asked to think about your position in relation to other community professionals. Who do you perceive as having the final say in what is best for this child or family? How might this way of knowing influence your interactions with other professionals?

Consider the Following Scenario: Donna

Donna worked at an elementary school providing emotional and social support to one of the students who presented with significant behavioural challenges. It was her first job as a Child and Youth Care Practitioner. After having worked with 12-year-old Jerome for several weeks, she had established an understanding of his needs for structure, routine, and frequent movement breaks. One particular day, his struggles ensued to the point he became aggressive. A meeting occurred with the school psychologist, vice-principal, social worker, and Donna. The psychologist, in reading over Jerome's previous reports, offered his opinion that Jerome may benefit from a smaller class setting and recommended a specialized behavioural program to meet his needs. In addition to reading Jerome's reports, the psychologist had met him once a few months ago, before Donna's involvement. Both the social worker and the vice-principal agreed with the psychologist. Donna remained silent, uncertain of what to do, as she did not agree that Jerome's needs would be best met in a behavioural program. She believed that this would only exacerbate his behaviours and would have a significant impact on his sense of self. Does she speak out and challenge their thinking by showing evidence of his progress from the structure and routine she implemented? Does she remain quiet because she is just a Child and Youth Care Practitioner? Does she ask them to provide a rationale for their thinking?

In this moment, Donna reconsiders her *just a Child and Youth Care Practitioner* position; she is a viable member of the team who has been working closely with Jerome for the past few months. She has established an understanding of his needs and has tested her hypothesis of his needs by observing his response to structure, routine, and movement breaks. She is aware that when these are missing from his day, his potential for behaviours is significantly higher. She considers this valuable information and shares with the team her experiences and Jerome's capacity to be successful with the structure and routines in place.

Reflection in Action involves rethinking one's way of knowing. Donna's shifting perspective of her role as "just" a Child and Youth Care Practitioner (having less value than the other team members to being valuable and important) influenced in-the-moment action (Schon, 1983), sharing a different perspective of Jerome with the others. Use the space below to identify any questions or comments you have about this scenario.

_____

_____

Give some thought to the perspective that other professionals with higher levels of education know what is best for the children, youth, and families you work with. Consider the frequency and nature of involvement between Child and Youth Care Practitioners and the children, youth, and families they interact with in practice. How does your role compare with those of other professionals? In considering these points, how does this connect with the idea that Child and Youth Care Practitioners are "just" Child and Youth Care Practitioners? What are the risks in assuming this mindset? What are the benefits in assuming this mindset?

_____

_____

For things to reveal themselves to us, we need to be ready to abandon our views about them.
—Thich Nhat Hanh

These moments of uncertainty will arise at different times in your learning and professional journey, notably regarding ethical dilemmas. We will return to ethical dilemmas in a later chapter. Not knowing, while discomforting as it is for some, allows the space for curiosity and considering the perspectives of the other (Bellefeuille & Ricks, 2010; Ricks & Bellefeuille, 2003; Krueger, 2004). Not knowing also creates the space to slow down thinking (Dewey, 1933) and for the opportunities to minimize the potential for reactive responses (Gharabaghi, 2008a) that can have detrimental impact for others. As you have learned throughout this book, the meaning you create from situations will influence how you think about self, others, and the profession. Feeling uncertain for some practitioners (including seasoned ones) can mean a loss of control, insecurity, a fear of failure, or a sense of being wrong (Gharabaghi, 2008a). Consider, for a moment, if these experiences fit for you and the meaning these have for you.

How have you responded to times of uncertainty? Do you do nothing? Do you seek clarity, explore options, or ask for support from others?

_____

_____

MOVING FORWARD

In the next chapter, you will advance your learning to develop the skills for critical thinking. Critical thinking involves a shift from reflective inquiry to an investigative, analytical query for effecting change.

_____

_____

CLOSING THOUGHTS

What did you learn about yourself from the concepts discussed in this chapter?

_____

_____

_____

How will your new learning influence your practice? From the learning in this chapter, what concepts do you anticipate will be most challenging to apply to your practice?

_____

_____

_____

What is required for you to shift your thinking from being "just" a Child and Youth Care student to a Child and Youth Care Practitioner?

_____

_____

_____

_____

What questions remain for you still?

_____

_____

NOTES

1. The Reflective Thinking Model is an adaptation of Gibbs' Reflective Cycle Model (1988) and Dewey's process model (1933).
2. The Reflective Process Model is based on distinct elements from the following models: Borton's (1970) What, So What, Now What; Dewey's (1933) reflective process model; Kolb's (1984) Experiential Learning Model; Kember et al.'s (2000) Reflective Learning Model.
3. The concept of relationship repair has been adapted from the Relationship Repair Wheel (jenmoff.com, 2018).

CHAPTER 8

Critical Thinking

The essence of the independent mind lies not in what it thinks, but in how it thinks.

—Christopher Hitchens

LEARNING OBJECTIVES

In this chapter, you will:

- define critical thinking and its relation to reflective practice
- describe the four phases of critical thinking
- distinguish between reflective thinking and critical thinking
- distinguish between implicit and explicit assumptions
- check the accuracy and validity of assumptions through research and inquiry
- be introduced to the concept of ethical dilemmas and the connection to reflective practice
- explain the Critical Thinking in Action process
- conceptualize case scenarios and written reports through a critical lens

The previous chapter introduced you to reflective thinking that involves questioning, analyzing, and evaluating aspects of your practice. Through questioning, greater insight and awareness of others' experiences can be established. Reflecting on your practice provides you with opportunities to analyze and evaluate your approach while identifying areas to improve. Developing the skills for reflective thinking will prepare you to think more critically about others and situations you will encounter. Thinking about the previous chapter concepts, what differentiates the Reflective Process Model from Schon's reflective model?

How do you distinguish between Schon's Reflection on Action and Reflection in Action? What is the connection between establishing the need for further action and relationship repair when reflecting on practice?

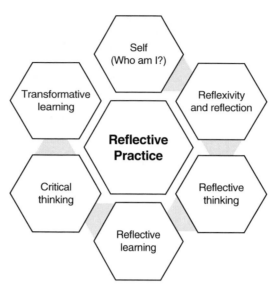

Figure 1: Reflective Practice Radial
Source: Recreated by author.

In this chapter, you will be introduced to critical thinking and exercises to support you in thinking critically about scenarios and your experiences during practice. The focus is on uncovering and checking out assumptions with others. You will engage in further group work to support your learning. This will involve an increase in checking out others' assumptions as they uncover your assumptions. Critical reflection is described as deep reflection, since it involves looking beyond the surface assumptions to explore the implicit truths that you operate from. Exploring your implicit truths, Brookfield (2012) asserts, cannot be done in isolation from a community of other practitioners. These hidden or implicit assumptions often mask personal beliefs, illusions of the way you believe things to be, and are influential in how practitioners make decisions and take action (Brookfield, 2012).

What Is Critical Thinking?

Critical thinking involves a process of uncovering and checking out assumptions, exploring alternative perspectives, and taking informed action as a result (Brookfield, 2012, p. xii). This process of uncovering and checking assumptions (implicit and explicit) occurs through inquiry and research (process-oriented) to measure the accuracy and validity of your assumptions to inform action (Brookfield, 2012). This exploring of and the questioning of assumptions and perspective underlie the key component of critical thinking. Mezirow (1991) describes critical reflection as the most significant learning experience enabling individuals to reexamine their ways of perceiving, knowing, believing, feeling, and doing—all of which shifts the way they think about problems (p. 8). Critical thinking and critical reflection are synonymous terms used throughout the literature (Brookfield, 2012; Mezirow, 1991).

Phases of Critical Thinking[1]

Brookfield (2012) identified four phases of critical thinking to guide practitioners in the critical thinking process:

1. Discovering the assumptions (implicit and explicit) that guide decisions, actions, and choices.
2. Checking out the accuracy of research and inquiry through reflective uncertainty (exploring different perspectives, viewpoints, and sources). Reflective uncertainty defies the either-or, right-or-wrong ways of thinking to consider alternative ways of knowing.
3. Interpretation (identifying the gaps between the assumptions and the research and inquiry) to make sense of the presenting issue. Interpretations involve identifying and exploring alternatives to existing ways of thinking.
4. Taking informed decisions that are based on the practitioner's interpretation.

Within critical thinking is the reflective uncertainty (willingness to consider alternative perspectives).

Because these assumptions are deeply embedded beliefs (Brookfield, 2012), they are not so easy to acknowledge as the assumptions you hold about others. Deep reflection requires you look beneath these beliefs and ways of thinking to identify the assumptions within, explore their origins, and then evaluate them through research and inquiry. Group processes are essential for challenging one's familiar ways of thinking and seeing.

Something to Think About

Consider the qualities you believe entail a good friend. These qualities are based on your assumptions of what makes a good friend. How might you evaluate the accuracy and validity of these assumptions? Consider the friends you have in your life. Do they measure up to the qualities you have identified?

Critical thinking requires practitioners to be open to identifying and exploring these hidden aspects of self, while defining the relevance to their own lives. This can be difficult at times, as it requires practitioners to look at the stark realities of their thinking.

Critical thinking occurs when practitioners challenge other assumptions, question others' decisions, practice, and social structures and relevant policies (Brookfield, 2012). When situations arise in your day-to-day interactions, it is important that you consider the practices of the different systems involved in the lives of children, youth, and families and question approaches that do not consider the lived experiences and histories of the individual, which can often lead to neglecting the best interests of others.

Exercise 50: Checking out Assumptions Exercise:[2] Revisiting Luca

Recall the scenario involving Luca (Chapter 6). Luca is the 15-year-old youth who was admitted to open custody for three months. He and three other boys were caught with alcohol in the recreation room. Despite his therapist's recommendations that you read the report about Luca, you declined. Your supervisor wants to meet with you to discuss this.

Review the following questions. Explore aspects of this scenario from a critical lens using the format below. Examples have been provided for you.

1. What assumptions underlie the scenario—both explicit (assumptions you as the practitioner are aware of) and implicit (influencing actions you are not aware of)? Identify two of each.

Explicit assumption: You assume that there is nothing to be learned from reading the report.

Explicit assumption:

_____

_____

_____

Implicit assumption: You assume no harm will come to Luca by not reading the report.

Implicit assumption:

_____

_____

_____

2. Identify assumptions that can be checked by simple research and inquiry. What is required?

    •   Explicit assumption: There is nothing to be learned from reading the report.
    •   Research and inquiry: Read the report to highlight any recommendations that would inform staff's actions (what learning, if any, resulted from reading the report?).
    •   Explicit assumption: _____

- Research and inquiry: _____
_____
_____

- Implicit assumption: Luca will not come to any harm.
- Research and inquiry: Luca was caught using alcohol with other boys. Luca's risk level is high when he is unsupervised.
- Implicit assumption: _____
_____

- Research and inquiry: _____
_____
_____

3. Provide an interpretation of this scenario (based on the events). For example: the practitioner's reluctance to read the report placed Luca at risk for engaging in high-risk behaviour. Supervision was inadequate as the practitioner believed Luca had the capacity to distinguish right from wrong behaviour.

   When you can uncover the assumptions and check them out, you identify areas that require change for the betterment of the children and youth you support.

_____
_____
_____

4. Informed Action: It is recommended that all youth reports be read by all staff members to ensure similar future situations do not happen. Interpretations have also revealed potential supervision issues that warrant reviewing.

   By examining scenarios and experiences in the workplace, you begin to see more clearly the multiple influences on children's lives, and the assumptions embedded within these larger sociocultural structures. In identifying these assumptions and the implications for children and youth, you recognize the importance your role has in advocating for others and becoming a voice for the young people you work with (Garfat & Ricks, 1995). Identify any questions or comments about this scenario in the space below.

_____
_____
_____

Exercise 51: Revisiting Debbie and Ji—Checking out Ty's Assumptions

Recall the case scenario from Chapter 3 involving Debbie, Ji, and Ty. Ty, a second-year Child and Youth Care student, recently secured a practicum at a community residential home for youth. As part of his orientation, he was given a file on a youth he would be working with on an individual basis. When he finished reading the file, he experienced an overwhelming sense of fear and anxiety and determined that the youth was dangerous and that he could be hurt. He told his professor that he felt unprepared to work in such a dangerous place and feared for his safety. Ty determined this practicum to be an unsafe and dangerous setting based on what he read from the case note.

Identify the assumptions Ty seemed to be operating from.

1. Explicit assumptions (overtly expressed, obvious):

    _____

    _____

    Implicit assumptions (not as clearly defined):
    For instance, he may assume Debbie is ill-equipped to manage the youth's behaviours.

    _____

    _____

2. Research and inquiry: Which of these assumptions could Ty check out through research and inquiry? What is required?

    _____

    _____

    Explicit assumption:

    _____

    _____

    Research and inquiry:

    _____

    _____

Implicit assumptions: Debbie is ill-equipped to manage the youth's behaviours.

Research and inquiry: Ty could inquire about Debbie's level of education and experiences. Ty should inquire about the program protocols for ensuring staff safety.

3. Provide an interpretation of the scenario (based on the assumptions/research and inquiry).

    _____

    _____

4. Informed action (based on the interpretation). What is required?

    _____

    _____

Something to Think About

The public assumes that all individuals working in the social services field have the child and family's best interests as the focus of their practice. Consider the assumptions of the agency practitioners in the diverse case scenarios you have read about throughout this book (e.g., Xandu's assumptions about Challah; Debbie's assumptions about Ji). How might the public assumption be challenged or confirmed through research and inquiry? What interpretation can be made as a result of the inquiry? How would this inform action? What is required?

Exercise 52: Checking out Systemic Structure Assumptions

Identify a situation from your practice to uncover the assumptions embedded in the systemic structure. Consider, for instance, the assumptions faculty/staff may have about support staff, children, or families. Ensure that you maintain an intentional approach to your inquiry and identify any bias or personal assumptions that may interfere with this exercise. The purpose of critical thinking is not to criticize another professional's approach, but to question and challenge the corporate, political, educational, and cultural organizations that attempt to influence you into thinking and acting in ways that serve their purposes (Brookfield, 2012, p. 2). What are the assumptions of the larger organizational structures that service children, youth, and families? This can be based on your own experiences or experiences of others.

1. List the assumptions (implicit and explicit).

_____

_____

_____

_____

2. Research and inquiry: Check these assumptions through research and inquiry. What is required?

_____

_____

_____

_____

3. Interpretation: Provide an interpretation consistent with your points above.

_____

_____

_____

_____

4. Informed action: What might be considered or is required based on what you have uncovered?

_____

_____

_____

Let your curiosity lead you down a road that is less traveled.
    —Asad Meah

Remembering When ...

During my experiences as a Family Support Counsellor for a children's mental health agency, I worked with a family whose son struggled with emotional regulation difficulties. He was described as dysregulated at times, presenting with fluctuations in mood, prone to engaging in aggressive outbursts at school and home. Previous reports included a diagnosis of ODD (oppositional defiant disorder) and ADHD (attention deficit hyperactivity disorder). Medication had failed to affect any changes, as indicated in reports. His parents reported that some days he was "fine," while other days he was a different child. They had changed his medication three times, to no avail. Over a few sessions, I noticed that he preferred to stand up while engaged in a game and often placed non-edible items in his mouth. When I shared my observations with his mother, she replied that he did that "all the time," chewing on pencils, paper, almost anything that he could get his hands on. She shared as well that when he was watching TV, he would sit upside down or in different positions that seemed out of the norm for others.

Being the reflective practitioner I was, I became curious about this and scheduled some sessions with the parents to learn more about the history and context for these behaviours. As it was impacting his school experiences, it was important that I speak to someone at the school to gather others' experiences and perspectives on his behaviour.

It is important that we don't confuse inquiry and considering different perspectives as an attempt to diagnose. Child and Youth Care Practitioners are not trained to diagnose; however, we can continue to be curious and reach out to those professionals who may have the knowledge we are seeking. Gathering further information from the relevant resources (people, books, educational website forums, articles) can support us in generating the information to further our understanding. As a result, new meaning begins to take shape; the context for the child's behaviours become the focus, as opposed to consequences of behaviour the child has no control over.

What might have been the implications for this child had I not noticed his oral fixation with non-edible objects? I would not have inquired further and may have resigned to the ADHD diagnosis on file. How different might this child's course of treatment been had I not embraced the curious mind that moves many practitioners from "what they think they know" to "what more is there to know"?

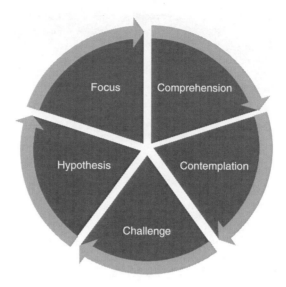

Figure 21: Critical Thinking in Action

Source: Created by author, adapted from Brookfield, 2012.

Critical Thinking in Action involves a more comprehensive approach to scrutinizing situations or events that have impacted the well-being of others.

Components of Critical Thinking[3]

- Emotions are central to the critical thinking process
- Practices, structures, and actions are context-dependent
- Identifying and challenging assumptions are central to critical thinking
- Consider and explore alternatives to ways of thinking and being
- Critical thinkers are skeptical investigators (Brookfield, 1987, p. 2)

CRITICAL THINKING IN ACTION

1. The Focus of Critical Analysis:

    Determine your focus based on the case scenario/situation.* Identify the who, what, where, when, and how aspects of the critical analysis.

    _____

    _____

    _____

2. Comprehension:

    Your perspective of the situation/experience—the focus for your critical analysis. How does your perspective align with professional practice? How do your perspectives differ from the other's?

    _____

    _____

3. Main Ideas/Key Points:

    List the key points or main ideas (from the critical analysis) that you are contemplating, analyzing, and questioning.

    _____

    _____

    _____

4. Deliberating Another's Idea or Argument:

    What is the basis for their perspective? Is there an aspect of objectivity in their ideas? What is the impact on the other?

    _____

    _____

    _____

5. Hypothesis:

    Create new meaning of the situation/experience and formulate a different perspective that aligns with Child and Youth Care practice. How does this new meaning compare to the other's perspective?

    _____

    _____

    _____

6. Challenge/Argue against the Other's Perspective:

    Identify the motives behind the other's perspective. Defend your position using theory. What aspects of the other's motives are you challenging and what is the basis for you?

    _____

    _____

    _____

7. Informed Action:

    What is required for a new outcome to occur?

    _____

    _____

    _____

*Alternatively, you may wish to identify a recent news article related to Child and Youth Care as a frame of reference for this exercise (for instance, consider the highly publicized case of Ashley Smith[4]).

In previous chapters you have learned about the impact of one's assumptions in practice and have engaged in different exercises that have enabled you to challenge these assumptions. This focus will continue throughout this chapter, with added emphasis on challenging other assumptions. You may have noticed the parallels between critical thinking and previous chapter concepts: assumptions, context, inquiry, and analysis were addressed in the previous chapter on reflective thinking. While similar, critical thinking and reflective thinking are different processes, which is important to address (Moon, 2008). Review Table 11 for a comparison of the two concepts.

Table 11: Comparison of Reflective and Critical Thinking

Reflective Thinking	Critical Thinking/Critical Reflection
Self, values, beliefs, experiences, social location	Assumptions, uncovering, checking for evidence, identifying values
Introspective: requires reflexive thinking	Analytical: critical analysis requires support of ideas
Influenced by values, beliefs Awareness of impact on the other	Considering alternative perspectives Challenging ideas
Self and other as object of inquiry: values, beliefs, assumptions, past experiences	Theories as object of inquiry: considering alternative views
What do I *think* I know?	What do I argue against? What is another way to understand this?
Our experience of the presenting issue Alternative perspectives	Alternative perspectives/theories
Thoughtful and contemplative: developing shifts from subjective to objective thinking	Objective process: considers theory to challenge thinking
Process of inquiry: questioning	Further inquiry: questioning
How am I meeting the best interests of the other: connect to learning	How does this idea conflict with the best interests of the other: connect to learning
Reflecting on experiences, impact of and identifying new learning to improve practice: essays, reflective journals, blogs	Presenting analysis and defense of approach; generating new knowledge; considering different conclusions supported by theory; working toward potential outcome: critical reports, reviews, essays
Insight-oriented, action-oriented (Reflection in Action)	Action-oriented (applying theory to action)

Comparison of Reflection and Critical Thinking[5]

In Chapter 3, you first learned about the concept of context as the internal and external factors that influence behaviour (Garfat & Fulcher, 2012). In the following case scenarios and throughout your professional career, you will continue to consider the context of situations as significant influential factors in exploring the meaning of experiences (Brookfield, 1987).

In previous chapters, you have explored the role that emotions, context, and alternative perspectives play in reflective practice. Emotions provide the foundation from which critical thinking occurs. Emotions are subjective, yet have a powerful influence on how one interprets and creates meaning of situations. Critical thinking, like reflexivity, reflection, and reflective thinking, begins with identifying the emotions in order to separate this subjective experience from influencing the practitioner's response and actions.

As you will discover throughout your practice and interactions with other community professionals, individuals have their own ways of thinking and seeing the world that are influenced by existing sociocultural systems, experiences, and previous learning. One way does not overrule the other; however, it is important to acknowledge the diversity of these values, beliefs, and experiences that will influence actions. Other systems that take a very different approach than you, yet profess to have the best interests of others at the core of their practices, will challenge you to consider these diverse perspectives and ways for working together.

It is important to explore the issue from diverse perspectives. When you review the reports later in the chapter, consider the perspectives of the author, their values, beliefs, and professional ideologies that may influence their perspectives. Considering the same situation from different points of view is fundamental to critical thinking. In deeper reflection, it is important to recognize that different people will see the same situation from different points of view (Mann, Gordon, & MacLeod, 2012), which are based on one's professional discipline and the theoretical frameworks within their discipline.

> Perspectives and assumptions are influenced by diverse sociocultural contexts.
> —Garfat & Ricks, 1995

The exercises and case scenarios in the text have provided you with opportunities to identify both implicit and explicit assumptions. Identifying implicit and explicit assumptions in others through direct interactions can often be challenging; however, as with each of the different concepts you learned throughout this book, practice is required to cultivate the diverse skill sets that underlie critical thinking and reflective practice.

The following exercise requires you to pair up with another student and will involve speaking about a specific topic, while the other person identifies the implicit and explicit assumptions within your discussion. After 15 minutes, switch roles.

Exercise 53: Pair and Identify Assumptions[6]

Share and discuss the role(s) you assume in your practice and identify three things that make you a fit for this position. As one person is talking, the other person looks for assumptions (implicit and explicit) in what is being said. When the speaking partner finishes, the other points out assumptions and engages their partner in the research and inquiry to measure the accuracy of these assumptions. Switch so both partners have a chance to speak and observe. Check in with each other about the process and reactions that you may have to the process. List your points below and the assumptions your partner identified. What research and inquiry are required to confirm or deny these assumptions?

_____

_____

_____

_____

_____

_____

_____

_____

_____

THEORETICAL FRAMEWORKS

Learning professionals are required to have an understanding of different theoretical frameworks that underpin their practice. This is not to suggest that one need only ascribe to one theory. This would be counterintuitive to practice, since many of the individuals you will work with present with their own unique needs. Table 12 includes some of the significant theories that underpin Child and Youth Care practice. It is not meant to imply these are the only ones learning professionals are to adopt; rather, it builds an awareness of why you do what you do in practice to acknowledge the inherent value and potential of each child, youth, and family you work with. Recall from Chapters 1 and 2, there is not any one approach that works with all children, youth, and families (Gharabaghi, 2008b).

Table 12: Theoretical Frameworks Explained

Theoretical framework	Overview	Questions
Maslow's Hierarchy of Needs	Hierarchy of five levels of basic needs: physiological, safety, needs of love, affection, and belonging; need for esteem; need for self-actualization.	Which need underlies one's behaviours? How might we understand the other's behaviours as an attempt to meet one of these basic needs? Have needs for safety, love/affection, and belonging been met?
Circle of Courage	A model of positive youth development that assumes a holistic approach for child-rearing and child development based on Indigenous philosophies, education, youth work, and resilience research (Brendtro, Brokenleg, & Van Bockern, 2002). The model is based on four universal growth needs of all children: belonging, mastery, independence, and generosity (Brendtro et al., 2009).	How does this child experience purpose, power, success, and love in their lives? How does this child experience a sense of belonging with others? How does this child problem-solve and take personal responsibility for their lives? What is required for this to occur?
Bronfenbrenner's Ecological Systems	Environmental elements of an individual's life affect their development (microsystem, macrosystem, mesosystem, chronosystem) and impact an individual's function.	How are each of the systems (micro-, macro-, meso-, chrono-) impacting the individual?
Relational Practice	The fundamental agent of change in Child and Youth Practice is the relationship between practitioner and individual.	How am I trying to establish rapport and trust? How am I supporting the individual achieve mastery over their experiences?
Attachment Theory	The presence or absence of key individuals in a child's life can impede or encourage their development.	Which relationships with the individuals' caregivers encourage or impede the emotional, social, and physical growth of the individual? How are relationships and social, emotional, and physical growth maintained?

(continued)

Table 12: Theoretical Frameworks Explained (*continued*)

Theoretical framework	Overview	Questions
Erikson's Developmental Theory	As children grow, they transition through distinct developmental stages that foster or inhibit their social, emotional, and physical growth.	Which developmental stage is this child at? Does their chronological age correspond with their developmental stage? (Note: Not all children's chronological ages align with their developmental ages. A recognition of this will inform best practice.)
Family Systems Theory	A systems approach to creating change. Difficulties are not isolated to the individual child; they are created and maintained by the interactions within the family. Changes in one aspect of the system create changes in other aspects of the system.	What is the quality of the interactions in a child's family? How do these interactions support or challenge a child's developmental, emotional growth? How do family members communicate with one another; solve problems; play together? What role does each family member play? What is important for me to know about this family in relation to this child? (It is important to note that considering the quality of interactions within the family does not suggest that the family is to blame for the child's issues.)
Trauma-informed Theory	Many individuals you will work with have experienced one sense of trauma or another that will impact their social, emotional, and developmental growth and require trauma-informed approaches to aid their development. Using behavioural approaches are not effective in supporting an individual reconcile their previous trauma.	How do I understand the individual's behaviours: as a reaction to previous traumatic experiences or as purposeful and manipulative? Am I concerned more with discipline and punishment to change the behaviour(s)? How am I supporting the individual to recognize their behaviours as a reaction to earlier trauma, or am I creating shame and humiliation for the individual to change their behaviours? Am I attempting to impose my own values and beliefs onto the individual?

As such, the practitioner's ability to conceptualize the presenting issues and needs of others will enable them to provide client-directed, competent, and ethical practice.

> We have a responsibility to ensure our actions are and have been consistent with our value.
> —Mezirow (1991)

REVISITING CHALLAH FROM A CRITICAL THINKING LENS

1. The Focus of Critical Analysis:
   Challah's frequent moves in the past two years. What supports were put in place at these placements before she was discharged? What is her experience of the many moves?

2. Comprehension:
   Challah may experience abandonment and trust issues with the different moves. She may expect to be moved again and will not invest in relationships with others. Child and Youth Care is about relationships, and every effort to support the child's emotional, social, and spiritual needs should be considered (relational practice; Garfat, 2003a). It is confusing that other practitioners are not operating from this same perspective.

3. Main Ideas/Key Points:
   Challah remained in the same foster home for four years. What impact did leaving this home have on her? Challah did not remain in foster care after her second foster home. What happened? (List other key points from the scenario that relate to the focus of analysis.)

---

4. Deliberating Another's Idea or Argument:
   Consider the other homes' reasons for discharging Challah. (This may require following up with the previous homes to seek further information.) The previous residential home seems to have operated from a Behavioral Modification Framework, as suggested by the evidence for her discharge (failure to comply with program rules). The program seems not to have been a fit for Challah, who may require a relational, individualized approach that meets her developmental needs for security and attachment (Curry et al., 2011; Steele & Malchiodi, 2012), and autonomy and control.

5. Hypothesis:
   The previous programs did not seem to meet the individual needs of Challah for security, attachment, and autonomy. Programs with rotating staff can threaten a youth's sense of safety (Steele & Malchiodi, 2012) when many individuals are involved. Challah's need for consistency, trust, and connections may have been challenged in homes with different personalities in the home. As you engage in critical thinking about these complex issues that arise in practice, it is important to point out that critical thinking is not about blaming or shifting responsibility, but rather identifying the contributing factor for multiple moves: a lack of fit between the needs of the child and the capacity of the program (Beck & Malley, 2003).

6. Challenge the Other's Perspective:

   Professional Child and Youth Care practice is grounded in relationships. The different moves Challah experienced may have threatened her sense of security and need to belong. How had the previous homes missed this crucial piece of Challah's development? What was missing for them to not have acknowledged her need for stable connections? Had they provided the necessary supports or recommendations to support her development, might she have had a different experience of residential care and relationships? If a different way of understanding Challah is not considered, she risks experiencing further moves and difficulties in establishing trusting relationships with others.

In order for Challah to experience secure relationships with adults in her environment, what is required? What additional supports may be necessary? Provide your responses in the space below.

_____

_____

> With a new day comes new strength and new thoughts.
> —Eleanor Roosevelt

The Critical Thinking in Action Process

Consider programs that use point systems to motivate behaviour. While these programs attest to possessing a high regard for safety and teaching responsibility (Henley, 2008), they often neglect to consider a key aspect of the Standards of Practice: the individual's unique experiences and the context in which they evolve (VanderVen, 1999, 2016).

Consider the Following Scenario: Tezique

Tezique is a 10-year-old child who has been residing in residential care for one month. He and his younger brother were apprehended from their home due to neglect and physical abuse; however, the boys reside in separate homes. The program Tezique resides in operates on a points system where children advance in privileges based on the number of points they acquire through demonstrating positive behaviour. Tezique seemed to have adjusted to the expectations of the home and had demonstrated his ability to follow rules and the house programming and had earned a late bedtime. He returned home from his first visit with his brother since their apprehension and yelled at Janyc, the Child and Youth Practitioner, to get out of his way. He threw his backpack at her and slammed the door so hard the glass panel broke. He ignored Janyc's directives to stop and proceeded up the stairs, kicking at items in front of him. Janyc called out to him to remind him that he would be expected to clean up the mess he created and recited the consequences of this behaviour, such as losing his late bedtime. He responded with a few expletives and slammed his door.

Situations like these invite opportunities for practitioners to set aside their assumptions, values, and beliefs and refrain from routine-focused responses (Schon, 1983) to consider the context for the behaviour. As you think about Tezique's reactions, engage the Critical Thinking in Action process as a framework to guide your thinking.

1. The Focus of Critical Analysis:
   What aspect of this situation are you questioning? Indicate the who, what, where, when, and how aspects of the critical analysis.

   _____

   _____

2. Comprehension:
   Your perspective of the situation/experience—the focus for your critical analysis. How does your perspective relate to professional practice? How is your perspective different from the other's perspective?

   _____

   _____

3. Main Ideas/Key Points:
   Identify the key points or main ideas (from the critical analysis) that you are contemplating, analyzing, and questioning.

   _____

   _____

4. Deliberating Another's Idea or Argument:
   What is the basis for their perspective? Is there an aspect of objectivity in their ideas? What is the impact on the other?

   _____

   _____

5. Hypothesis:
   Create new meaning of the situation/experience and formulate a different perspective that aligns with Child and Youth Care practice. How does this new meaning compare with the other's perspective?

   _____

   _____

6. Challenge/Argue against the Other's Perspective:
    Identify the motives behind the other's perspective. Defend your position using theory. What aspects of the other's motives are you challenging and what is the basis for your argument? Identify and connect a theoretical framework to the situation.

    _____

    _____

7. Informed Action:
    What is required for a new outcome to occur?

    _____

    _____

The heart of critical thinking is the ability to understand one's assumptions more accurately by seeing them from multiple points of view (Brookfield, 2012). When practitioners demonstrate an awareness of and a willingness to explore these assumptions (Garfat & Ricks, 1995) and program policies through critical inquiry (as above), their understanding of others expands and the potential to respond with routine-oriented responses will decrease (Bellefeuille et al., 2008; Dewey, as cited in Rodgers, 2002).

Something to Think About

What is your role in challenging program policies similar to those above, which do not account for the context or living experiences of children in care?

Remembering When ...

In my earlier days as a Child and Youth Care Practitioner, I worked in a classroom supporting six latency-aged boys who presented with emotional regulation and impulse control issues. I worked alongside another Child and Youth Care Practitioner to support them in developing their social and emotional skills over a four-month period; however, I realized that each Monday when they returned to class, it was like starting all over with them. Why do you think this might have occurred? My experiences working in this classroom taught me the importance of including the parents in this skill-based work; however, due to the nature of the program and the tenuous relationships between the school and the parents, it proved difficult to engage the parents in supporting the gains the boys made each week. This experience taught me the value and necessity of systemic collaboration. A shared and balanced perspective of these boys' needs was required that was based on mutual respect. How does a Child and Youth Care Practitioner challenge this?

Use the space below to note your thoughts and questions about this.

_____

_____

_____

CRITICAL SHIFTS

The perspectives of parents as the enemy and the cause of problems for children (Garfat & McElwee, 2001) once dominated professional practice, but has shifted immensely over the past several years (Garfat & Charles, 2012). It was once believed that children's "bad behaviour" was a result of poor parenting. This thinking was reinforced when children who returned to the care of their parents after residential care soon resorted to former patterns of behaving. It was common practice to blame parents for this regression, since children made gains in care. Adopting a critical lens to explore other potential reasons children did not manage well after care revealed that many of the parents did not receive the essential support prior to their children returning home. Essentially, parents were set up to fail. In viewing the parents as the enemy and to blame for their children's difficulties was reflective of a rigid and power-infused understanding about change.

Parental and family support is widely recognized as essential to effecting change in the child's life (Garfat & Charles, 2012). While family is now recognized as the single-most important influence in a child's life (Garfat & Charles, 2012), there remains the potential and reality for practitioners to assume this earlier way of thinking that dominated Child and Youth Care practice if they do not maintain a high level of awareness of the influence that self can have in their interactions with others.

ETHICAL DILEMMAS

Another aspect of critical thinking is the ethical dilemmas that can arise when working with children, youth, and families presenting with complex issues. Complex issues are often wrought with uncertainties and require practitioners to engage in an ongoing process of critical reflection. Critical reflective practitioners possess a high level of morale and commitment to ensuring the best interests of the individuals they work with (Bellefeuille & Ricks, 2010; Brookfield, 2012; Ricks, 1997). They demonstrate an openness to considering multiple perspectives, maintain clear boundaries, and adapt their approaches to meet the individualized needs of children, youth, and families (Fook, as cited in Bolton, 2009).

Children's and families' ways of thinking about the world can be understood as a representation of the complex experiences they have encountered. These complex experiences require a consideration of context and an openness to interpretation and alternative perspectives from which to understand these experiences. Failure to do so risks creating assumptions that can result in ineffective interventions, which fail to acknowledge the children's or families' social, emotional, and spiritual developmental needs.

Ricks (1997) described ethical dilemmas as situations where the Child and Youth Care Practitioner's own values compete with the ethical codes for practice and the practitioner must select one over the other to resolve the dilemma. For example, in Chapter 1, you were asked to reflect on the meaning of *do no harm* from the Code of Ethics, responsibility to the child, youth, and family. Do no harm has many different connotations and requires practitioners to consider the context it implies. Do no harm is not limited to physical harm, but encompasses emotional and psychological harm that practitioners can unwittingly create when the individual's needs and their life space experiences are not considered (Gharabaghi, 2008b; Phelan, 2005). Often, when practitioners consider the context in which situations arise, the concept of do no harm can be fraught with ethical dilemmas.

Ethical dilemmas will arise where learning professionals are challenged by the systemic policies that govern their practice as they try to address individual needs and the best interests of others.

The store of one's wisdom is the result of the extent of one's reflection.
—Rodgers, 2002, p. 853

Review the following scenario and identify the ethical dilemma embedded in this scenario and how you might respond.

Exercise 54: A Duty to Report?

Beatrice is a recent graduate who has begun working as a community outreach counsellor. She is currently working with a single mother of two, who has recently had her two young children returned to her care after they were placed in the care of her brothers for one year. Prior to the children's return, the mother had completed a six-month treatment program for her addictions. She had started seeing Beatrice for counselling support to prepare herself for the busy demands of parenting. In meeting with Beatrice one session, she disclosed that she had relapsed one night. She spoke of the stress she had been under in managing work and the demands of parenting and her fears of failure. She expressed her fear that the children would be removed again and vowed she would not do it again. Beatrice is aware that Mom is high-risk for relapse and she is concerned about Mom's stress levels. What does she do?

When responding to the questions below, explain the rationale for your thinking.

Does Beatrice tell Mom of her responsibility to call?

_____

_____

Does she excuse herself from the room and call child welfare without telling Mom?

_____

_____

Does she support Mom in making a call to the worker in the morning?

_____

_____

Use the space below to identify any question or other comments that arise for you.

_____

_____

Exercise 55: A Question of Emotional Harm

Emotional harm as a subjective experience (Phelan, 2005) requires practitioners to consider the unique experiences of individuals in order to determine the best course of action. How might you understand the experiences of this mother, who may have had several adversarial experiences with service providers prior to Beatrice's involvement? Having established a sense of trust with Beatrice to support her and her children, what might be the implications for this mother and her ability to trust or reach out to service providers in the future if Beatrice were to contact child welfare without involving her in this decision?

_____

_____

What is the context for her relapse? What are the implications for her and her children if she determines that social service professionals cannot be trusted?

_____

_____

_____

"Resistant," "disregard for authority," and "uncooperative" are often terms used to describe individuals and families who are not as willing to engage with community partners for different reasons. This warrants consideration of context and past experiences.

What is your responsibility to this woman, her children, and to the agency you are employed by? Whose needs take precedence?

_____

_____

Having explored further this mother's previous experiences as context for understanding her current behaviours, how might this influence the practitioner's response?

This scenario illustrates an example of an ethical dilemma. Using the space below, note any thoughts or questions from this scenario.

_____

_____

When you encounter ethical dilemmas, it is important to:

- Gather your facts
- Define the ethical dilemma
- Establish which values are in opposition
- Identify the best interests of children, youth, and families
- Identify your options and make a decision

Following this, however, is the additional responsibility to monitor, evaluate, and provide feedback related to the outcome of the ethical dilemma (Garfat & Ricks, 1995). This ensures accountability of your actions and sharing the learning that has occurred from this with others.

As you proceed through this chapter, be mindful of the decisions you come to and the rationales behind them. When others question your actions, be prepared to defend your thinking with theory, as theory provides the anchor from which effective practice occurs. Without such an anchor, practitioners risk reacting out of impulse, emotions, and judgement. That being said, such reactions provide a point of reference to further reflect and explore with others in the reflective group.

In doing so, learning professionals demonstrate alternative ways of knowing that are integral to reflective practice (Bellefeuille & Ricks, 2010; Brockbank & McGill, 2007; Gharabaghi, 2008a; Moon, 2008; White, 2007). New learning opportunities evolve from your questions, engaging in inquiry, challenging assumptions, and considering diverse perspectives (White, 2007).

Something to Think About

Recall the scenario involving Tezique and Janyc. As Janyc reflected on Tezique and the context for his behaviours, she realized that her response about consequences risked causing him emotional harm. Given his situation and the experience of just having seen his brother for the first time in over a month, she understood his reactions as an overt expression of his hurt, anger, and frustration. How could she consequence him for what she and the other staff were responsible for—supporting him in regulating his emotions? She realized that her value for relationships and emotional development was in contrast with the agency's philosophy of change. She would not implement a consequence nor remove his late bedtime. This, she realized, would challenge the other children who had lost late nights and points for their behaviour.

In reviewing the Standards of Practice, Janyc noted it states a responsibility to the child in recognizing the individual needs of children; however, her responsibility to the employer is upholding the commitments to the program (points system). What does she do? Which takes precedence: the needs of Tezique or her commitments to the program? Which perspective aligns with Child and Youth Care practice?

Share your thoughts in the space below.

_____

_____

_____

Having predetermined rules and regulations about who, when, and with whom we do our work presents us with some significant practice dilemmas that cannot be easily resolved and warrant further attention (Gharabaghi, 2008b).

Ricks (1997) recommends that practitioners examine, reflect, consider, and reason the situation through until an option becomes clear. Sit with the uncertainty and explore it. How much of the uncertainty is related to doing the right thing? Reflect on your values, your sense of right and wrong when addressing this ethical dilemma (Garfat & Ricks, 1995). Ask yourself, "what harm might my actions create for the other(s)?"

A QUESTION OF CONSENT

Children 12 and over can consent to receiving their own mental health services from community organizations without parental consent. Schools, however, require children to be 16 and over to receive counselling support without parental consent. How is it that this difference exists? Children spend most of their time in school and yet cannot access supports available to them within the school setting without parental consent.

Exercise 56: Critical Thinking in Action: A Matter of Ethics

As the school Child and Youth Care Practitioner, Mathew had been supporting an eight-year-old girl, Charly, in processing her experiences of her parents' divorce. Prior to his involvement, Charly had begun to withdraw and isolate herself from peers and social activities. Her doctor placed her on medication to support her in coping with the sadness; however, her mother felt she would benefit by meeting with someone at school, where she spent most of her time. Consents were received from both parents. Charly seemed receptive and her mood and isolation shifted; she began to engage with others more. One day, the father contacted Mathew to revoke consent and expressed that Charly didn't need to see him any longer. This was communicated to Charly by Mathew and the school principal, and further contact with Mathew halted. During one lunch hour, Charly locked herself in the washroom, crying, and refused to speak to anyone but Mathew.

As a Child and Youth Practitioner, Mathew has an obligation to meet the best interests of the child and to do no harm, yet he is also responsible for abiding by the school board's consent policies. If he does not respond and meet with Charly, he risks negating his responsibility to her as a Child and Youth Care Practitioner. If he does respond, he is refuting the father's revoked consent and the school board's policy. This reflects an ethical dilemma because of the competing values when considering the best interests of Charly. Refer to the Critical Thinking in Action framework and focus on points 5–7.

5. Hypothesis: Create new meaning of the situation/experience and formulate a different perspective that aligns with Child and Youth Care practice. How does this new meaning compare with the other's perspective?

_____

_____

_____

6. Identify the motives behind the other's perspective. Defend your position using theory. What aspects of the other's motives are you challenging and what is the basis for your argument? Identify and connect theoretical frameworks to the situation.

_____

_____

_____

When presented with complex situations involving ethical dilemmas, it is important to consult with colleagues and your supervisor or professor.

7. Who else might you access support from in the Child and Youth Care field to address the ethical focus of this situation?

_____

_____

_____

Critical thinking involves more of a focus on the relevance to theory (Dewey, as cited in Moon, 2008) and requires the practitioner to analyze the information presented and identify how this information relates to Child and Youth Care practice (consider the Standards of Practice, relational practice, and the other key frameworks presented in Table 10). As you continue to progress in your learning and experiences during practice, you will begin to reframe problems as opportunities to further explore, question, analyze, and challenge inconsistencies that inhibit the development of others from a critical lens. You will discover that the more you approach situations from a critical thinking lens, the more your need for a solution or obtaining a right answer will diminish.

This being said, however, developing the skills necessary for critical thinking takes time and will continue for the duration of your career. Refer to Chapter 10 (Reflective Tools) to select one of the tools to support you in conceptualizing your experiences during practice. The templates in the appendices will further support you in developing your skills as a reflective practitioner. You will learn in Chapter 10 that there are other tools for capturing your reflection if writing is not a fit for you. Determine which is a better fit for you and use those tools to continue reflecting on practice. In capturing as much detail of your experience as possible, you provide the context necessary to engage in critical thinking.

EXPANDING YOUR CRITICAL THINKING LENS

Another way to practice critical thinking is to read articles from the field and other disciplines on topics that relate to your practice. Additionally, reading reports, case studies, and news articles related to the field will assist you in developing your critical lens. Remember, however, that this is not about critiquing others' ideas nor imposing your own ideas as fact; rather, it is an opportunity to identify and challenge assumptions, to consider alternative perspectives, and to expand your ways of knowing, thinking, and doing. This will require you to share these ideas with others, which will assist you in developing the necessary skills of communication, receiving and providing feedback, working in groups, managing conflict, and demonstrating accountability to others (Ash & Clayton, 2009) by defending your position with theory, which in turn leads to a more informed, action-oriented approach (Moon, 2008; Schon, 1983). Additional opportunities to engage in this collaborative approach to practice will be introduced in the following chapter.

The following report will provide you with an opportunity to demonstrate your critical thinking skills, following the Critical Thinking in Action process. Read through the report and make any notes or questions you have about the content of the report in the space below (alternatively, you may wish to note your comments directly onto the report). This report is a sample intake report that was completed for a mother involved with social services who attempted to reestablish custody of her eight-year-old daughter. Pay attention to the content and tone of the report and to your reactions (notably the internal reactions) and assumptions. The questions below are more specific than the questions from the critical thinking model; however, they are still designed to support your critical thinking skills.

When additional questions come up from reading the initial report, it is common practice to request previous reports to gain a better understanding of the family's history and needs. Remember our request for further information often comes from our critical analysis of the presenting information and demonstrates intentionality and the importance in examining context. Social histories provided on request from the child welfare agencies provide the historical information that is not included in the initial referral/intake form.

As you read further about this family in Figure 23 (Cat and Alice), identify aspects of the report that would warrant further exploration.

Therapeutic Services Intake Report

Date of Intake: Apr. 7, xxxx   **Intake completed by:** Joshua B

Name of Referring agency: xxxx   **Worker's Name:** Cally T

Date of Admission: January 10, xxxx

Child's Information

Child's Name: Alice N   **D.O.B:** Jan. 10, xxxx

Foster Home: G. and J. Battuli   **Address:** xxxx   **Phone number**: xxxx

Status: Temporary Care Agreement   **Children's Service Worker:** J. V.

Reason for referral:
Worker is requesting therapy for Alice to help her deal with the mom's mental health behaviours. To facilitate access visits between mother and child.

Presenting concerns:
Alice acts out when she doesn't get her own way. She is sexual toward her foster father and foster brothers. The worker thinks she was sexually abused while living at home. She doesn't follow morning routines, taking a long time to get ready in the morning. She doesn't listen and is defiant toward her teacher and the foster parents. She is very possessive. She does a lot of screaming and whining. The foster mom gets frustrated with Alice, especially in the morning when she takes forever to get ready. Foster mom rules the household like a drill sargent. Foster parents need help to manage Alice's aggressive behaviour.

Family history:
Alice was living with her mother until November xxxx, when she was apprehended due to mom's mental health behaviour. Mom is fighting for custody. There has been no access since July xxxx. Alice made an allegation against the foster parents. Mom has tried to convince Alice that something is happening to her. Mom is very paranoid. The referring agency put a hold on visits since the investigation of allegation against the foster parents. Visits with mom have not occurred for 6 months. The father is not involved. No known information on the father is available. Mom is trying to see Alice and wants information on her whereabouts. She has threatened the agency if she doesn't receive information about her daughter. The worker has refused her access visits at this time because of her mental health behaviour. Mom feels she should know where her daughter is, what supports she has, and who is involved in her care.

Mom has recently retained a lawyer to regain custody of her daughter.

Additional information:
The worker is requesting copies of all the access visit notes and wishes to be notified each time the mother is late or absent. She has requested that all access visits start and end on time, and that if mom is late three times, the next session will be cancelled.

Figure 22: Carla's Therapeutic Services Intake Report

Source: Adapted from https://www.sampleforms.com/counseling-intake-forms.html.

Exercise 57: Reviewing Reports through a Critical Lens

What are the assumptions of the author? What is the emotional tone of the report? What is the importance of acknowledging the emotional tone?

_____

_____

Who is the author of the report? What is their relationship to the family?

_____

_____

What is the author's philosophy about children, youth, and families? (Consider the greater social structure to which they belong.) How does this compare to the philosophy of Child and Youth Care practice?

_____

_____

Have the individual or family's perspectives been captured in the report?

_____

Deliberating Another's Idea or Argument

What is the basis for their perspective? How does this compare to your perspective as a Child and Youth Care Practitioner?

_____

_____

What are the motives of the author of the report?

_____

_____

How are the recommendations related to the needs of the family?

_____

_____

Questioning different details is beneficial in establishing objectivity when reading reports written by other professionals. Analyzing aspects of the report will assist you in maintaining objectivity and prevent you from being influenced by the author's impression. Identify any questions you have from the content of the report.

Hypothesis

Create new meaning of this author's perspective. How does this new meaning compare to the author's perspective?

Challenge the other's perspectives. Defend your position with theory. Example: Professional practitioners operate from a strength-based and relational approach to practice. Families develop new skills in an environment that conveys respect and acceptance and provides the support for families to experience success. Adopting a directive approach that does not acknowledge the family's individual needs is not conducive to promoting change or opportunities for new ways of experiencing. Attachment theory states that when individuals are connected with others and provided the opportunities to build on their strengths and encouragement to thrive, individuals will grow (Golding & Hughes, 2012).

How do the perspectives of this author compare with Child and Youth Care practice?

Informed Action

What is required for you to proceed with this family/this worker?

Identify additional comments or questions you have and list them below.

Social History of the Child

SOCIAL HISTORY DETAILS

Name: Alice N   **Worker:** J.V.   **Date of Report:** xxx. xx, xxxx

IDENTIFYING INFORMATION

Name: Alice N   **Date of Birth:** Jan. 10, xxxx   **Language:** English

Ethnic Origin: Caucasian   **Religion:** Catholic

Place of Birth: Orillia, ON

OCCURRENCE HISTORY

Removal   **Removal Type:** Apprehension

Start Date: Nov. xx, xxxx   **Days in Care:** 185

PRIMARY PLACEMENT

Provider: Carla's Therapeutic Service Homes, G. and J. Battuli

---

LEGAL STATUS

Agency: **Legal Status:**

Children's Aid Society   Temporary Care and Custody

Significant Events:

One year ago, Alice was placed in a residential group home for support with the level of aggression Alice had been demonstrating at school and home. Her mother, Cat, contacted the agency for support with her daughter's behavioural difficulties. It was deemed that placing Alice in a residential program could provide further support in shifting the behaviours. During an on-site visit with the mother, staff alleged that the mother had struck Alice across the face. The mother denies this occurred and has not taken any responsibility for her behaviour. It was at this point that the agency determined Alice's custodial agreement needed to be extended given the physical abuse the mother inflicted on her.

Supervised access visits were arranged in the agency office for weekly one-hour visits. The mother was often redirected as she would attempt to engage Alice in conversations about her care status. The mother often presented as angry and belligerent toward staff, accusing the agency of ruining her family.

The agency had requested a psychological report for Alice as it was suspected that she might have been subject to sexual abuse. Medication was recommended to support Alice in managing her impulses; however, the mother declined and as such Alice's medical needs were not provided for. Recommendations were also indicated for Alice to receive therapy as she transitioned into foster care.

As the mother's behaviour escalated, Alice's safety was deemed a priority. She was moved into a foster home 3 hours away. The mother was made aware of this in a letter to avoid potential retaliate behaviours against the agency. The mother had demanded to know the whereabouts of Alice and often threatened to damage property if she was not given information.

Figure 23: Alice's Social History Report

Source: Adapted from Toronto Children's Aid Society agency forms.

Alice was moved to a foster home with three of the parents' biological sons. Visits were placed on hold between the mother and Alice for 6 months. Alice had no contact with her mother during this time. The agency withheld all contact until the mother dealt with her mental health issues.

In the foster home, Alice has difficulties with routine, transitions, and interacting with others. The foster parent is required to supervise her at all times, as she will engage in proactive behaviours with the sons (ages 2, 10, 12). Alice engages in tantrums daily. The foster parent has indicated several incidents of sexually inappropriate behaviour from Alice. She has been reminded about privacy and boundary issues and once told the foster parent that she used to run around naked at home. The agency suspects sexual interference; however, this has not been confirmed.

At school, she struggles to complete the school tasks and will engage in aggressive behaviours to get her own way. The school often will remove her from the classroom to sit with the school CYCP, where she plays games and refuses to complete homework.

When she was first placed in foster care, she often asked about her mother and when she would see her again. Alice was told that mom was very ill, and it would be a longer time before her mom could see her.

Family History:

Cat is a single mother who once worked as a legal administrative assistant for a lawyer's office. She became ill with significant physical health issues that required her to stop working. Mother has bipolar disorder and would often not take her medication. The agency initially tried to set the mother up with a therapist; however, because of the mother's paranoid delusions, she refused. There is no known information on Alice's father.

Cat comes from a wealthy extended family whom she has no contact with. It is suspected that she was molested as a young child by a family member; however, this has not been verified. The foster mother has described Alice as highly emotional and does not listen. She will not follow routines and demonstrates significant difficulty with routines, transitions.

Primary Permanency Plan: Extended Society Care

Permanence Plan Details:

The mother has requested to have her daughter back in her care; however, she has not been responsive to the agency's or her daughter's medical needs. The mother has not consented to participate in a psychological assessment to determine her ability to parent.

Describe the child's personality and behaviour

Alice is an active child who likes to make and follow her own rules. She does not like to be told what to do and will often ignore the adults' directives. She can be helpful in the home at times. She enjoys making things, however, she struggles with cleaning up afterwards. She has few friends at school.

Describe the child's aptitudes and abilities

Alice has few interests other than making things. She enjoys her arts and crafts.

Alice is a curious child who enjoys reading and creating. She likes playing with toys and has not shown any interest in attending community recreational activities. She requires individual supports in school and has a difficult time in completing academic tasks.

Figure 23: (*continued*)

Exercise 58: The Social History Report: A Focus for Critical Analysis

Use the space below to record any questions or thoughts that come up for you. Identify the influential factors that have impacted this family (consider Bronfenbrenner's ecological systems theory).

_____

_____

_____

In considering the different theories, it is important to evaluate any discrepancies on which you are basing your argument. Provide evidence of and evaluation of your approach (while linking to theory). Critical thinking requires you to look beyond the surface behaviours to argue against, question, and consider diverse perspectives to achieve new outcomes. Continue to identify any assumptions or judgements that arise. Ask yourself what this is based on: past experiences, others' perspectives, values, beliefs?

Asking "do I know this to be true?" will support you in challenging and setting aside those assumptions.

Identify areas in the social history that you have questions about and seek to challenge.

_____

_____

_____

What perspectives might inform the agency author's frame?

_____

_____

_____

Defend your argument with examples.

_____

_____

_____

Based on what you have read in the social history and in the referral report, what are your next steps?

_____

_____

_____

_____

_____

What are the needs you have determined for this family? How might this differ from the author of the report?

_____

_____

_____

_____

_____

We don't see things as they are, we see things as we are.
    —Anaïs Nin

Students may express feeling intimidated by challenging the opinions of other professionals, which provides opportunities to engage in reflective thinking and explore the meaning this holds for them. It is these situations that call for reflective dialogues to support them in discussing, sharing, and exploring the beliefs that underlie their thinking. This will be further explored in the following chapter on reflective learning.

Practice applying the Critical Thinking in Action framework to issues of concern that occur over the next few weeks. Pay attention to current events or situations during your practice and the assumptions that underlie these. Use the template in Appendix XII to guide your thinking.

We become critically reflective by challenging the established definition of a problem by seeing the individual through a different, less muddied lens that allows for new insights.
    —Jack Mezirow, 1991

Practice, practice, practice, practice. Each of the processes you have engaged in throughout this book has prepared you in developing as a reflective professional practitioner.

It is important to continue applying the different concepts you have learned into your daily life and practice. Remember that learning occurs through experiences. It will be beneficial to review concepts from previous chapters to support your learning.

CLOSING THOUGHTS

What new insight did you discover from this chapter? About yourself? Child and Youth Care practice?

_____

_____

_____

How will adopting a critical thinking lens assist you in maintaining a balanced perspective of other community professionals and their involvement with children, youth, and families?

_____

_____

_____

Identify aspects of this chapter that you require further support or clarification with.

_____

_____

_____

NOTES

1. Phases of Critical Thinking has been taken from Brookfield (2011).
2. The "checking out assumptions" exercise is adapted from Hall, McWeeny, and Brookfield (2012).
3. "Components of Critical Thinking" was taken from Brookfield (1987).
4. *The Fifth Estate* outlines the life and death of Ashley Smith, a highly publicized case in 2010 about the prevalent systemic failures to address her mental health needs. Available at: https://www.cbc.ca/fifth/blog/the-life-and-death-of-ashley-smith.
5. The Reflective Thinking and Critical Thinking Comparison (Table 11) was taken from Mann, Gordon, and MacLeod (2009).
6. The "identify your assumptions" partner exercise has been adapted from Brookfield (2012).

CHAPTER 9

Reflective Learning

Individuals are the agents of their own learning.
—Ference Marton, 1975

LEARNING OBJECTIVES

In this chapter, you will:

- reflect on your learning to date
- define reflective learning as a holistic approach to learning
- distinguish between the different learning styles
- describe your experiences from your practice utilizing reflective tools
- document your observations during practice using the observation log

In the previous chapter you learned about critical thinking as an advanced process of reflective practice. In assuming a critical thinking lens for practice, practitioners identify and challenge assumptions that underlie professional practice, consider diverse perspectives, and demonstrate a greater understanding of the systemic barriers that children, youth, and families experience. Critical thinking leads to new ways for *thinking about and doing* Child and Youth Care practice that aligns with professional practice. Practice will be required for you to integrate a critical thinking lens into your approach.

In this chapter, you move forward to reflective learning, which will introduce you to the theoretical concepts of reflective learning. The ensuing chapters introduce different writing tools to further guide you in reflective practice, and reflective dialogue or, more aptly, collaborative reflection. Collaborative reflection brings to light the importance and value group reflections have for thinking critically about your practice, while identifying opportunities for further learning. At this point, I invite you to reflect on your learning to identify how this has affected your development as a professional practitioner.

Reflect on your learning to this point in the text. What have you learned about yourself that you may not have been aware of before?

_____

_____

What has shifted for you? What remains the same, a struggle, or an uncertainty?

_____

_____

What further learning is required in terms of the different concepts you have learned about in the previous two chapters?

_____

_____

What shifts have you noticed in your practice as a result of reflecting on practice?

_____

_____

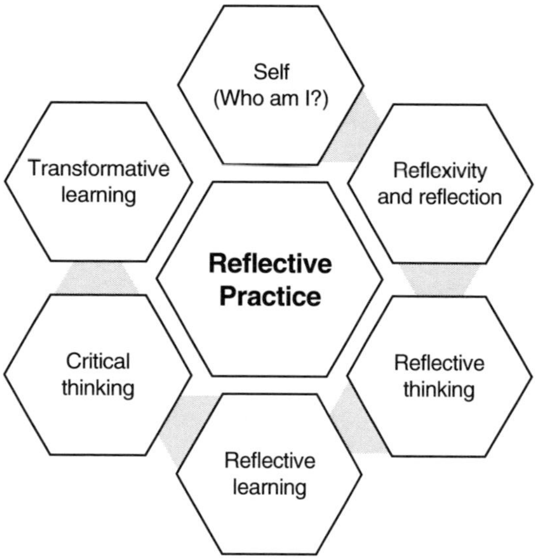

Figure 1: Reflective Practice Radial

Source: Recreated by author.

WHAT IS REFLECTIVE LEARNING?

Reflective learning has been described across the reflective practice literature as a process of reflecting on key issues of concerns that are triggered by experiences and lead to different perspectives (Brockbank & McGill, 2007; Brookfield, 1987; Johns, 2009; Moon, 2004). Reflective learning occurs through both writing and reflective dialogue with others in order to transform learning (Brockbank & McGill, 2007). New learning is the central focus for reflective learning (Moon, 2004), which occurs from knowledge and through learning experiences that assist practitioners in reexamining their understanding of issues (Moon, 2004). Learning is less about the acquisition of the material and more about your ability to integrate aspects of the material into your practice.

Learning Styles

What have you discovered about the way you learn? Your learning style represents another aspect of self and the formats you may require for further learning. This will enable you to acquire, process, and apply that learning to daily practice in a way that fits for you (Brockbank & McGill, 2007; Tsingos, Bosnic-Anticevich, & Smith, 2015).

Reflecting on the style of one's learning and applying that way of learning into day-to-day experiences will provide a greater chance for new learning to take effect (Brockbank & McGill, 2007; Tsingos et al., 2015) and for you to integrate it into your daily practice. Of the different exercises in this book, which ones have resonated with you most? The case scenarios, where the concept of reflection is broken down into specific steps? The case scenarios where you applied your knowledge and ideas to discover possibility and connections? The exercises that involved visual images or demonstrations? Or class discussions and lectures that highlight and explain information? Do you prefer to follow the sequential steps that many of the reflective processes have included, or do you prefer to look at the larger picture and determine your understanding of what it means for you?

An alternative way of thinking about your style of learning is to think about which aspects of these exercises and case scenarios have assisted you in developing your skills as a reflective practitioner. If you feel that nothing has helped and that this material remains confusing to you, it is important to step back and consider your role in this learning. What have you done to ascertain the material is connecting with you? Have you addressed your concerns with the professor? Reflect on the challenges you have had with the learning and consider what has prevented you from reaching out to address these challenges. How might your challenges in reaching out to seek support influence your practice with children, youth, and families and day-to-day interactions in your practice? These are important questions to ask at this point in your learning. Use the space below to respond to the questions above and include comments or questions you may wish to follow up on.

_____

_____

_____

_____

_____

Felder and Solomon (2008) defined these distinct types of learners:

- Active learners
- Reflective learners
- Sensing learners

- Intuitive learners
- Visual learners
- Verbal learners
- Sequential learners
- Global learners

The purpose of introducing you to the different learning styles is to provide you with an opportunity for further developing an understanding of your learning needs, which will assist you in your reflective practice moving forward. If you have identified yourself as having a specific learning style, it is important for you to share this understanding with others so that you remain responsible for your learning. Identifying your learning style can also assist you in recognizing what you need from your work and learning environments for optimal learning.

If you're not sure how you learn best, you can complete a free online questionnaire to discover what type of reflective learner you are. You can find one at www.webtools.ncsu.edu/learningstyles/.

Table 13: Learning Styles[1]

Learning style	Description	Example	Challenges	Consideration for further action
Active Learners	Active learners tend to retain and understand information best by doing something active with it: discussing or applying it or explaining it to others.	Active learners tend to like group work. Experiential: doing first.	Learning that involves note-taking during lectures. Active learners can react first without thinking through aspects of the situation.	You have a greater chance of retaining the information if you find ways to do something with it. When you think about presenting your cases, consider how you will involve others' feedback and input.
Reflective Learners	Reflective learners prefer to think about it quietly first and often prefer working alone.	Thinking through first.	Working in groups during reflective dialogues may be difficult as you think about the information presented. You might find it helpful to write short summaries of readings or class notes in your own words. Doing so may take extra time but will enable you to retain the material more effectively.	During case presentations, write down questions or comments you have about the information presented.

Learning style	Description	Example	Challenges	Consideration for further action
Sensing Learners	Sensing learners often prefer to obtain facts. They may tend to rely on "the right" way of doing things through specific methods.	Obtaining knowledge about others and having a plan of what they will do.	They may doubt their own judgement without a specific method or strategy to rely on. Thinking and actions may present as rigid and routine-oriented.	During case presentations, it can be helpful to ask others to explain their reasoning as opposed to determining what did or didn't work. Asking for examples will support you in making connections about cases.
Intuitive Learners	Intuitive learners often prefer discovering possibilities and interactions between the material to arrive at their own conclusion.	Considering novel ways of responding to situations.	Intuitive learners will struggle if they are told to follow one way for doing things. May make careless mistakes by not considering the key aspects of information.	During case presentations, asking questions to support others in making connections will be beneficial.
Visual Learners	Visual learners prefer graphic images or diagrams to represent learning concepts.	Create visuals of the information they are being presented.	May struggle without visual context to integrate the learning. May become distracted with an overload of verbal or written information.	Present case information in a visual format and offer to create this format for others (the mind mapping tool discussed in Chapter 10 can be helpful in this area).
Verbal Learners	Verbal learners have a preference for information that is delivered in written or spoken form.	You may wish to make notes and create information questions about the children, youth, and families you will work with at practicum.	Visual representations without the explanations may pose challenges. You may doubt your thinking if the information is not presented first. You may be challenged by not having the information presented to you first about a child or youth you will be working with.	Create a list of questions about those you will be working with if no other information is provided. During case presentations, it can be helpful to make notes of what others present. You may prefer to provide others with a written summary of your case to present with others.

(continued)

Table 13: Learning Styles (*continued*)

Learning style	Description	Example	Challenges	Consideration for further action
Sequential Learners	Sequential learners learn and gain knowledge through step-by-step instructions.	Following a particular model or way of doing things. Solution-oriented.	May become stuck on the right way of doing things. May be challenged in slowing down their impulse to find a solution.	Having cheat-sheets or notes that outline ways of doing things. For instance, having a copy of the reflective models may support you in integrating your learning about these different reflective models. (See Appendices for templates.)
Global Learners	Global learners consider the larger picture first without acknowledging the context or individual aspects of the situation.	Focuses on solving problems. May defer to the rules and policies as the solutions.	May be challenged in seeing the connections in situations. May attempt to offer solutions based on what you think you know.	During case presentations, break down your thinking into smaller chunks. Ask questions to assist you in connecting your previous knowledge to the presentation. You may prefer to have a succinct focus for the presentations first. For instance, ask the presenter, what is the focus of their presentation and make notes of their comments.

Exercise 59: Your Learning Style

When you have identified with a learning style that best represents you, think about how this way of learning influences your interactions with others and the ways you take in information from others. What have you noticed? When presented with new information, what format do you learn from best? Do you learn best from reading, hearing, or seeing the information? How has this impacted your ability to absorb the information? How do you make your needs known to others if you require a different format for learning?

What is the connection between your learning style, absorbing information, and applying that learning into practice? What are the implications if you do not communicate with others? What methods for sharing information do you require?

_____

_____

_____

_____

_____

Checking In

Where are you with understanding the concepts and exercises in this chapter thus far? How do they connect with your learning from the previous chapters? What questions do you have that warrant further exploration to support your learning in this chapter?

The content and conditions in which learning occurs is paramount to the degree of autonomy the learner experiences (Brockbank & McGill, 2007). Previous chapters have focused on individual-based learning to develop the foundational skills of reflective practice. Developing the skills necessary for reflective thought and developing a sense of self and awareness of one's own experiences and others have provided the foundation from which reflective learning occurs.

Brockbank and McGill (2007) purport that social process is critical to learning, and it is social relations that are necessary for the advanced skills of critical thinking, reflective dialogue, and collaborative reflections to develop (Kahnet et al., as cited in Brockbank & McGill, 2007). Didactic and group-based reflections enable practitioners to review, re-think, and reconsider their ways of knowing and the impact this has on practice. Your previous group experiences, which may have created angst, will have prepared you for this moment. Working in teams is a significant aspect of Child and Youth Care practice, whether you are directly or indirectly involved with those teams. Upholding your responsibility to the community and colleagues within your workplace necessitates professional behaviour when working with others, irrespective of personal feelings toward them. How does this expectation for professional practice apply to your relationships in the academic environment? What differences exist between your interactions at school and those in the working environment? How do you explain the difference?

_____

_____

_____

Establishing the Conditions for Further Learning

Share your reflective journals and the other reflective tools you use with others to further develop your reflective practice skills. Sharing with others provides you the opportunity to receive feedback that will assist you in identifying assumptions or judgement present in your writing. Reflective writing will prepare you for participating in reflective dialogues and collaborative reflections. Group-based reflective processes are not to be confused with venting about your experiences. The guidelines will be explained in the latter part of this chapter.

Schon (1983) introduced the concept of the "reflective practitioner" as one who uses reflection as a tool for learning from past experiences and for acknowledging the uncertainties within professional practice. Similarly, reflective learning involves the processing of experience in a variety of ways. Learners explore their understanding of their actions and experience, and the impact of these on themselves and others. Meaning is constructed within a reflective community with others (Allard et al., 2007; Carson, Tesluk, & Marrone, 2007).

> Learning from experience is key to reflective learning.
> —Brockbank & McGill (2007)

The focus of reflective learning is not what you have achieved or succeeded at in your practice, but your ability to create meaning of your experiences with others and the result this has on your learning. It is through reflective dialogues and collaborative reflections that reflective learning develops. This requires more than reading, thinking, and talking about cases to include the practitioner's ability to reflect on their experiences and to defend their theory-grounded practice, while remaining open to continued forms of enquiry that lead to new ways of thinking about practice.

Take a _mmm_ Moment

Take five minutes from what you are doing and notice where you are in the space and time; I mean _really_ notice. Where are you situated in this room? Where are your feet in relation to the rest of your body? Where is your head space at? Notice what you are thinking about at this very moment. What is the impact of this thinking on you? Is something distracting you? Are you feeling bored, consumed, or overwhelmed by the knowledge and information you are taking in? Are you taking it in or are you going through the motions of learning and doing the bare minimum to earn your grades? What is and what is not working for you in your stage of learning?

Uncertainty yields opportunities for reflection.
—Author Unknown

RECONSIDERING FEEDBACK: A SOURCE OF ANGST OR OPPORTUNITY?

No two people will perceive a situation the same way (Gharabaghi, 2008b) and engaging in opportunities to consider diverse perspectives is pivotal for working with others, notably your team members or classmates. When you can consider diverse perspectives and the values and beliefs that underlie them, opportunities to grow and develop as practitioners will occur. This too makes room for new learning, new possibilities, and reinforces the importance of working in teams. Giving and receiving feedback is an essential aspect of reflective learning, as you will discover when you are introduced to reflective dialogues (or collaborative reflection; Brockbank & McGill, 2007). Reflective inquiry provides opportunities to enhance one's learning and capacity to look beyond the surface of the presenting issue or concern in order to consider different perspectives and new ways of looking at things.

Feedback is essential for learning and enables practitioners to consider different ways of thinking about and responding to situations. However, the concept of feedback is often associated with a negative connotation and, for some individuals, feedback can imply "what you are doing wrong." This way of thinking is often based on past experiences with individuals who have not provided feedback in a manner intended to support growth and professional development. This should always be the aim of feedback.

Recall the case scenario involving Xandu, where zir coworker Lauren suggested zi reflect on zir interactions with Challah. Being challenged or *called out* on one's behaviour, while seemingly unsettling at first, requires that you withhold judgement of the other to consider personal responsibility for your professional behaviour. When practitioners react or become defensive when another colleague questions their practice, there is an opportunity to reflect on the meaning this holds. What is required to make this less about *you* and more about improving practice as a professional practitioner? Pay attention to your internal reactions, since feelings can influence the degree to which new learning can occur (Moon, 2004). Recall from previous chapters that one's emotions can also influence the meaning of the experiences. This is not to suggest that your feelings are not valid; rather, you should be aware of them and reflect on the meaning experiences hold for you. When you shift your meaning, the experiences shift too, creating the space for further learning to occur. As you continue to reflect on your experiences, you create the necessary space to *get out of the way of yourself*, which allows for this learning and growth to occur. The more attuned and present you are to the other, the greater the learning and the greater the impact this new learning will have for the other (Moon, 2004).

Transparency diminishes the space for judgement.
—Pharrell Williams, 2008

Something to Think About

What is your current comfort level in giving and receiving feedback? What supports your ability to give and receive feedback? What prevents you? What is required for you to develop the skills necessary for giving and receiving feedback?

Use the space below to respond to the questions above.

_____

_____

_____

_____

Exercise 60: Assessing Your Skills

Review the list of skills related to reflective practice you have learned from the previous chapters to identify areas you are developing in and areas that require additional practice or clarification. For areas that you require additional practice in, list the ways you will achieve this practice.

_____

_____

_____

_____

Table 14: Assessing Your Skills in Reflective Practice

Reflective practice skill	Under-developed	Requires further development	Refining through daily practice	Support with examples
Use of Self: • Awareness of values • Beliefs • Assumptions, social locations • Awareness of implications on practice				

Reflective practice skill	Under-developed	Requires further development	Refining through daily practice	Support with examples
Reflexivity: • Awareness and under-standing of social location and connection to privilege and power • Awareness of and comfort in expressing emotions • Ability to consider how actions meet the best interests of the individual				
Reflection: • Ability to reflect on experience, identify the impact on self and others • Ability to determine what is required to be different for next time • Ability to consider alternative perspectives • Ability to discern between transference and counter-transference and implications on practice				
Reflective Thinking: • Ability to apply the reflective thinking model to situations • Ability to differentiate between Reflective Process Model and Schon's reflective process models • Awareness and ability to reflect on action and in action				
Critical Thinking: • Ability to distinguish between implicit and explicit assumptions • Ability to defend thinking with theory • Ability to consider alternative perspectives				

(continued)

Reflective practice skill	Under-developed	Requires further development	Refining through daily practice	Support with examples
Reflective Learning: • Ability to participate in collaborative reflections and reflective dialogues • Ability to give and receive feedback as areas for learning • Ability to engage in reflective journal writing as means to reflect on practice				

CLOSING THOUGHTS

You may have noticed that the concepts are repeated throughout the text and some of the exercises may seem similar. Remember that reflective practice is a process that requires ongoing practice and is a core aspect of professional practice. The more you practice, the more seamless opportunities and new learning become. *Practice makes better.*

How are you integrating the aspects of reflection into your day-to-day experiences?

_____

_____

What concepts are you finding difficult to integrate? What is this about? Your discomfort or fear in trying something new?

_____

_____

What is it that you require in order to embrace new learning concepts in your practice?

_____

_____

What questions remain for you from this chapter?

_____

_____

NOTE

1. The learning styles table has been adapted from Feldman and Solomon (2008).

CHAPTER 10

Reflective Tools for the Reflective Practitioner

Tell me and I'll forget, show me and I'll understand, involve me and I'll remember.

—Chinese Proverb

LEARNING OBJECTIVES

In this chapter, you will:

- be introduced to diverse media for engaging in reflective practice
- be introduced to the concept of metaphors as alternative means for engaging in reflective practice
- demonstrate the ability to critically reflect on issues addressed in practice
- demonstrate your ability to reflect on practice

Reflective tools provide you with different ways to explore your thinking about aspects of your practice. You may already be using some of these tools to support your learning in reflective practice. Pause for a moment to identify the impact these tools have had in shifting or expanding your thinking about your practice.

Written reflections and group discussions provide valuable means for engaging in reflective practice; however, there are many other ways to reflect on practice, which will appeal to the visual learner. There is much value in providing experiential creative means for practitioners to express their experiences of practice. The use of metaphors and sensorial or experiential exercises can assist practitioners in *getting out of the way of themselves* to be in the present moment. You may find that you connect more readily to one tool than an another and may use this to support your reflections throughout your learning journey. This said, however, it will be important that the focus of reflections guide this process.

Writing, blogging, recording, and art media are different tools that can be used to support your ability to reflect on practice:

- Small moments
- Guided reflections
- Mind mapping
- Creative imagery
- Social media
- Reflective blogs

There are important points to consider for using the reflective tools to guide your thinking:

- Establish a focus—what issue of concern are you basing your reflections on?
- What reflective model will inform your reflection?
- What connections or new insights have you developed from this process?
- How will these connections/insights inform your action?
- What further learning have you identified?

SMALL MOMENTS

Small moment reflections capture one aspect of the learning professional's experience as they provide structure and focus of one experience as opposed to several (Bleicher & Correia, 2011; McCormick Calkins & Oxenhorn-Smith, 2003). The exercises in the initial part of the book are similar to small moment reflections, designed to introduce learning professionals to the reflective process.

Writing about your small moments provides you with opportunities to reflect on your experiences and to prepare you for writing in reflective journals, which you will be introduced to in the following section. Small moment reflections can be completed daily or weekly and focus on one experience that you identify as a concern or issue of struggle. Small moments are brief reflections that ask you to:

- Briefly identify the issue of concern
- Briefly describe your reactions (feelings and thoughts) and your interpretation of the experience and your response to this
- Identify the risks/benefits of your response (impact on others)
- Identify questions you have or insight that may influence further action

Writing about your emotions and thoughts related to starting out in your practice or the different class concepts are examples of small moment reflections. You will identify potential key learning in these small moments (Bleicher & Correia, 2011), experiences that will assist you in identifying and exploring your assumptions and the what-if thinking often associated with new experiences (Bolton, 2009).

GUIDED REFLECTIONS

Guided reflections are reflective prompts used to facilitate individual and group reflective discussions (Moon, 2004). The closing thoughts at the end of each chapter are examples of guided reflections. Guided reflections can prepare students for the more advanced process of reflective journals by prompting them to reflect on their feelings or thoughts related to different scenarios or day-to-day experiences. This can be beneficial when students first begin their practice. Many of the exercises in this book are guided reflections.

The reflective prompts listed in Table 15 can support students in guiding their thinking when they first meet in their reflective dialogue groups. Reflective prompts are intended to encourage students to respond to one another in ways that prompt further reflection and discussion. Guided reflections provide a beginning step for reflective dialogues or collaborative reflections. The reflection prompts offer the emotional distance from sharing about oneself or personal experiences until safety has been established in the group.

Table 15: Reflective Prompts

I am worried about …	I am most eager to …	Something hard for me to do is …
What I need from others to feel safe is …	I want to …	I am nervous that …
What if I ….	What if I don't …	Something important to me is …
I believe that …	My perceptions of others are that …	I expect that others will …
Others most appreciate that I …	My greatest strength in working with others is …	My greatest challenge in working with others is …
My most challenging experience was …	If I could turn back time, I would …	My proudest moment of being in this program so far is …
My greatest learning moment is …	What I value most is …	What I fear most is …
I should know …	Others should …	When others are upset with me, I think …
I think that …	What I bring to this work is …	When working in groups, it is easy for me to …
When working with groups, it is difficult for me to …	Something I'd like to get better at is …	Others would describe me as …
If I could, I would …	My approach to conflict is to …	When others are upset at me, I …

The following types of questions encourage reflection and critical thinking (Morgan & Saxon, as cited in Moon, 2004):

- "I wonder" questions
- Questions that focus on feelings, e.g., what frustrates you most …
- Future-oriented questions
- What-if questions
- How can we …?

They provide students with opportunities to reveal aspects of themselves, which then allows for opportunities to discuss and consider the impact of their thinking on others. This exercise provides a rich opportunity for students to realize the similarities in thinking in the group, which can lend to the safety and inclusiveness required for reflective groups. It is important to establish ground rules at the beginning to ensure that the sentence prompts are used to guide reflections for learning experiences and not as opportunities to share and discuss past personal experiences. It is also important that students do not jump to provide solutions for one another. These groups will provide students with the opportunity to monitor internal reactions, demonstrate curiosity and presence, and examine context while practicing those key communication skills (active listening, summarizing, paraphrasing) that will prepare you for the reflective dialogues.

REFLECTIVE PROMPTS

Mind Maps

Mind maps are visual representations of ideas and connections between those ideas (Stevens & Cooper, 2009). They can be a useful way of organizing your thoughts and formulating questions that can assist you in determining informed action. Mind maps are beneficial for identifying the presenting issue as the central idea and related ideas for questions and answers from your inquiry to better understand the issue by considering the *what, who, where, when* to determine next steps. These also appeal to visual learners in analyzing a situation or experience. The social location exercise you completed in Chapter 2 is a version of a mind map, as it illustrates the connected aspects of your personal and professional identity.

Mind maps can be used in a number of ways:

- To explore the worldviews of others
- To uncover and check out assumptions
- To explore internal reactions (emotions and thoughts) related to specific experiences
- To explore self as a focus for analysis

- To provide a framework for the reflective dialogue
- To provide a framework for observation logs

The middle circle represents the main focus for reflection.

The outer circles represent any assumptions, questions, or thoughts related to the issue to reflect on (as identified in the middle circle). You will notice that further questions will emerge for you and shifts in your thinking will occur as a result.

Mind maps can be used in reflective dialogues as a means to keep you focused on your ideas and the question you seek clarification on. They can also support you with journal writing. Journal writing can often be an arduous task, notably if articulating your thoughts is a challenge for you. You can recreate the format of the mind map to provide you with additional space to capture your points for consideration. The outer circles represent facts (what you know) relating to the issue and points of inquiry to support your understanding of this issue.

Mind Map Reflection Tool

The following mind map is an example of challenging one's assumptions about children in care. The example is provided to support your understanding of using mind maps. This example gives the practitioner an opportunity to note any points of reference to their understanding of children in care. Points are brief, yet offer an opportunity for the practitioner to question their assumptions and identify gaps in knowledge about the reasons children are placed in care.

Figure 24: Mind Mapping Reflection Tool

Source: Adapted from Stevens & Cooper, 2011.

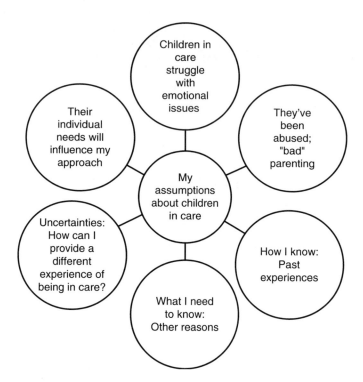

Figure 25: Sample Mind Map
Source: Created by author.

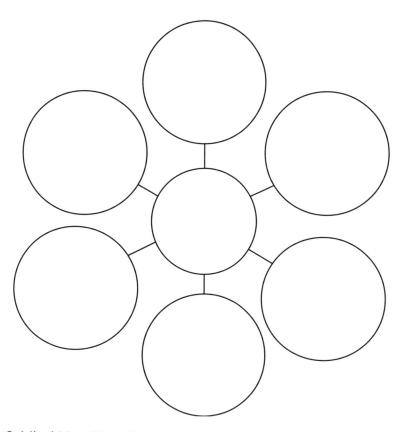

Figure 26: Mind Map Template
Source: Created by author.

This sample mind map revealed for the practitioner that his personal experiences may have influenced his thinking about children in care. Through reflective inquiry, the practitioner realized that each child's experiences are unique and tailoring one's approach to meet these needs is important. Mind maps provide a succinct way of capturing one's thinking about issues of concern to them and can be beneficial for starting out in writing reflective journals.

Exercise 61: Personal Learning Analysis

As with previous concepts you have been introduced to, I invite you to experiment with the mind map first. Use the mind map template (Figure 26) or recreate the template on larger paper should you wish for additional space.

The middle circle represents the presenting issue for analysis.

The first few outer circles represent key aspects/personal characteristics you embody as a Child and Youth Care Practitioner.

The next few circles represents key areas of your practice you wish to develop in or require further learning in.

The last set of circles represents your course of action to acquire this learning.

If there is further learning or questions you have about any of the concepts, add in an extra shape.

Exercise 62: Mind Map Analysis

Think about one of the children, youth, or families you support in your practice as the basis for this next mind map. Be mindful of confidentiality and only use first and last initials. The middle circle: Their initials and the question or presenting issue of concern you have about them.

The second few circles: What you know about them based on presenting facts.

The next few circles: What you think you know about them, based on your observations and impressions.

The next few circles: What you are inquiring about or wish to know about them.

One circle: Your hypothesis.

Last circle: Your action steps to consider (your plan based on your hypothesis).

When you review this mind map, notice any connections between the points you have listed.

Checking In

Where are you with understanding the concepts and exercises in this chapter thus far? How do they support your learning style and understanding of others? How do they not? What is it about these tools thus far that do not fit for you and your learning? What questions do you have that warrant further exploration to support your thinking about this chapter?

Creative Reflective Tools

Reflective tools need not be limited to writing. Visual learners may be better able to reflect on ideas and situations through abstract forms, such as art and imagery media (Moon, 2004). Creative imagery can be used to represent a concept or to represent an experience (Moon, 2004).

Exercise 63: Capturing Your Experience through Art

Using the space below or on a separate sheet of paper, create an image using art or other visual media to illustrate your understanding of (select one): (1) a child or family's worldviews; (2) a family's experiences of engaging with service providers; or (3) your understanding of the individual needs of children and families in your practice (you can also refer to any of the case scenarios from this book). The use of metaphors in reflective practice is beneficial in generating thought processes about one's experiences (Moon, 2004). Sharing one's imagery/metaphors with others can further facilitate an awareness of different perspectives.

Exercise 64: Collages

Collages are another way of representing individual perspectives of practice. Decide upon a focus for the collage. You can try one of these ideas, or come up with your own theme.

- Your identified or personal style as a Child and Youth Care Practitioner
- Your philosophy as a practitioner
- A learning concept

Create a collage to represent the distinct aspects of the issue you have identified above.

Take turns sharing your art piece with a partner to highlight key aspects that relate to the identified focus. Students are encouraged to ask questions about one another's art that prompt further reflection. (Remember, questions are to be intentional in nature and lead to greater understanding about your partner.)

Recalling experiences through storytelling and sharing with others improves an individual's ability to engage in reflections.

—Hargreaves & Page, 2013

SOCIAL MEDIA

The popularity of social media provides students with additional opportunities to engage in reflective practice. Students can create a Facebook page that is only for school use, designed in a way that reflects their values, beliefs, and philosophies as a professional practitioner. Quotes or brief articles can be uploaded and posted that relate to the focus of their "issue." Use the space provided to outline your idea and consider the following questions.

Guidelines

- What are you attempting to communicate about this topic or theme?
- How do you create opportunities for online discussion, questions, and reflective periods?

_____

_____

_____

_____

_____

REFLECTIVE BLOGS

Blogs are an alternative to writing in journals and assist in developing critical thinking. Blogging meets the interest of students and presents opportunities to share and challenge diverse perspectives with others. Using a similar method to above, students will be required to post questions, engage in discussion, and lead reflective discussion. As students develop in their skills, they will be required to engage in more critical analysis of points for discussion or elements of the news media to facilitate reflective practice. It will be important for students to be mindful of the confidentiality and privacy policy by refraining from posting and identifying information of the others they are discussing. Sharing reflections in a public forum allows for further learning and professional growth (Stevens & Cooper, 2009). The physical barriers social media provides seem to offer a sense of security and distance for others to share their experiences and comment on others' posts. Reflective blogs are also another venue for engaging in reflective dialogues with small groups.

Use the space below to record ideas for questions or content you will post in your blog.

_____

_____

_____

_____

_____

AUDIO RECORDINGS

Audio recordings provide another means for capturing reflective moments. Record your thoughts about any of the case scenarios, your day-to-day interactions, or experiences from your practice to reflect further on. Use a USB that you can share with your professor for any submissions you are responsible for.

FURTHER INSIGHT AND QUESTIONS

Return to your reflections at a later time (no longer than a week) to include any insight or additional questions that may have emerged (refer to the Code of Ethics for support). Note the outcome from your actions. How has this outcome led to new experiences or shifts in your practice, for self, and others? If you did not follow through on your action identified above, describe your reasons for not doing so.

CLOSING THOUGHTS

What reflective tools resonate with you?

_____

_____

Which of the reflective tools challenges your familiar ways of doing things?

_____

_____

How might this new learning influence your practice and future learning? Your relationships and interactions with others?

_____

_____

CHAPTER 11

Reflective Journals

Challenges are what make life interesting and overcoming them is what makes life meaningful.

> —Joshua J. Marine

LEARNING OBJECTIVES

In this chapter, you will:

- identify the rationale for reflective journals
- be introduced to the format for reflective journaling
- distinguish between daily journals and reflective journals
- distinguish between reflective journal entries and report writing
- develop and practice the skills of critical reflective writing
- journal about experiences from your practice
- describe your most significant moment of learning

The previous chapters have introduced you to the different processes needed for reflective practice to develop. Through exploring self, you have identified those aspects that influence your ways of knowing and thinking and the impact this can have on practice. You have explored the key characteristics of Child and Youth Care practice that play a significant role in your ability to reflect on experiences. The reflective models in Chapter 7 gave you a framework for reflecting on your experiences. How you think about these experiences is the essence of reflection and what you identify as needing to be done differently for next time (and following through) is essential to reflective practice. Your willingness and ability to engage in inquiry, challenge the assumptions of self and others, and consider different perspectives are indicators of critical thinking that you will continue to demonstrate as a reflective practitioner.

REFLECTIVE JOURNALS

The focus of this chapter is to introduce you to the reflective journal. Up to now, you have reflected on your experiences through the structured exercises within the chapters. The focus for reflective journals is for you to write about your experiences, following a structured template to guide your thinking. Following a structure for writing about your experiences will enable you to remain focused and concise (Moon, 2004). Journal entries should be no longer than one page.

Bolton (in Hargreaves & Page, 2013) believes that writing down the reflection (beneficial for beginning and developing practitioners) is an essential starting point for developing reflection and provides further clarity about one's thinking about an experience. Writing may influence one's way of viewing experiences. What you initially perceived may change significantly after writing about the situation (Bolton, as cited in Hargreaves & Page, 2013, p. 14).

The benefits and impact that reflective journals have on student learning have been widely documented (Kuhn, Keeley, & Shenmberg, in Moon, 2008; Mann et al., 2009; Moon, 2008; Richardson & Van Manen, as cited in Krueger, 1997; Stevens & Cooper, 2009). While they reveal the learning professional's narratives of their experiences, these extend beyond simply retelling an event (Sutherland, 2007). Reflective journals represent the reflective processes (feeling, thinking, interpreting, making sense of; Moon, 2004), knowledge, and evaluation of application to practice.

The objectives of journals are to establish continuity between experience, reflection, and learning (Stevens & Cooper, 2009). Reflective journals are structured and follow a format to ensure that the student's thinking is focused on one particular issue as the basis for the reflection. Daily journals are beneficial for communicating about your experiences from your practice (Moon, 2004; O'Connell & Dyment, 2013) and focus on the details of the day. This is different from reflective journals that focus on the practitioner's experience of one particular issue. Learning is an experiential process that requires interactive experiences from which to apply, examine, and analyze the outcome of the learning. Embedded in these day-to-day experiences are rich learning opportunities to create meaning of, reflect upon, and identify any further learning that may be required. It is also important to continue noticing your reactions and assumptions that unfold from these experiences as learning opportunities to rethink your ways of thinking. Writing in a journal offers one of several ways to reflect on and in practice and assist students in assessing their ability to engage in critical reflective thinking.

Table 16: Benefits of Reflective Journals

Fosters personal insight	Reveals evidence of Schon's (1983) Reflection in Action and Reflection on Action models
Enhance understanding of others	Includes evidence of critical thinking
Provides means for students to maintain control of their learning	Requires students to provide evidence of key skills
Provides students a means to evaluate and monitor their growth and development	Requires students to connect experience to theory
Provides students a means to identify key skills that require further learning and development	Supports students in achieving deeper meaning and understanding required for critical thinking
Can reveal themes and patterns in thinking process	Provides way for professors to guide and develop reflective practice in students

REFLECTIVE JOURNAL GUIDELINES[1]

Clearly identify the focus of your reflection describing the situation, issue, or topic you are struggling with. This needs to be succinct and can include any of the following:

- The focus of my reflection is to explore …
- The focus of my reflection is to explore my reaction toward …
- The focus of my reflection is to explore alternative actions …
- The focus of my reflection is to explore the impact of my interactions …

Your focus for the entry will become clearer to you as you write about your issue of concern and it may change after you complete it.

When you start writing in your journal, it is important to follow this template as it will support you in maintaining a focus for your writing. Over time, however, as you develop in your confidence and your skills in writing reflectively you may wish to write without this template. The template, as shown in Figure 27, has five parts.

Return to your journal later in the day or the following day and pay attention to the emotional tone of your entry. Writing from an emotionally heightened place can influence the way you see and write about your experiences. You may discover new insight that you did not think of before. Returning to your journal entries enables you to see them through an objective, curious, meaning-making lens that will lead to new insights and new learning (Allard et al., 2007; Carson et al., 2007; Moon, 2004; Stevens & Cooper, 2009). Add feedback from others and any new information you may have discovered at the bottom of the page. If feedback from others or the additional information you have leads to any changes, it will be important to include this in your journal. A blank copy of the journal page is located in Appendix XIII.

Your Name: _____   **Date:** _____

Focus:

Briefly state the nature of your reflection. Is this to evaluate your approach with others? To develop further clarity about another's behaviours? To develop insight about your experience? To question why things occurred as they did? Or something else?

The experience:

A brief description of what happened and who was involved with your observations to support this. Include a comment about your reactions and feelings and a comment about your interpretation (meaning) and context for the other's behaviours.

Your actions:

A brief description of what you did and reasons for doing so (connect theory to support your action).

Your evaluation:

What was the impact of your actions on the other? (Note their actions/potential perspectives of you.)

What worked and what did not?

What needs to be different for next time? What impact will this have on practice moving forward?

Establishing further action:

Based on your evaluation, what further action may be required?

Return to the journal later to review and identify further insight and additional questions you may have.

What have you realized from this experience? What questions still remain for you?

Figure 27: Reflective Journal Guidelines

Source: Adapted from Moon, 2004.

Table 17: Comparison of Critical Reflective Journals and Written Reports

Critical Reflective Journals	Written Reports
Focus is on *you* and *your* experience	Focus is on the *child, youth,* or *family*
Personal narrative: "I"	*This writer*
References to emotional experiences of the individual	Refrains from including personal emotional and cognitive experiences
Personal reflection of an experience	Factual documentation of the other
Includes your personal previous experiences	Captures the experiences of the other
Opportunities to contemplate the impact of your role on the child's history, development based on your subjective experience	Captures history, development, strengths and resources, recommendations of the other based on fact and objective observations

Critical Reflective Journals	Written Reports
Opportunities to identify previous learning and relevant theory as it relates to the case	Identifies relevant theory to support your written points
May include goal for self or identified area to improve on	Goals for the other
Acknowledgement of further personal growth and opportunities to improve on practice	Recommendations to support the social, emotional, and developmental growth of others

It is important to note that reflective journals are different from written reports and, while they share some similar concepts in terms of considering context and meaning-making, the purpose for writing each differs significantly. Table 17 outlines these differences.

The following case scenario will provide you with some context for the journal entries that follow. As you review each sample entry, consider the feedback provided on each entry and compare these entries to the guidelines outlined in Figure 27.

Consider the Following Scenario: Bethunia

Bethunia is a second-year student who has begun her practicum at an elementary school. She had initially resisted completing a practicum in a school setting as she had always struggled in following the rules of school as a young child and was concerned she may be triggered by the experience. However, she relented and considered that this would be a learning experience in which to develop as a practitioner. The following entry represented her first day at practicum. What do you notice about the emotional tone of her entry? How might you understand the connection between her past experiences and her journal entry?

Reflective Journal Entry

Name of person completing this journal: *Bethunia*

Date: *xxx. xx, xxxx*   **Time:** *5:00pm*

Practicum was brutal. Too many kids, too many people yelling at the kids. The supervisor kept telling me what to do and what I shouldn't do and would not listen to me when I tried to explain what I wanted to do. Felt mad and stupid. There's nothing I could have done. Why does this always happen to me? I always seem to get people who are idiots for supervisors. Nothing will change if I stay and I know myself better than anyone, I'll lose it, and end up getting let go so better to leave before it happens. I'm requesting a new practicum.

Figure 28: Sample Reflective Journal Entry 1

Source: Created by author.

Compare Bethunia's entry to the guidelines above. The risks of writing without a structured format to follow is well-illustrated here. It would appear that Bethunia's emotions took over her ability to write about her experience from a reflective position. She didn't use the journal template to structure her thinking and, as a result, missed several components of the reflective journal. This does not meet the criteria for a reflective entry. When she returned to the entry a few hours later, Bethunia was able to identify how emotionally activated she had been from the experience and the connection to her previous school experiences. Having identified the connection and acknowledging writing from an emotional reactive place was not conducive to new learning, she rewrote her entry following the guidelines in Figure 27.

Reflective Journal Entry

Name of person completing this journal: *Bethunia*

Date: *The following day to first entry.*   **Time:** *4:00pm*

Focus: *To relay my experiences of first day of practicum.*

Experience: *My first day at practicum was challenging. I took an instant dislike to my supervisor. When I approached a child in the office who was crying, he told me to ignore him, stating that the child just does that for attention. I can't stand that when someone prejudges another; it's disrespectful, and I felt humiliated. As I think about what it was that put me off, I realized that it was more than just being told what to do. He didn't support my CYC approach to connect with another. Attuning to another is essential for relationship-building as we have learned in class. This killed me; it's so unCYC-like to not acknowledge a sad child. He reminds me of other supervisors I have had in the past: the micromanagers who questioned everything I did. I felt so stupid each time he told me what to do. He told me to go and talk to another child who clearly wanted his space. I just knew I would make the child more mad, but the supervisor kept insisting that I talk to him.*

Actions: *I did as the supervisor told me to. I ignored the one child and went to speak to another child who clearly wanted his space. I am so mad at myself for going against my better judgement.*

Evaluation: *The child I went to speak with threw a book in my face. I should have left him and given him his space, but I didn't want to get into trouble for not listening to my supervisor. I should have stood my ground and told the supervisor that the child appeared to need his space and seemed too emotional to engage in conversation. We learned this in class. I always seem to do this, discount my own knowledge and instincts to appease others. Because they are older, I think they are smarter. I felt humiliated and stupid and realize how little faith he has in me. Even though it was my first day, wouldn't he have assumed I had some previous learning? I remember feeling this way in the past and vowed I would not ever let myself feel this way again. The supervisor must think I am a push-over and the child must think I'm an idiot and a push-over for not standing up to my supervisor.*

Establishing further action: *I am going to meet with the principal to review my learning contract and discuss my hopes and learning needs for this practicum to be successful for me. I will also be meeting with the child I upset to validate his frustrations (establishing further action). It's like the Prof says, my experience, my learning.*

Further insight and questions: *I have to stop second-guessing myself and begin to assert myself more. I am not sure though, will I get in trouble for asserting myself with the supervisor?*

Figure 29: Sample Reflective Journal Entry 2

Source: Created by author.

Sample Journal Entry

This entry captures the elements of the reflective journal. There is a clear focus for her journal, and she reflects on her experiences at practicum in a way that includes her awareness of her feelings, assumptions, and values as a Child and Youth Care Practitioner. She clearly indicates the implications her actions have had on practice and has identified necessary next steps to improve her experience at practicum and areas for further growth.

Exercise 65: Journal Entry Review

In reviewing these journal entries, consider the following questions:

- What is the focus of the entries?
- What is the emotional tone of these entries?
- What meaning did Bethunia make of her experiences?
- What context has she identified?
- What is the connection to theory?
- What opportunities has she identified for further learning and what she requires to improve?

What other differences do you notice between Bethunia's first and second entry?

It is important to remember that journaling is not about recording your daily events, or details of *what happened* during your practice or what *others have done* to cause a reaction in you. Rather, they are about reflecting on your experiences and connecting to the theory that underlies your practice and development as a Child and Youth Care Practitioner (O'Connell & Dyment, 2013). Reflective journals provide you with opportunities to write from a narrative perspective that fosters a process of becoming a reflective practitioner (Sutherland, 2007) through learning, knowing, and doing.

Reflective writing expands on the thinking process through the use of visual (written journals) or audio media (your recordings of your reflections) as a representation of the reflection (Moon, 2004) for learning professionals to return to and identify key themes, patterns of thinking, and questions that can prompt a further course of action.

Through interaction with the world we both change it and are changed by it.
—Schon, 1983

Checking In

Where are you with understanding the concepts and exercises in this chapter thus far? How do these concepts connect with your role as Child and Youth Care Practitioner and your learning from the previous chapters? What concepts remain unclear to you and require further exploration to support your learning from this chapter?

Checking In

Where are you with understanding the purpose of reflective journals thus far? How will reflective journals enhance your ability to engage in reflective practice? What questions do you have that warrant further exploration to support your learning in this chapter?

CRITICAL REFLECTIVE WRITING

Journaling your experiences as a student provides many benefits, one of which is the chance to engage in introspection, to focus within. Engaging in introspection will support you in exploring the reactions you have toward others. While you will not connect with each person you meet, it is important to acknowledge that not liking someone does not give cause for not working with them (classmates, professors, children, youth, and families). The reality of Child and Youth Care practice is that you are not going to connect with everyone you meet for many different reasons, children included. However, it is important to understand *what that is about* and what you can do to separate your personal issues from your professional responsibility through the processes of reflective practice.

Boud et al. (1985) assert that critical thinking is developed when students have the opportunity to reflect critically on their own practices, rather than through prescriptions of good learning practice (p. 16). Good learning practice is not about doing or saying the right thing or writing about what you think you should have done. Similar to reflective thinking, critical thinking requires experiences from your practice to apply and reflect on in relation to others.

Critical thinking, if you recall, is about uncovering and checking out the implicit and explicit assumptions of practice through research and inquiry. When you connect your action to the theory that underlines your actions, it is important to critically reflect on your thinking behind the theory and actions and its relevance to the children, youth, and families and share your thinking with others (your classmates, your professor, and team members from your practice). How do you know for certain that this theory best relates to this individual? What aspects of their presentation would suggest this? Critical reflective writing is also about identifying key patterns in your thinking and connecting this to previous experiences.

> Sharing your journals with colleagues, peers, supervisors, and professors will support you in acknowledging different perspectives, while considering the risks and benefits of your thinking and enabling you to generate new ideas.
> —Donicka Budd

Reviewing Your Journal Entries

Reviewing your journal entries can assist you in identifying key themes or patterns in your writing and thinking and provide opportunities for developing your skills as reflective practitioners.

- Does the focus of your entries remain the same or is there variation that provides for different learning experiences? If they remain the same, reflect on the meaning of this to question if this is related to uncertainty, lack of confidence, or something else.
- Are there similarities in your reactions and interpretations of others? What is the meaning of this? Are you stuck in habitual ways of responding? What role do past experiences play in your responses?
- Are you incorporating insight and further learning from your past journal entries into your current entries?
- Identify shifts and new patterns in your entries.
- Which theoretical framework underlies your actions? Are these the same for each experience? Have you considered the unique needs of others when you connect theory to practice?

CLOSING THOUGHTS

What are the key points you have learned from this chapter that you will apply in your practice?

_____

_____

What key points of reflective journals are or are not fitting with your learning about reflective practice?

_____

_____

What questions remain for you from this learning?

_____

_____

NOTE

1. The guidelines for journal entries have been adapted from Moon (2004).

CHAPTER 12

Establishing a Community of Practice

It takes a village to raise a child.

—African Proverb

LEARNING OBJECTIVES

In this chapter, you will:

- be introduced to the process for reflective dialogues
- establish the conditions for reflective dialogues to occur
- develop an understanding of the learning professionals' roles and responsibilities in reflective dialogues
- learn to support peers in developing their skills in giving and receiving feedback
- assess the experience of reflective dialogues through group debrief

COMMUNITY OF PRACTICE[1]

Collective reflections, collaborative reflections, and reflective dialogues are terms that have been used throughout the literature to mean a process for enhancing professional development through reflecting on practice with others (Allard et al., 2007; Brockbank & McGill, 2007). For the purpose of this book, the term reflective dialogue will be used to represent this community of practice. Note: Reflective dialogues are not meant to duplicate a group therapy session, revisit past or current experiences involving personal issues, or to vent about other students, work, or personal life. These reflective groups are intended to support practitioners in developing their ability to reflect on practice, to identify their assumptions, and to reflect collectively as a group (Allard et al., 2007).

Dewey (1933) believed that reflection needs to happen in community and during interactions with others while valuing personal and intellectual growth of oneself and others.

It is important to acknowledge that reflective dialogues are not synonymous to advice-giving or reassuring others; rather, they are about supporting one another in considering their assumptions, the rationale for their approach, and diverse perspectives through reflective questioning. (Allard et al., 2007; Lee & Barnett, 1994). Reflective questioning is specific to reflective dialogues, as it encourages other practitioners to explore their knowledge, skills, experiences, attitudes, beliefs, and values, which broadens and deepens the other's understanding of self and practice (Lee & Barnett, 1994, p. 16). Offering solutions and acknowledging challenges, difficulties, or how hard someone has been working does not generate new insight or lead to new learning (Allard et al., 2007); asking reflective questions allows the necessary space for practitioners to enhance their skills for reflective thought and generate new insights. We will discuss reflective questions later in this chapter.

Dewey (1933) believed that the practitioner's attitudes could block or facilitate the reflective process. That is important to be aware of as, when working in reflective dialogues and collaborative reflective groups, there is an aspect of vulnerability. It is therefore essential that safety be established during these groups in order for members to actively demonstrate these attitudes with each other (see Establishing Conditions for Reflective Dialogues below). When you are working individually in isolation from others, it is easy to become complacent in your own ways of thinking (Garfat & Ricks, 1995). Gharabaghi (2008b) asserts that teams provide opportunities for practitioners to assume greater accountability for their decisions through questioning and critical evaluation of one another's actions.

> Effective questioning brings insight, which fuels curiosity, which cultivates wisdom.
> —Chip Bell

Reflective dialogues stimulate purposeful and structured discussions that aid in learning while enabling practitioners to share their knowledge, their sense of self, and their meaning of experiences. At the same time, practitioners are open to being challenged or questioned by others, which can lead to new understanding (Brockbank & McGill, 2007). These experiences enable you to consider alternative ways of thinking (Bleicher & Correia, 2011) that you may not have considered before and allow you to refocus on the needs of others (Gharabaghi, 2008b), as opposed to a righteous way of thinking. Within the process of sharing multiple perspectives is the collaborative meaning-making process that is central to Child and Youth Care practice (Bellefeuille & Ricks, 2010).

Further to the new understanding and insights that individuals will develop is the heightened potential for critical reflective learning to occur (Brockbank & McGill, 2007; Brookfield, 2012). This process for sharing and challenging one another, however, requires a certain vulnerability from the group members. With the students as the focus of the dialogue, there is a greater emphasis for establishing the necessary conditions in which students can grow and risk being vulnerable.

BENEFITS OF REFLECTIVE DIALOGUES[2]

- One's experience and understanding broadens
- Peer support provided in sharing the space for experiences
- Develops communication and problem-solving skills
- Promotes professionalism by being accountable to others
- Provides additional opportunities to demonstrate CYC characteristics and core conditions
- Provides opportunities to further develop critical thinking skills
- Student engagement heightened

Establishing the Conditions Necessary for Reflective Dialogues

Consider your first meeting with a child, youth, or family. How might you attempt to establish safety during your first meeting? What is the importance of engaging in rapport-building as a means to establish safety in the group? How will you know when safety has been established? Establishing safety, if you recall, is a collective experience between the practitioner and others; others can include other practitioners or team members with whom you work.

Although working in groups offers opportunities for learning professionals to further their skills, it can also present a source of angst, much of which can be related to past experiences. It is therefore integral to the effectiveness of the group that safety be established (Pearson & Smith, as cited in Boud, Keogh, Petersen, & Seligman, 2004) prior to engaging in reflective dialogues. The size of the group is another factor to consider that can influence the group effectiveness. Students are required to have ample and equal opportunity to share their ideas without having to fight for air time. Groups of four to six people are ideal for reflective dialogues. Students will be accountable for determining what they need for these group experiences to be successful, yet this requires a certain level of vulnerability that cannot, and should not, be expected to occur without having established safety first. Safety in groups will enable students to take risks, to challenge and encourage one another to reconsider their thinking in different situations—all of which is necessary for growing and developing as a reflective practitioner (Boud et al., 1985).

The following exercises are intended to establish safety and trust between group members in order for reflective dialogues to be effective. You might wish to select a few of the exercises to try for the initial group meetings.

Exercise 66: Establishing Safety 1[3]

Group members will spend 5–10 minutes creating a list of things they have in common with each other, excluding physical features and details related to Child and Youth Care practice. When you are finished, review the list and identify the theme of the similarities identified. Discuss as a group.

Exercise 67: This Is Me[4]

Each person in the group is to find one item in their possession or from the classroom that best represents who they are. (These can include any aspect of the room that is representative of you.) Metaphors can enable you to perceive self from a different perspective, can create an emotional distance from talking about self (Stevens & Cooper, 2009), and can reveal different aspects of yourself that others may not otherwise know about you. Take turns describing your item with the group and share what you bring to the group (aspects of you, skills, character traits, etc.).

Exercise 68: Me and Groups

The purpose of this exercise is to share past experiences, perspectives of, and group experiences and hopes for this group experience. On a scale of 1 to 10, 10 being very positive and 1 being not so, each group member is to rate their past experiences of group work. Discuss how your past experiences may potentially impact your current group experiences. What is required for this group experience to be different? (If you experience discomfort in sharing, reflect afterwards—what contributed to the discomfort? How might you understand this? What role do past experiences play in this discomfort? What role do you play in this experience?) If we want to create new experiences, we have to learn to let go.

Letting go isn't about having the courage to release the past; it's about having the wisdom and strength to embrace the present.
—Steve Maraboli

Exercise 69: Creating Connections

Establishing connections is essential for practitioners to risk being vulnerable in reflective dialogues (Brockbank & McGill, 2007). This exercise provides students with opportunities to establish safety and take risks through a process of anonymity.

Everyone selects one to three index cards to write a question(s) they have about Child and Youth Care practice or concepts related to reflective practice. Questions are placed in a box, and each person selects one question to read aloud and respond to during the group. Scripted questions provide necessary

structure that many new groups can benefit from while promoting communication, vulnerabilities, and connecting with others. The questions below are ideas
to build from:

- What are you most worried about when you begin practice?
- What do you anticipate will be a challenge for you beginning practice?
- What is something you will require support with during class?
- How will others know you need support?
- If you need support from others will you reach out or stay silent?

There are many different activities that will support you in establishing rapport,
perspective taking, and developing the communication essential for reflective dialogues.
For the initial part of the reflective dialogue process, students may wish to select and facilitate their own exercises to demonstrate their responsibility to the group. Safety, trust, and
rapport are established through experiences such as these and are essential for engaging in
reflective dialogues with others. Each time your group meets, it will be important to spend
the initial 10 minutes doing a check-in. Check-ins are powerful exercises to gage the tone
of the group and to challenge any assumptions that members may present. It is important
to clarify that these groups are designed to foster your reflective thinking and critical
thinking skills, which includes receiving feedback from others and identifying areas for
further growth and development (Brockbank & McGill, 2007).

Preparing for the reflective dialogues requires students to review the distinct roles and
process outlined below. Reflective dialogues involve four distinct roles:[5] The presenter, the
enabler, the reporter, and the seeker.

The presenter will share their issue of concern and reflect on their experiences from
practice (based on their observation log). Brockbank and McGill (2007) have identified
the following statements to include in the presenter's description of their experience: *I
think ... I want ... I realized ... I know ... I found out ... I thought I knew ... I was unaware ...
I knew ... I felt ... I was overwhelmed by ... I went blank ... I wanted ... I am feeling ... I am
wondering about ...*

The enabler will assist the presenter in ensuring the question or concern is clearly
identified (from the copy of the observation log). It is the enabler's responsibility to ensure
that the presenter remains on task and does not divert from the experiences outlined in the
observation log. The enabler (with practice and experience) will also identify any judgement, assumptions, or underlying emotions that have not been expressed by the presenter.

The reporter is the observer and focuses on the other members of the group. It is the
reporter's responsibility to ensure that the other group members are asking questions and
providing feedback in response to what the presenter has shared. When reflective dialogues first begin, it is common for the group to remain quiet, as if uncertain about which
questions to ask. The reporter will call on individuals to query or share their thinking as it

relates to the content of the presenter's discussion. It is also the reporter's responsibility to point out when others are offering solutions, as this conflicts with the process of reflective dialogues (Brockbank & McGill, 2007).

The seekers are the remaining group members, responsible for clarifying their understanding of the presenter's issues of concern by asking reflective questions. They are required to ask the presenter questions to establish further understanding of the presenter's experience and to point out areas for the presenter to reflect on their experience and identify their ways of thinking.

The presenter will be required to complete and bring their observation logs[6] each week and to identify a succinct question or concern they are struggling with. The observation logs provide a structure for the presenter when sharing their experiences with others. Use some of the reflective prompts identified above or, alternatively, students can use one of the reflection tools as the format to present their concern or question.

The following template serves as a guideline for group members to follow when they first begin their reflective dialogues. As they become more familiar with the process, students may not need to refer to the template.

Reflective Dialogue Process

The Presenter
- Presents their issue of concern and reflects on their experiences from their practice (based on their observation log).

The Enabler
- Assists the presenter in ensuring the question or concern is clearly identified (from the copy of the observation log).
- Ensures the presenter remains on task and does not divert from the experiences outlined in the observation log.
- Identifies any judgement, assumptions, or underlying emotions that have/have not been expressed by the presenter.

The Reporter
- Ensures the seekers are participating and their questions are in response to what the presenter has shared.
- Ensures the seekers do not offer solutions or advice.
- Ensures the seekers' questions promote reflection and feedback, based on what the presenter has shared.

The Seekers
- Summarize the presenter's issue of concern.
- Ask questions related to the presenter's experience.

> •   Establish better understanding of the presenter's experiences and perspectives.
>
>   The debrief allows the group to question the member's experiences, their feelings, new insights or learning, and what is required to be different for the next time.

Checking In

Where are you with understanding the concept and process of reflective dialogues? How might these enhance your understanding of reflective practice? What might challenge you about this process? What questions do you have that warrant further exploration to support your thinking about reflective dialogues?

REFLECTIVE QUESTIONS

Lee and Barnett (1994) identify three types of questions that form the basis of reflective questions: clarifying questions, purpose and consequence questions, and linking questions that are essential to the reflective process.

Clarifying questions are the who, what, where, when, how questions:

- How would you describe ...
- What happened when you ...

Purpose and consequence questions allow practitioners to consider the cause-and-effect connections of their actions:

- What were you hoping to accomplish?
- What did you/are you anticipating ...?

Linking questions support the practitioner in connecting their actions to the concepts and theory learned in class:

- How does that connect to what we learned in class?
- How does that connect to trauma-informed theory?

These are a few examples of the questions that the seekers will ask the presenters during the reflective dialogue process.

The following scenario is an example of an initial reflective dialogue, involving third-year student Julip. Review his observation log to give some context to his reflection.

Observation Log

Name: Julip P   **Date:** xxx. xx, xxxx

Setting: After School Program   **Time:** 3:30–4:30

Who was involved? What did you observe? Where and when did this observation occur? What did you see? (Describe specific behaviours.) Who was involved? What was the nature of the interactions?

I observed a group of children aged 6 to 10 years engaged in an art activity. They seemed to be having fun, until one of the program leaders told them it was time to clean up. One of the kids screamed and threw the markers. I froze; I didn't know what to do or say, so I just sat there (challenging experience). I felt horrified and stupid (emotion), like I should be doing something, but didn't know what to do. As I watched the leader approach, she calmly picked up the markers and said in a low, quiet voice, "Let's clean up and come to the table for snack." She did not respond or react to the boy's behaviour. She always does this, like the other time when …. (diverting to another issue). It freaked me out (reaction), and I think she should have done more to address the boy's behaviours (judgement), like consequence him for his behaviour (reaction). I wanted the CYCP to do something more so he would learn from his behaviour. I felt so mad that she didn't do anything that I left the room (response).

Follow up: Based on your observations and discussions with others, what is your next step?

Figure 30: Julip's Observation Log
Source: Created by author.

Consider the Following Scenario: Julip

Julip, the presenter, briefed his observation log with Jack, the enabler. Cierra, the reporter, reviewed the expectations of the group with the other group members. Julip briefly described the setting and his role as a practitioner. He shared that he struggled to understand the interactions between the full-time Child and Youth Care Practitioner and the children and is requesting feedback and support in understanding his reactions from practice (identified concern, established question).

As the enabler, Jack reminds Julip to remain focused on this one experience and brings his attention to the present issue. He points out to Julip the judgement in his comment about the full-time practitioner and asks Julip to identify how he felt based on her response to the boys. Jack reminds Julip that the group is not to provide a solution or advice to Julip and asks him to speak more to his interpretation of this experience.

Cierra (the reporter) notices the group is quiet after Julip has shared and asks one of the group members to share their thinking, while reminding them not to provide solutions or advice. She encourages the group to ask open-ended questions to assist in clarifying understanding of the experience. One of the seekers summarizes Julip's experience by stating that he was thrown off by both the boy's behaviour and the practitioner's response to the behaviour. Another seeker asks Julip what he thought would happen when he first noticed the boy throwing markers (open-ended question). Another asked Julip what he thought the boy was feeling at the time (reflective question to seek different perspective). Another seeker asks Julip to consider the context for the child's behaviours.

Through this process of sharing perspectives and feedback with Julip, he acknowledged that his own values of respect and control were underlying his reactions in his practice and it was important for him to debrief his experience further with the full-time Child and Youth Care practitioner to better understand her reactions to the boy (follow up). At this point, Julip would add this to his observation log and would bring it with him to his meeting with the full-time practitioner.

THE DEBRIEF[7]

The importance of debriefing group experiential-based learning exercises has been documented throughout the literature (Boud et al., 1985; Brockbank & McGill, 2007; Coulson & Harvey, 2013) and provides additional opportunities to enhance the reflective experience. Pearson and Smith (as cited in Boud et al., 2004) defined debriefing as a process that occurs after an experience and the deliberate decision to reflect on that experience (p. 70). Facilitating debriefs after the reflective dialogues provide opportunities for the group members to reflect on their experiences by acknowledging how they felt, identify new learning (Pearson, as cited in Boud et al., 1985), and identify areas of improvement for next time. Pearson and Smith (1985) emphasize the importance of trust and acceptance and a willingness to be vulnerable as essential conditions in order for this sharing to occur. Questions can be general to the experience of reflective dialogues or specific to the different roles individuals assumed. The following questions[8] are directed toward feelings, reactions, and observations and provide a structure for the debrief experience.

General Questions

- How did you feel about that? (feeling)
- What happened for you during this experience? (reaction)
- Who else had the same experience? Who had a different experience?
- What did you learn from this experience?
- What can be different for next time?
- I noticed when you ... and wonder what you were feeling at the time? (observation)

Questions specific to the roles in the reflective dialogue can be beneficial as well, since they support group members in assuming responsibility for their learning and to the group process. It is important to avoid asking "why" questions as they risk conveying judgement, which contradicts the purpose of the debrief. The debrief questions will enhance the group members' reflective skills, while identifying any concerns or uncertainties they may have experienced. Further to this is the importance of documenting the debrief questions and responses of the members and the recommended changes for next time. See the template below.

Role-specific Questions

Questions to the Presenter
- What was it like for you to share your experiences from practice?
- How did you feel when others were not willing to give you a solution or advice for next steps?
- How did this help you during this reflective experience?
- What new learning or insight did you realize from this group experience?

Questions to the Enabler
- What was the experience like for you in having the responsibility to track the presenter?
- How did you feel when … ?
- What made it difficult or easy for you to … ?
- What were the benefits and challenges of your role?
- What new learning or insight did you realize from this group experience?

Questions to the Reporter
- What made this experience easy or difficult for you in calling on other members to ask questions?
- What were the benefits and challenges of your role?
- What new learning or insight did you realize from this group experience?

Questions to the Seekers
- What was your experience as the observer?
- What made this experience easy or difficult for you?
- How did you feel when … ?
- What new learning or insight did you realize from this group experience?
- How can we improve this process?
- What needs to be different for next time?

It is important to ensure that the responses are reviewed and implemented at the next session.

Effective reflective dialogue experiences require practitioners' willingness to engage in this process, which requires open communication, giving and receiving feedback, sharing perspectives, and challenging other assumptions. Ricks (1997) highlights the importance of practicing the cognitive and interpersonal skills that are required in team-based settings.[9] Students may wish to opt out of meeting as a means to avoid the potential conflict or discomfort that can occur in these groups. Consider the implications that this can have on your own practice, learning, and for other group members. Child and Youth Care focuses on connections and relationships (Garfat & Fulcher, 2012; White, 2007) that occur through experiences, from learning and knowledge (Garfat & Fulcher, 2012).

Follow the template below to debrief the reflective dialogues.

The Group Debrief

Group Member Names: **Debrief Facilitator:**

Date:

What happened during this experience? Who had similar/different experiences?

How did people feel? Emotional experiences of members:

New insights or learning: What did you learn from this experience?

Recommendations for next time: What can be different?

Figure 31: Debrief Template

Source: Created by author.

CLOSING THOUGHTS

What did I learn about myself from participating in reflective dialogues?

_____

_____

How did my group help me to learn or improve my ability to reflect on practice?

_____

_____

What questions remain for me from this chapter?

_____

_____

NOTES

1. A community of practice highlights the significance of teams that is reflective of the core competency of Professionalism.
2. Benefits of Reflective Dialogues is adapted from Dewey (as cited in Rodgers, 2002).
3. Establishing Safety 1 icebreaker is adapted from "Similar and Different: An Ice-breaker Activity That Builds Community" (Drake, n.d.).
4. This Is Me icebreaker is adapted from "Boundary Breaking Activity" (Pack, n.d.).
5. The roles involved in reflective dialogues have been taken from Brockbank and McGill (2007).
6. Templates for observation logs are located in Appendix VIII.
7. The debrief process is one aspect of the core competency of Professionalism, during which practitioners reflect and evaluate their performance and provide and receive constructive feedback from others (CYCCB, 2018).
8. Questions for the debrief have been adapted from Pearson and Smith (as cited in Boud et al., 1985).
9. Teamwork represents one aspect of the core competency of Relationship and Communication, which necessitates practitioners to establish and maintain effective relationships with team members.

CHAPTER 13

Transformative Learning

To be useful, knowledge has to be transformed.

—Gould & Taylor, 2016

LEARNING OBJECTIVES

In this chapter, you will:

- define transformative learning
- identify the essential components for transformative learning to occur
- connect transformative learning to professional practice

The previous chapter focused on the elements of reflective learning—reflective tools, reflective journals, and reflective dialogues—each of which have assisted you in transforming your ways of knowing and doing Child and Youth Care practice. These shifts in perspectives and doing are reflective of transformative learning. This chapter will provide an overview of transformative learning, while identifying those core components that facilitate transformative learning.

This chapter marks the final step in reflective practice and while transformative learning is an aspect of critical thinking, the measure of your learning is truly your ability to integrate your learning into practice. Compare your initial stage of learning to where you are now. What shifts have you experienced in your practice that embody the distinct aspects of reflective Child and Youth Care practice? How do your values and beliefs influence your practice? Do these have the same influence as before or have these shifted throughout your practice? What feedback have you received that supports your ability to apply theory to practice?

The theoretical constructs you have learned over your studies as a practitioner will become the framework from which you make choices that will guide your practice. However, one needs to remember that the meaning one makes of their experiences through and with others is required for critical thinking and transformative learning to develop.

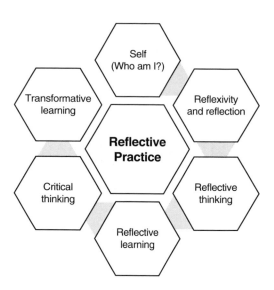

Figure 1: Reflective Practice Radial

Source: Recreated by author.

Transformative learning has to do with making meaning out of experiences and questioning assumptions based on prior experience (and leads to an altered sense of self as a practitioner; Cranton, 2016, p. 7). Transformative learning occurs when you have reached a point of discovery, or an "a-ha moment," in your learning that results in new perspectives or a new meaning of an experience (Mezirow, 1991). This new meaning, however, needs to lead to new ways of doing that will translate consistently into all aspects of your practice. As these new insights are applied to practice, the opportunities for new experiences and further learning increase (Dewey, as cited in Rodgers, 2002). Recall Xandu and Challah's case scenario for instance. When zirs perspectives of Challah shifted to consider her experiences of loss and need for security, zi adapted zirs approach with her. This shift in thinking to adapt to new ways of practicing moving forward illustrates an example of transformative learning (D'Cruz et al., 2007).

You will notice as you become more proficient in reflective practice, your ability to identify areas for your own learning as opposed to relying on *feedback* from others will increase. Presenting and deliberating differing points of views with others is a vital aspect for developing transformative learning (Cranton, Meziros, & Taylor, as cited in Kroth & Cranton, 2014). It is not enough to say one realizes something; practitioners need to apply that learning to action on a consistent basis. Otherwise, it remains a passing a-ha moment that has no bearing on one's practice.

The previous chapters have provided you with a framework to develop as reflective practitioners. It is up to you to apply that learning to your practice on a consistent basis that shifts your ways of knowing and doing. The reflective moments and check-ins throughout the book have provided you with opportunities to monitor your own learning by considering the key points in your learning that fit for you or have challenged you. It is through these moments that you determine how you will integrate this learning into your practice on a consistent basis.

When we maintain a commitment to growth and learning, we disengage from judgement. In asking yourself what each experience teaches you about yourself, others, and what additional learning there is to be had, you move away from judgement and embody the reflective practitioner philosophy.

—Donicka Budd

Brockbank and McGill (2007) purport that congruity between acquired knowledge and practice is required for transformational learning to occur; essentially, you consistently incorporate the concepts from your learning into your practice to reflect the foundation of Child and Youth Care (White, 2007). This reiterates the importance of demonstrating your understanding of the learning that has developed from an ongoing process of self-monitoring, self-awareness, and reflecting on your experiences, more so than memorizing and reciting knowledge from the text.

Checking In

How have the previous chapter reflections, group discussions, reflection journals, and different exercises supported you to demonstrate your learning of the concepts from this chapter? From this book thus far? What areas of this chapter thus far do you require further clarification about? What questions do you have about transformative learning in relation to reflective practice?

Reflect on the experiences from your practice to identify those a-ha moments that have influenced your approach to practice. How did they occur? How did you connect them to your learning? What were the shifts that occurred, and has this remained consistent?

Exercise 70: Personal Review

Return to the earlier self-exploration exercises in Chapter 2 and redo the values, beliefs, assumptions, and strengths exercises (templates of the values and beliefs exercises are in Appendices III and IV).

What changes, if any, have you identified?

_____

_____

What has contributed to these changes?

_____

_____

How have these changes influenced your ways of knowing and doing?

_____

_____

How have these a-ha moments changed your experiences of the situation; and your learning, experiences with others, in class and from practice?

_____

_____

What challenges do you anticipate moving forward in your practice?

_____

_____

TRANSFORMATIVE LEARNING IN ACTION[1]

- Actively demonstrates critical thinking skills in practice that leads to new ways of thinking and doing
- Actively takes feedback from group reflections and applies to practice that leads to new ways of doing practice
- Achieving greater autonomy in decision-making
- Ability to take risks in practice and considers alternative approaches to practice as opposed to the routine-oriented responses
- Integrates different perspectives into practice
- Actively questions assumptions and perspectives
- Actively engages in reflective dialogues and integrates feedback into practice

Transformative learning continues throughout one's professional career. Despite this, it is important to recognize that falling into habitual ways of doing provides an opportunity to reflect on the assumptions that underlie your response. This in itself is reflective of transformational learning as you consider alternative perspectives for why you do what it is you do (Bellefeuille & Ricks, 2010).

Exercise 71: The Critical Thinking Self-assessment[2]

Where are you in this space and time of your academic journey?

_____

_____

What concepts from this book have influenced your ways of knowing and doing the most?

_____

_____

What assumptions about others—your colleagues, other professional members, children, youth, and families you work with—have you held onto or let go of?

_____

_____

Are you more aware of when you do make assumptions of others?

_____

_____

How has this influenced your practice?

_____

_____

What key points of your learning have you integrated into your daily practice as a Child and Youth Care Practitioner?

_____

_____

What further learning or aspects of reflective practice do you struggle with or require further development in?

_____

_____

What questions still remain for you about reflective practice?

_____

_____

CLOSING THOUGHTS

Where have you progressed the most in your journey as a reflective practitioner?

_____

_____

What concepts or exercises resonated with you the most to support the learning that you will take forward in your continued journey of reflective practice?

_____

_____

NOTES

1. Transformative learning in action is adapted from Mann et al. (2009) and Cranton (2016).
2. The Critical Thinking Self-assessment was adapted from Brookfield (2012).

Conclusion

And suddenly you know … it's time to start something new and trust the magic of beginnings.

    —Meister Eckhart

Reflective practice, as identified earlier in the text, is a cyclic, dynamic process that evolves over time through experiences. Understanding why you do what you do is not possible without considering the distinct aspects of reflective practice. As you have learned throughout this text, reflective practice embodies more than thinking about *what happened* to thinking about *your experience* of what happened. It is your experience of events that provides the basis for reflective practice. Through the moment-to-moment interactions with others, further learning and knowledge is achieved (Bellefeuille & Ricks, 2010; Garfat, 1992). When you are able to step away from judgement and allow for other ways of knowing, this learning will occur.

    Your interactions with others will continue to provide you with many opportunities to develop your skills as reflective practitioners. These experiences can challenge your ways of knowing (beliefs, values) that are embedded in ways of being in and seeing the world (Garfat & Fulcher, 2012; Moon, 2004). These challenges will only enhance your learning experience, if you remain open to the opportunity these experiences allow.

Change and growth occurs when we are willing to let go of what is familiar to allow for what may be.

    —Donicka Budd

Remember that learning is a lifelong journey and does not end with the diploma or other educational credentials you may receive. In continuing to reflect on practice, you demonstrate your commitment to the profession, your role, and the many individuals and families you will meet. It is important to return to the basics of your learning when judgement or other previous ways of knowing and doing occurs. Revisiting your values and beliefs and acknowledging your assumptions are important to consider throughout the duration of your career. In doing so, you create the space necessary for reflective Child and Youth Care practice to continue evolving.

Moving forward in your academic and professional experiences, creating a community of practice is crucial to your effectiveness as a practitioner (Allard et al., 2007). Who will you consult with when you realize your own values and beliefs are impeding your practice? What additional reading, courses, and training are required for you to further develop in meeting the complex needs that others will present? What ideals have you or will you continue to ask about to ensure children, youth, and families continue to receive the most optimal care? How will you continue to ensure you are meeting your own personal, emotional, and spiritual needs to provide this optimal care? These questions are important to consider throughout the duration of your career.

To this, I leave you with a quote sometimes attributed to Maya Angelou and my sincerest warm thoughts and energetic positive vibrations as you continue forward in your journey:

> People will forget what you said,
> People will forget what you did,
> But people will never forget how you made them feel.

May peace be with you today, tomorrow, and always. May you continue to view every experience as a learning opportunity and every new person you meet as someone to learn from.

    —Donicka Budd

APPENDICES

The following templates are intended to guide your thinking in the reflective/critical thinking process. You may find as you progress through your studies that you no longer need the structure to follow and that it begins to come naturally.

APPENDIX I

Standards for Practice of North American Child & Youth Care Professionals (ACYCP, 2018)

The Standards of Practice for Child and Youth Care Professionals provides a framework to guide ethical thinking and behaviour as Child and Youth Care Professionals promote the well-being of children, youth, and families. Working with vulnerable populations requires that we maintain responsibility to these individuals while demonstrating ethical behaviour and encouraging this behaviour in others.

PRINCIPLES AND STANDARDS

I. Responsibility for Self

A. Demonstrates high standards of integrity and professional conduct
B. Develops knowledge and skills necessary to benefit children, youth, and families
   1. Participates in education and training for ongoing professional development
   2. Engages in ongoing supervision and/or counsel as appropriate
C. Maintains physical and emotional well-being
   1. Aware of personal values and their implication for practice
   2. Mindful of self as a growing and developing practitioner
   3. Understands the importance of self-care and the responsibility to seek guidance, counseling, and support

II. Responsibility to Children, Youth, and Families

A. Does not cause harm
   1. Encourages safe and ethical practice
   2. Does not disrespect, exploit, or intimidate others
B. Maintains privacy and confidentiality as appropriate to role
C. Ensures services are culturally sensitive and non-discriminatory (regardless of race, color, ethnicity, national origin, national ancestry, age, gender, sexual orientation, marital status, religion, mental or physical capacity/ability, medical condition, political views, or socioeconomic status)
D. Provides protection and advocacy
   1. Recognizes, respects, and advocates for the rights of the child, youth, and family
   2. Supports individuals in advocating for their own rights and safety
E. Fosters self-determination and personal agency
F. Encourages a child or youth's participation within a family and community, and facilitates the development of social networks
G. Recognizes the life space of young people involves physical, emotional, mental and virtual domains (including social media, messaging, gaming, etc.)

H. Respects the diversity of life patterns and expectations
   1. Affirms that there are differences in individual and family needs and meets those needs on an individual basis
   2. Ensures interactions reflect developmental age, status, understanding and capacity
   3. Adapts to individual needs when designing and implementing plans and programs (including psychological, physical, social, cultural, and spiritual needs)
I. Values collaboration with colleagues and those from other disciplines
   1. Makes referrals to other professionals as necessary and seeks assistance to ensure access to needed services
   2. Observes, assesses, and evaluates services/treatments prescribed or designed by other professionals
J. Ensures appropriate boundaries between professional and personal relationships
   1. Recognizes and adjusts for dynamics related to power, authority, and position
   2. Does not engage in harassment or sexual misconduct with a child, youth, or family member

III. Responsibility to the Employer and/or Employing Organization

A. Responds to employer in a professional manner and seeks to resolve differences collaboratively
B. Treats colleagues with respect, courtesy, and equity
C. Models flexibility and inclusiveness in working with colleagues and family members
D. Respects the commitments made to the employer or employing organization

IV. Responsibility to the Profession

A. Acts in a professional manner toward colleagues
   1. Seeks arbitration or mediation with colleagues as appropriate
   2. Reports ethical violations to appropriate individuals or boards when informal resolution is not appropriate or sufficient
B. Encourages collaboration among professionals, children, youth, family and community to share responsibility for outcomes
C. Ensures professional practice in training and research activities
   1. Ensures education and training programs are competently designed and delivered
   2. Ensures research is of high quality and is designed, conducted, and reported in accordance with quality and ethical standards
D. Ensures that practitioners, supervisors and administrators lead programs according to high-quality and ethical practice

V. Responsibility to the Community

A. Promotes awareness of the profession and the needs of children, youth, and families to the community

B. Models ethical behavior in relationships and interactions with community members

C. Promotes respect and appreciation of diversity, racial equality, social justice and cultural humility

D. Encourages informed participation by the public in shaping social policy and decisions affecting children, youth, and families

© 2017 Child and Youth Care Certification Board. (2018). Association for Child & Youth Care Practice. https://cyccb.org/CYCcertification@youthworkacademy.org.

Competencies for Professional Child & Youth Work Practitioners (ACYCP, 2010)

The CYC Competencies are organized across five domains:

1. Professionalism
2. Cultural & human diversity
3. Applied human development
4. Relationship & communication
5. Developmental practice methods

I. PROFESSIONALISM

Professional practitioners are generative and flexible; they are self-directed and have a high degree of personal initiative. Their performance is consistently reliable. They function effectively both independently and as a team member. Professional practitioners are knowledgeable about what constitutes a profession and engage in professional and personal development and self-care. The professional practitioner is aware of the function of professional ethics and uses professional ethics to guide and enhance practice and advocates effectively for children, youth, families, and the profession.

    A. Foundational Knowledge
- History, structure, organization of Child and Youth Care Work
- Resources and activities of CYC
- Current and emergent trends in society, services, and in CYC
- Structure and function of Codes of Ethics applicable to practice which includes the Code of Ethics, Standards for Practice of North American Child and Youth Care Professionals (www.acycp.org)
- Accepted boundaries in professional practice
- Stress management and wellness practices
- Strategies to build a professional support network
- Significance of advocacy and an array of advocacy strategies
- Relevant laws, regulations, legal rights and licensing procedures governing practice

    B. Professional Competencies
        1. Awareness of the Profession
            a. access the professional literature
            b. access information about local and national professional activities

    c. stay informed about current professional issues, future trends and challenges in one's area of special interest

    d. contribute to the ongoing development of the field

2. Professional Development and Behavior

    a. Value orientation

      (1) state personal and professional values and their implications for practice including how personal and professional beliefs, values and attitudes influence interactions

      (2) state a philosophy of practice that provides guiding principles for the design, delivery, and management of services

    b. Reflection on one's practice and performance

      (1) evaluate own performance to identify needs for professional growth

      (2) give and receive constructive feedback

    c. Performance of organizational duties

      (1) demonstrate productive work habits

        (a) know and conform to workplace expectations relating to attendance, punctuality, sick and vacation time, and workload management

        (b) personal appearance and behavior reflect an awareness of self as a professional as well as a representative of the organization

    d. Professional boundaries

      (1) recognize and assess own needs and feelings and keeps them in perspective when professionally engaged

      (2) model appropriate interpersonal boundaries

    e. Staying current

      (1) keep up-to-date with developments in foundational and specialized areas of expertise

      (2) identify and participate in education and training opportunities

3. Personal Development and Self Care

    a. Self awareness

      (1) recognize personal strengths and limitations, feelings and needs

      (2) separate personal from professional issues

    b. Self care

      (1) incorporate "wellness" practices into own lifestyle

      (2) practices stress management

      (3) build and use a support network

4. Professional Ethics

    a. describes the functions of professional ethics

    b. applies the process of ethical decision making in a proactive manner

    c. integrates specific principles and standards from the relevant Code of Ethics to specific professional problems

    d. carries out work tasks in a way that conforms to professional ethical principles and standards

5. Awareness of Law and Regulations
   a. access and apply relevant local, state/provincial and federal laws, licensing regulations and public policy
   b. describe the legal responsibility for reporting child abuse and neglect and the consequences of failure to report
   c. describe the meaning of informed consent and its application to a specific practice setting
   d. use the proper procedures for reporting and correcting non-compliance
6. Advocacy
   a. demonstrate knowledge and skills in use of advocacy
   b. access information on the rights of children, youth and families including the United Nations Charter on the Rights of the Child
   c. describe the rights of children, youth, and families in relevant setting/s and systems advocate for the rights of children, youth, and families in relevant settings and systems
   d. describe and advocate for safeguards for protection from abuse including institutional abuse
   e. describe and advocate for safeguards for protection from abuse including organizational or workplace abuse
   f. advocate for protection of children from systemic abuse, mistreatment, and exploitation

II. CULTURAL AND HUMAN DIVERSITY

Professional practitioners actively promote respect for cultural and human diversity. The Professional Practitioner seeks self understanding and has the ability to access and evaluate information related to cultural and human diversity. Current and relevant knowledge is integrated in developing respectful and effective relationships and communication and developmental practice methods. Knowledge and skills are employed in planning, implementing and evaluating respectful programs and services, and workplaces.

A. Foundational Knowledge
   The professional practitioner is well versed in current research and theory related to cultural and human diversity including the eight major factors which set groups apart from one another, and which give individuals and groups elements of identity: age, class, race, ethnicity, levels of ability, language, spiritual belief systems, educational achievement, and gender differences.
   • Cultural structures, theories of change, and values within culture variations
   • Cross cultural communication
   • History of political, social, and economic factors which contribute to racism, stereotyping, bias and discrimination
   • Variations among families and communities of diverse backgrounds
   • Cultural and human diversity issues in the professional environment

B. Professional Competencies
1. Cultural and Human Diversity Awareness and Inquiry
    a. describe own biases
    b. describe interaction between own cultural values and the cultural values of others
    c. describe own limitation in understanding and responding to cultural and human differences and seeks assistance when needed
    d. recognize and prevent stereotyping while accessing and using cultural information
    e. access and critically evaluate resources that advance cultural understandings and appreciation of human diversity
    f. support children, youth, families and programs in developing cultural competence and appreciation of human diversity
    g. support children, youth, families and programs in overcoming culturally and diversity based barriers to services
2. Relationship and Communication Sensitive to Cultural and Human Diversity
    a. adjust for the effects of age, cultural and human diversity, background, experience, and development on verbal and non verbal communication.
    b. describe the non verbal and verbal communication between self and others (including supervisors, clients or peer professionals)
    c. describe the role of cultural and human diversity in the development of healthy and productive relationships
    d. employ displays of affection and physical contact that reflect sensitivity for individual development, cultural and human diversity as well as consideration of laws, regulations, policies and risk
    e. include consideration of cultural and human diversity in providing for the participation of families in the planning, implementation and evaluation of services impacting them
    f. give information in a manner sensitive to cultural and human diversity
    g. contribute to the maintenance of a professional environment sensitive to cultural and human diversity
    h. establish and maintain effective relationships within a team environment by:
        (1) promoting and maintaining professional conduct;
        (2) negotiating and resolving conflict;
        (3) acknowledging and respecting cultural and human diversity; and
        (4) supporting team members
3. Developmental Practice Methods Sensitive to Cultural and Human Diversity
    a. integrate cultural and human diversity understandings and sensitivities in a broad range of circumstances
    b. design and implement programs and planned environments, which integrate developmental, preventive, and/or therapeutic objectives into the life space, through the use of methodologies and techniques sensitive to cultural and human diversity

        (1) provide materials sensitive to multicultural and human diversity

        (2) provide an environment that celebrates the array of human diversity in the world through the arts, diversity of personnel, program materials, etc.

        (3) recognize and celebrate particular calendar events which are culturally specific

        (4) encourage the sharing of such culture specific events among members of the various cultural groups

  c. design and implement group work, counseling, and behavioral guidance with sensitivity to the client's individuality, age, development, and culture and human diversity

  d. demonstrate an understanding of sensitive cultural and human diversity practice in setting appropriate boundaries and limits on behavior, including risk management decisions

III. APPLIED HUMAN DEVELOPMENT

Professional practitioners promote the optimal development of children, youth, and their families in a variety of settings. The developmental-ecological perspective emphasizes the interaction between persons and their physical and social environments, including cultural and political settings. Special attention is given to the everyday lives of children and youth, including those at risk and with special needs, within the family, neighborhood, school and larger social-cultural context. Professional practitioners integrate current knowledge of human development with the skills, expertise, objectivity and self awareness essential for developing, implementing and evaluating effective programs and services.

  A. Foundational Knowledge

      The professional practitioner is well versed in current research and theory in human development with an emphasis on a developmental-ecological perspective.

- Lifespan human development
- Child and adolescent development as appropriate for the arena of practice (including domains of cognitive, social-emotional, physiological, psychosexual, and spiritual development)
- Exceptionality in development (including at-risk and special needs circumstances such as trauma, child abuse/neglect, developmental psychopathology, and developmental disorders)
- Family development, systems and dynamics

  B. Professional Competencies

    1. Contextual-Developmental Assessment

      a. assess different domains of development across various contexts

    b.   evaluate the developmental appropriateness of environments with regard to the individual needs of clients

    c.   assess client and family needs in relation to community opportunities, resources, and supports

2.   Sensitivity to Contextual Development in Relationships and Communication

    a.   adjust for the effects of age, culture, background, experience, and developmental status on verbal and non-verbal communication

    b.   communicate with the client in a manner which is developmentally sensitive and that reflects the clients' developmental strengths and needs

       (1) recognize the influence of the child/youth's relationship history on the development of current relationships

       (2) employ displays of affection and physical contact that reflect sensitivity for individuality, age, development, cultural and human diversity as well as consideration of laws, regulations, policies, and risks

       (3) respond to behavior while encouraging and promoting several alternatives for the healthy expression of needs and feelings

    c.   give accurate developmental information in a manner that facilitates growth

    d.   partner with family in goal setting and designing developmental supports and interventions

    e.   assist clients (to a level consistent with their development, abilities and receptiveness) to access relevant information about legislation/regulations, policies/standards, as well as additional supports and services

3.   Practice Methods That Are Sensitive to Development and Context

    a.   support development in a broad range of circumstances in different domains and contexts

    b.   design and implement programs and planned environments including activities of daily living, which integrate developmental, preventive, and/or therapeutic objectives into the life space through the use of developmentally sensitive methodologies and techniques

    c.   individualize plans to reflect differences in culture/human diversity, background, temperament, personality and differential rates of development across the domains of human development

    d.   design and implement group work, counseling, and behavioral guidance, with sensitivity to the client's individuality, age, development, and culture

    e.   employ developmentally sensitive expectations in setting appropriate boundaries and limits

      f.   create and maintain a safe and growth promoting environment

      g.   make risk management decisions that reflect sensitivity for individuality, age, development, culture and human diversity, while also insuring a safe and growth promoting environment

   4. Access Resources That Support Healthy Development

      a.   locate and critically evaluate resources which support healthy development

      b.   empower clients, and programs in gaining resources which support healthy development

IV. RELATIONSHIP AND COMMUNICATION

Practitioners recognize the critical importance of relationships and communication in the practice of quality child and youth care. Ideally, the service provider and client work in a collaborative manner to achieve growth and change. "Quality first" practitioners develop genuine relationships based on empathy and positive regard. They are skilled at clear communication, both with clients and with other professionals. Observations and records are objective and respectful of their clients. Relationship and communication are considered in the context of the immediate environment and its conditions; the policy and legislative environment; and the historical and cultural environment of the child, youth or family with which the practitioner interacts.

   A. Foundational Knowledge

- Characteristics of helping relationships
- Characteristics of healthy interpersonal relationships
- Cultural differences in communication styles
- Developmental differences in communication
- Communication theory (verbal and non-verbal)
- Group dynamics and teamwork theory
- Family dynamics and communication patterns, including attachment theory as it relates to communication style

   B. Professional Competencies

     1. Interpersonal Communication

       a.   adjust for the effects of age, cultural and human diversity, background, experience, and development of verbal and non-verbal communication

       b.   demonstrate a variety of effective verbal and non-verbal communication skills including

          (1) use of silence

          (2) appropriate non-verbal communication

          (3) active listening

          (4) empathy and reflection of feelings

          (5) questioning skills

(6) use of door openers to invite communication, and paraphrasing and summarization to promote clear communication

(7) awareness and avoidance of communication roadblocks

c. recognize when a person may be experiencing problems in communication due to individual or cultural and human diversity history, and help clarify the meaning of that communication and to resolve misunderstandings

d. assist clients (to a level consistent with their development, abilities and receptiveness) to receive relevant information about legislation/regulations, policies/standards, and supports pertinent to the focus of service

e. provide for the participation of children/youth and families in the planning, implementation and evaluation of service impacting them

f. set appropriate boundaries and limits on the behavior using clear and respectful communication

g. verbally and non-verbally de-escalate crisis situations in a manner that protects dignity and integrity

2. Relationship Development

a. assess the quality of relationships in an ongoing process of self reflection about the impact of the self in relationship in order to maintain a full presence and an involved, strong, and healthy relationship

b. form relationships through contact, communication, appreciation, shared interests, attentiveness, mutual respect, and empathy

c. demonstrate the personal characteristics that foster and support relationship development

d. ensure that, from the beginning of the relationship, applicable procedures regarding confidentiality, consent for release of information, and record keeping are explained and clearly understood by the parent/caregiver and by the child, as appropriate to his/her developmental age. Follow those procedures in a caring and respectful manner

e. develop relationships with children, youth and families that are caring, purposeful, goal-directed and rehabilitative in nature; limiting these relationships to the delivery of specific services

f. set, maintain, and communicate appropriate personal and professional boundaries

g. assist clients to identify personal issues and make choices about the delivery of service

h. model appropriate interpersonal interactions while handling the activities and situation of the life-space

i. use structure, routines, and activities to promote effective relationships

j. encourage children, youth and families to contribute to programs, services, and support movements that affect their lives by sharing authority and responsibility

    k. develop and communicate an informed understanding of social trends, social change and social institutions. Demonstrate an understanding of how social issues affect relationships between individuals, groups, and societies

    l. identify community standards and expectations for behavior that enable children, youth and families to maintain existing relationships in the community

3. Family Communication

    a. identify relevant systems/components and describe the relationships, rules and roles in the child/youth's social systems and develop connections among the people in various social systems

    b. recognize the influence of the child's relationship history and help the child develop productive ways of relating to family and peers

    c. encourage children and families to share folklore and traditions related to family and cultural background. Employ strategies to connect children to their life history and relationships

    d. support parents to develop skills and attitudes which will help them to experience positive and healthy relationships with their children/youth

4. Teamwork and Professional Communication Skills

    a. establish and maintain effective relationships within a team environment by: promoting and maintaining professional conduct; negotiating and resolving conflict; acknowledging individual differences; and, supporting team members

    b. explain and maintain appropriate boundaries with professional colleagues

    c. assume responsibility for collective duties and decisions including responding to team member feedback

    d. use appropriate professional language in communication with other team members, consult with other team members to reach consensus on major decisions regarding services for children and youth and families

    e. build cohesion among team members through active participation in teambuilding initiatives

    f. collect, analyze and present information in written and oral form by selecting and recording information according to identified needs, agency policies and guidelines. Accurately record relevant interactions and issues in the relationship

    g. plan, organize, and evaluate interpersonal communications according to the identified need, context, goal of communication, laws/regulations, and ethics and involved. Choose an appropriate format, material, language, and style suitable to the audience

    h. acknowledge and respect other disciplines in program planning, communication and report writing using multidisciplinary and interdisciplinary perspectives. Communicate the expertise of the profession to the team

    i.   establish and maintain a connection, alliance, or association with other service providers for the exchange of information and to enhance the quality of service

    j.   deliver effective oral and written presentations to a professional audience

    k.   demonstrate proficiency in using information technology for communication, information access, and decision-making

V. DEVELOPMENTAL PRACTICE METHODS

Practitioners recognize the critical importance of developmental practice methods focused in CYC practice: Genuine Relationships, Health and Safety, Intervention Planning, Environmental Design and Maintenance, Program Planning and Activity Programming, Activities of Daily Living, Group Work, Counseling, Behavioral Guidance, Family (Caregiver) Engagement, Community Engagement. These are designed to promote optimal development for children, youth, and families including those at-risk and with special needs within the context of the family, community and the lifespan.

    A. Foundational Knowledge
- Health and safety
- Intervention theory and design
- Environmental design
- Program planning and Activity Programming including:
  - Developmental rationales
  - Basic strategies of program planning
  - Specific developmental outcomes expected as a result of participating in activities
  - Principles of activity programming, e.g., activity analysis, adaptation, strategies for involving youth in activities
  - Relationship of developmental processes to the activities of daily living (eating, grooming, hygiene, sleeping and rest)
  - The significance of play activities
  - Community resources for connecting children, youth and families with activity and recreational programs
- Behavioral Guidance methods including conflict resolution, crisis management, life space interviewing
- Behavior Management methods
- Counseling Skills
- Understanding and Working with Groups
- Understanding and Working with Families
- Understanding and Working with Communities

    B. Professional Competencies

       1. Genuine Relationships

a. recognize the critical importance of genuine relationships based on empathy and positive regard in promoting optimal development for children, youth, and families (as fully described in Section III)

b. forming, maintaining and building upon such relationships as a central change strategy

2. Health and Safety
   a. environmental safety
      (1) participate effectively in emergency procedures in a specific practice setting and carry them out in a developmentally appropriate manner
      (2) incorporate environmental safety into the arrangement of space, the storage of equipment and supplies and the design and implementation of activities
   b. health
      (1) access the health and safety regulations applicable to a specific practice setting, including laws/regulations related to disability
      (2) use current health, hygiene and nutrition practices to support health development and prevent illness
      (3) discuss health related information with children, youth and families as appropriate to a specific practice setting
   c. medications
      (1) access current information on medications taken by clients in a specific practice site
      (2) describe the medication effects relevant to practice
      (3) describe the rules and procedures for storage and administration of medication in a specific practice site, and participate as appropriate
   d. infectious diseases
      (1) access current information on infectious diseases of concern in a specific practice setting
      (2) describe the components relevant to practice
      (3) employ appropriate infection control practices

3. Intervention planning
   a. assess strengths and needs
   b. plan goals and activities which take agency mission and group objectives, individual histories and interests into account
   c. encourage child/youth and family participation in assessment and goal setting in intervention planning and the development of individual plans
   d. integrate client empowerment and support of strengths into conceptualizing and designing interventions
   e. develop and present a theoretical/empirical rationale for a particular intervention or approach
   f. select and apply an appropriate planning model
   g. select appropriate goals or objectives from plans, and design activities, interactions, and management methods that support plans in an appropriate way

h. work with client and team to assess and monitor progress and revise plan as needed

4. Environmental Design and Maintenance
    a. recognize the messages conveyed by environment
    b. design and maintain planned environments which integrate developmental, preventive, and interventive requirements into the living space, through the use of developmentally and culturally sensitive methodologies and techniques
    c. arrange space, equipment and activities in the environment to promote participation and prosocial behavior, and to meet program goals
    d. involve children, youth and families appropriately in space design, and maintenance

5. Program Planning and Activity Programming
    a. connect own childhood activity experiences and skills, and adult interests and skills, to current work
    b. teach skills in several different domains of leisure activity
    c. assist clients in identifying and developing their strengths through activities and other experiences
    d. design and implement programs and activities which integrate age, developmental, preventive, and/or interventive requirements and sensitivity to culture and diversity
    e. design and implement challenging age, developmentally, and cultural and human diversity appropriate activity programs
        (1) perform an activity analysis
        (2) assess client's interests, knowledge of and skill level in various activities
        (3) promotes client's participation in activity planning
        (4) select and obtain resources necessary to conduct a particular activity or activity program
        (5) perform ongoing (formative) and outcome (summative) evaluation of specific activities and activity programs
    f. adapts activities for particular individuals or groups
    g. locate and critically evaluate community resources for programs and activities and connect children, youth, and families to them

6. Activities of Daily Living
    a. integrate client's need for dignity, positive public image, nurturance, choice, self-management, and privacy into activities of daily living
    b. design and implement, and support family members and caregivers to implement, activities of daily living, which integrate age, developmental, preventive, and/or interventive requirements and sensitivity to culture and diversity
        (1) age and cultural and human diversity appropriate clothing
        (2) pleasant and inviting eating times that encourage positive social interaction

        (3) age and developmentally appropriate rest opportunities

        (4) clean and well maintained bathroom facilities that allow age and developmentally appropriate privacy and independence

        (5) personal space adequate for safe storage of personal belongings and for personal expression through decorations that do not exceed reasonable propriety

  c. design and maintain inviting, hygienic and well maintained physical environments and equipment and supplies which positively support daily activities

  d. encourage client development of skills in activities of daily living

        (1) personal hygiene and grooming skills

        (2) developing and maintaining of areas related to daily living, e.g., maintaining living space, preparing and serving meals, cleanup

        (3) socially appropriate behavior in activities of daily living: respecting other's privacy, expected grooming and dress for various occasions

7. Group Process

  a. assess the group development and dynamics of a specific group of children and youth

  b. use group process to promote program, group, and individual goals

  c. facilitate group sessions around specific topics/issues related to the needs of children/youth

  d. mediate in group process issues

8. Counseling

  a. recognize the importance of relationships as a foundation for counseling with children, youth and families (as fully described in Section III, Relationships and Communication)

  b. has self awareness and uses oneself appropriately in counseling activities

  c. able to assess a situation in the milieu or in individual interaction and select the appropriate medium and content for counseling

  d. able to make appropriate inquiry to determine meaning of a particular situation to a child

  e. assist other adults, staff, parents and caregivers in learning and implementing appropriate behavioral support and instruction

  f. employ effective problem solving and conflict resolution skills

9. Behavioral Guidance

  a. assess client behavior including its meaning to the client

  b. design behavioral guidance around level of client's understanding

  c. assess the strengths and limitations of behavioral management methods

  d. employ selected behavioral management methods, where deemed appropriate

  e. assist other adults, staff, and parents and caregivers in learning and implementing appropriate behavioral guidance techniques and plans

    f. give clear, coherent and consistent expectations; sets appropriate boundaries

    g. evaluate and disengage from power struggles

    h. employ genuine relationship to promote positive behavior

    i. employ developmental and cultural/diversity understandings to promote positive behavior

    j. employ planned environment and activities to promote positive behavior

    k. employ at least one method of conflict resolution

    l. employ principles of crisis management

        (1) describe personal response to crisis situations

        (2) describe personal strengths and limitations in responding to crisis situations

        (3) take self protective steps to avoid unnecessary risks and confrontations

        (4) dress appropriately to the practice setting

        (5) employ a variety of interpersonal and verbal skills to defuse a crisis

        (6) describe the principles of physical interventions appropriate to the setting

        (7) conduct a life space interview or alternative reflective debriefing

10. Family and Caregiver Engagement

    a. communicate effectively with family members

    b. partner with family in goal setting and designing and implementing developmental supports and/or interventions

    c. identify client and family needs for community resources and supports

    d. support family members in accessing and utilizing community resources

    e. advocate for and with family to secure and/or maintain proper services

11. Community Engagement

    a. access up to date information about service systems, support and advocacy resources, and community resources, laws, regulations, and public policy

    b. develop and sustain collaborative relationships with organizations and people

    c. facilitate client contact with relevant community agencies

APPENDIX III

Beliefs Exercise

The future is determined by one's past.	Children, youth, and families do the best they can with the resources they have.	When I am upset, it is because of something someone has said or done.
The future is determined by experiences yet to occur.	Children, youth, and families are our greatest teachers.	Behaviours are good or bad.
I am responsible for my actions and …	The higher the grade, the better the CYCP you will be.	Behaviours represent an unmet need the child is attempting to meet.
Others are responsible for how I think and act.	Education is the most important asset anyone can have.	The more friends one has, the more likeable one is.
When you trust others, you will experience disappointment.	Showing emotions is a sign of weakness.	Children, youth, and families who argue with the CYCP should be transferred to another practitioner.
Everything happens for a reason.	Family shapes who we become.	The past defines who you are.
When others are nice to you, they usually want something from you.	When we do nice things for others, others will do nice things in return.	Mistakes are opportunities in disguise.
I am responsible for how others feel.	Creativity is about artistic expression.	Children and youth have a right to express how they feel.
Life is meaningful when accomplishments are achieved.	It is the parent's responsibility to teach children right from wrong.	Children should know right from wrong.
Experiences are meaningful regardless of the outcome.	Children do the best that they can with what they have.	When people struggle, it is because of a lack of faith.
Rules should be the same for everyone in order to be fair.	Children and youth should listen to adults.	Individuals' struggles are a result of a disconnection from others.

APPENDIX IV

Values Exercise. Version 1

Accountability	Achievement	Adventure
Being responsible for one's behaviour.	Experiencing success by completing goals, tasks, or mastering new skills.	Taking risks to explore new ideas. Appreciating new experiences to feel rewarded by.
Appreciation	**Authenticity**	**Autonomy**
Acknowledging the qualities of others or what life has to offer.	Being honest, genuine, and sincere.	Exercising freedom to direct one's own behaviour, free from the controls and restraints of external forces.
Balance	**Communication**	**Community**
Devoting time in life to work, leisure, and/or faith.	Dialogue or written expressions between people.	A group of people that share like-minded thinking and interests.
Conformity	**Creativity**	**Education**
Demonstrating behaviour as dictated by social standards, practices, and attitudes.	Acknowledging that there are different ways of doing things.	Diverse learning experiences to gain knowledge.
Fairness	**Faith**	**Family**
A measure of how others should be treated. Everyone should be treated equally regardless of their circumstance.	Appreciating spirituality or religion.	Appreciating the relationships within the family (blood relatives or close friends and team members) and demonstrating one's commitment to improve these relationships.
Fun and play	**Growth and development**	**Honesty**
Taking time to engage in leisure activities.	Engages in new learning experiences to develop skills and knowledge base.	Being truthful about what is occurring. Acknowledging personal strengths and challenges.

Independence	Individuality	Integrity
Relying on one's resources to complete tasks. Working individually without the influence of others.	Appreciating one's unique strengths and challenges.	Demonstrating what is right and just over policy.
Justice	**Loyalty**	**Patience**
Treatment of others that reflects their individual needs.	A sense of commitment to the other.	Taking the time to complete tasks. Accepting the time others take to achieve tasks.
Perseverance	**Predictability**	**Relationships/ Connections**
Commitment to seeing things through, regardless of the challenges.	Bound by routine and structure. Knowing what to expect is important.	Individuals who are important to you.
Responsibility and accountability	**Safety**	**Self-care**
Acknowledging and assuming ownership for one's actions.	The space and freedom to express yourself without fear of judgement.	Emotional, spiritual, and physical wellness practices on body, mind, and soul.
Success	**Teamwork**	**Tolerance**
Being acknowledged for your achievements.	Working with others to reach a common goal. A sense of camaraderie and cohesion within a group.	Willingness to accept another's opinion or behaviour that you do not necessarily agree with. Allowing for openness.

Note: The blank spaces are for you to add in additional values that you have identified to be important to you.

Values Exercise. Version 2

Identify two or three responses for each of the questions below. When you are finished, review your list and circle each repeating or similar word with a different coloured marker. Select the top three most common (indicated by the number of similarities). Refer to Chapter 3.

1. What do you fill your personal or professional space with most?
2. How do you spend your time?
3. What energizes you most?
4. What do you spend your money on that has meaning for you?
5. What areas of your life do you feel most organized or structured in?
6. What areas of your life are you most disciplined and focused in?
7. What do you think about most that you aspire to have or be?
8. What do you imagine or envision most for how you would love your life to be that is already happening or starting to happen?
9. What does your dialogue with self consist of that is meaningful to you?
10. What does your dialogue with others (friends, family, co-workers) consist of that is meaningful to you?
11. What or who inspires you most?
12. Which goals do you commit to working on each day?
13. Which topics inspire you most, that you are most interested in learning more about?

APPENDIX V

Reflective Inquiry Questions

Self-inquiry	Reflective Inquiry
Who am I?	Who is this person? What do I know about this other person?
Am I operating from an assumption or from cues I am observing in others?	What do I know about this situation?
What am I basing this knowledge on? My values, beliefs, my social location?	What is the nature of their familial interactions? Interactions with others?
What previous experiences have contributed to my thinking this way?	What is important for me to know that will assist my understanding of their experiences?
What do I need to know that will enable me to better understand this situation?	What is the other's experience of me? How have their perspectives of me influenced their response?
How have I contributed to the other's experience?	What purpose does their behaviour serve them?
What is my role to engage the other? How might I encourage their involvement?	What about this discussion is contributing to their behaviour?
What aspects of my presentation might be influencing the other's behaviours?	What about the day, the dynamics, the … is contributing to the behaviour?
How are aspects of self influencing my approach here?	What aspects of the other's self is influencing their behaviours?
What is another way for me to understand this situation?	What systems are involved with this individual that may be influencing their behaviours?
What aspects of this situation are similar to other situations I have encountered? What do these similarities mean for me?	How is this individual's sense of self influencing their interactions with others?
What shifts in my approach are necessary to influence a different outcome?	What do they require to have a different experience of helping professionals?
How will shifts in my approach benefit me?	How will shifts in my approach benefit the other?
What am I missing? What am I not seeing that is important to see?	How much of their past experiences/relationships are influencing their current interactions?

APPENDIX VI

Bronfenbrenner's Ecological Systems Template

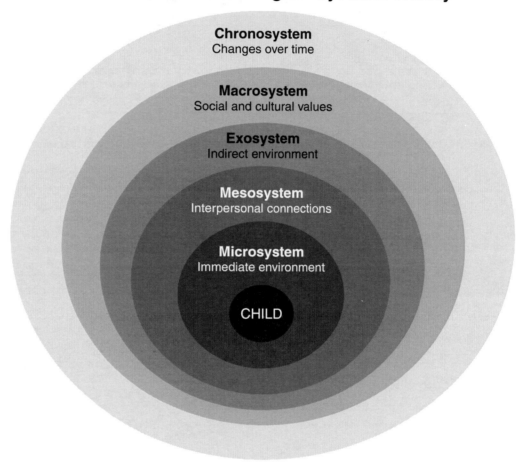

Bronfenbrenner's Ecological Systems Theory

Source: The Psychology Notes Headquarters. https://www.PschyologyNotesHQ.com.

APPENDIX VII

Iceberg Template

APPENDIX VIII

Observation Log Template

Observation Log

Name of the individual completing the form: **Date:**

What happened? What did you see? (Describe specific behaviours.) What did the other do? What is the evidence to support what you saw?

Who was involved? Adults, children? What was the nature of the interactions?

Where did this observation take place?

When did this observation take place?

How (if so) did you come to observe this situation? What is your understanding of what you observed (based on fact, not on your opinions)?

Reflection of the experience to include any of the following prompts as it relates to your experience: I think … I want … I realized … I know … I found out … I thought I knew … I was unaware … I knew … I felt … I was overwhelmed by … I went blank … I wanted … I am feeling … I am wondering about.

Remaining questions/Next steps:

Signature

Source: Created by author.

APPENDIX IX

Reflective Process Model

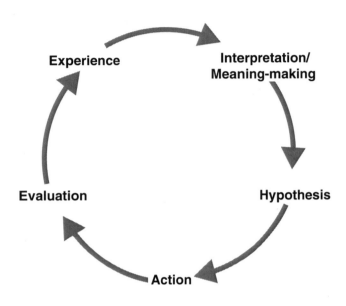

Source: Adapted from Borton (1970), Dewey (1933), Kolb (1984), Kember et al. (2000).

APPENDIX X

Schon's Reflection on Action/in Action Guidelines

Reflection on Action Process: Reflection on the experience after it has occurred

What happened? What did I do? How am I feeling?

What assumptions influenced my reactions?

What was the impact of my actions on others?

What are the other perspectives of me?

What was the context for the other's or my behaviours?

What can I do differently next time?

What further learning or action is required? What do I do now?

Reflection in Action Process: Reflecting during the experience

You monitor your internal reaction

Consider the context for the situation (yours and others' behaviours)

Recreate meaning

Determine the best response for the situation and respond at that moment

Source: Created by author.

APPENDIX XI

Key Theoretical Frameworks of Child and Youth Care Practice

Theoretical framework	Overview
Maslow's Hierarchy of Needs	Hierarchy of five levels of basic needs: physiological, safety, needs of love, affection, and belonging; need for esteem; need for self-actualization.
Circle of Courage	A model of positive youth development that assumes a holistic approach for child-rearing and child development based on Indigenous philosophies, education, youth work, and resilience research (Brendtro, Brokenleg, & Van Bockern, 2002). The model is based on four universal growth needs of all children: belonging, mastery, independence, and generosity (Brendtro et al., 2009).
Bronfenbrenner's Ecological Systems	Environmental elements of an individual's life affect their development (microsystem, macrosystem, mesosystem, chronosystem) and impact an individual's function.
Relational Practice	The fundamental agent of change in Child and Youth Care Practice is the relationship between practitioner and individual.
Attachment Theory	The presence or absence of key individuals in a child's life can impede or encourage their development.
Erikson's Developmental Theory	As children grow, they transition through distinct developmental stages that foster or inhibit their social, emotional, and physical growth.
Family Systems Theory	A systems approach to creating change. Difficulties are not isolated to the individual child; they are created and maintained by the interactions within the family. Changes in one aspect of the system create changes in other aspects of the system.
Trauma-informed Theory	Many individuals you will work with have experienced one sense of trauma or another that will impact their social, emotional, and developmental growth and require trauma-informed approaches to aid their development. Using behavioural approaches are not effective in supporting an individual reconcile their previous trauma.

APPENDIX XII

Critical Thinking in Action

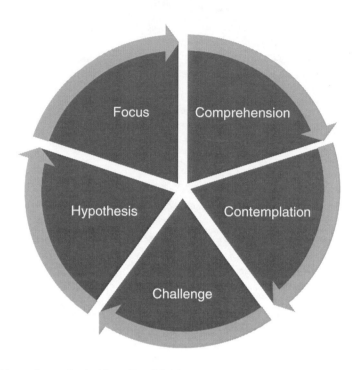

Source: Created by author, adapted from Brookfield, 2012.

APPENDIX XIII

Reflective Journal Guidelines and Template

Your Name: ----------------------   **Date:** ------------------

Focus:

Briefly state the nature of your reflection. Is this to evaluate your approach with others? To develop further clarity about another's behaviours? To develop insight about your experience? To question why things occurred as they did? Or something else?

The experience:

A brief description of what happened and who was involved with your observations to support this. Include a comment about your reactions and feelings and a comment about your interpretation (meaning) and context for the others' behaviours.

Your actions:

A brief description of what you did and reasons for doing so (connect theory to support your action).

Your evaluation:

What was the impact of your actions on the other? (Note their actions/potential perspectives of you.)

What worked and what did not?

What needs to be different for next time? What impact will this have on practice moving forward?

Establishing further action:

Based on your evaluation, what further action may be required?

Return to the journal later to review and identify further insight and additional questions you may have.

What have you realized from this experience? What questions still remain for you?

Source: Adapted from Moon, 2004.

APPENDIX XIV

Legislation Governing Child and Youth Care Practice

Convention on the Rights of the Child	The Convention on the Rights of the Child (CRC) is the first legally binding international instrument to incorporate the full range of human rights—including civil, cultural, economic, political, and social rights for children. https://www.ohchr.org
Child and Family Services Act (These are provincially governed. Refer to the distinct provincial websites for further information.)	In Ontario, for example, the *Child and Family Services Act* (CFSA) governs many of the province's programs and services for children and youth, including: • Child welfare; • Youth justice services; • Secure treatment; • Children's developmental services; • Residential services; • Community support services; • Indigenous child and family services; and • Adoption within the provinces.
Youth Criminal Justice Act	The federal law that applies to all young people in Canada charged with an offence under the Criminal Code of Canada. https://laws-lois.justice.gc.ca
Indigenous Justice, Recognition and Reconciliation	Policy and law reform to renew relationships with First Nations, Inuit, and the Métis Nation based on the recognition of rights, respect, and partnership. https://www.justice.gc.ca
Charter of Rights and Freedoms	Part of the 1982 Constitution, the highest law in Canada to protect rights and freedoms of individuals. www.justice.gc.ca
Ministry of Children, Community and Social Services (Ontario) (See individual provinces for similar ministries.)	Lists different services the ministry is responsible for providing to children and youth.
Constitution Act • *Education Act* • *School Act* • *Inclusive Education*	The 1982 *Constitution Act* gives the provinces the power to decide how public schools in their jurisdiction will be run and funded. Each province then enacts a law related to education and schools, often called the *Education Act* or the *School Act*. The provisions governing a child's rights to education are outlined and vary from province to province.

REFERENCES

Addison, J. T. (1992). Urie Bronfenbrenner. *Human Ecology, 20*(2), 16–20.

Allard, C. C., Goldblatt, P. F., Kemball, J. I., Kendrick, S. A., Millen, K. J., & Smith, D. M. (2007). Becoming a reflective community of practice. *Reflective Practice, 8*(3), 299–314.

Anglin, J. (1999). The uniqueness of child and youth care: A personal perspective. *Child and Youth Care Forum, 28*(2), 143–150.

Anning, A., Cottrell, D., Frost, N., Green, J., & Robinson, M. (2010). *Developing multi-professional teamwork for integrated children's services* (2nd ed.). London: McGraw-Hill Education.

Ash, S. L., & Clayton, P. H. (2009). Generating, deepening, and documenting learning: The power of critical reflection in applied learning. *Journal of Applied Learning in Higher Education, 1*(1), 25–48.

Association for Child and Youth Care Practice. (2017). www.acycp.org.

Balmer, B. (2018). Lutheran Seminary, Wilfrid Laurier University.

Basol, G., & Gencel, I. E. (2013). Reflective thinking scale: A validity and reliability study. *Educational Sciences: Theory & Practice, 13*(2), 941–946.

Beck, M., & Malley, J. (2003). A pedagogy of belonging. *E-Journal of the International Child and Youth Care Network (CYC-Net), 50*. Retrieved from https://www.cyc-net.org/cyc-online/cycol-0303-belonging.html.

Bellefeuille, G., Hedlin, C., & McGrath, J. (2011). Evidence-based practice informed by relational-centered inquiry. *International Journal of Interdisciplinary Social Sciences, 6*(4), 131–142.

Bellefeuille, G., & Jamieson, D. (2008). Relational-centered planning: A turn toward creative potential and possibilities. In G. Bellefeuille & F. Ricks (Eds.), *Standing on the precipice: Inquiry into the creative potential of child and youth care practice* (pp. 35–72). Calgary, AB: MacEwan Press.

Bellefeuille, G., McGrath, J., & Jamieson, D. (2008). A pedagogical response to a changing world: Towards a globally-informed pedagogy for child and youth care education and practice. *Children and Youth Services Review, 30*(7), 717–726.

Bellefeuille, G., & Ricks, F. (2010). Relational inquiry: A child and youth care approach to research. *Children and Youth Services Review, 32*(10), 1235–1241.

Bleicher, R. E., & Correia, M. G. (2011). Using a "small moments" writing strategy to help undergraduate students reflect on their service-learning experiences. *Journal of Higher Education Outreach and Engagement, 15*(4), 27–56.

Bolton, G. (2005). *Reflective practice: Writing and professional development.* London: Sage Publications.

Bolton, G. (2009). *Reflective practice: Writing and professional development* (2nd ed.). London: Sage Publications.

Borton, T. (1970). *Reach, touch and teach.* London: McGraw-Hill.

Boud, D. (1999). Avoiding the traps: Seeking good practice in the use of self assessment and reflection in professional courses. *Social Work Education, 18*(2), 121–132.

Boud, D., Keogh, R., & Walker, D. (1985). *Reflection: Turning experience into learning.* London: Kegan Paul.

Boulton, J., & Mirsky, L. (2006). Restorative practices as a tool for organizational change. *Reclaiming Children and Youth, 15*(2), 89–91.

Brendtro, L., Brokenleg, M., & Van Bockern, S. (2002). Reclaiming youth at risk: Our hope for the future. Bloomington, IN: Solution Tree Press.

Brockbank, A., & McGill, I. (2007). *Facilitating reflective learning in higher education* (2nd ed.). New York: McGraw-Hill Education.

Brookfield, S. D. (1987). *Developing critical thinkers: Challenging adults to explore alternative ways of thinking and acting.* San Francisco: Jossey-Bass.

Brookfield, S. D. (1995). *Becoming a critically reflective teacher.* San Francisco: Jossey-Bass.

Brookfield, S. D. (2012). *Developing critical thinkers* (2nd ed.). Teachers College. Retrieved from https://static1.squarespace.com/static/5738a0ccd51cd47f81977fe8/t/5750ef2d62cd947608165cf2/1464921912225/Developing_Critical_Thinkers.pdf.

Carroll, L., Gilroy, P. J., & Murra, J. (1999). The moral imperative: Self-care for women psychothera-pists. *Women & Therapy, 22*(2), 133–143.

Carson, J. B., Tesluk, P. E., & Marrone, J. A. (2007). Shared leadership in teams: An investigation of antecedent conditions and performance. *Academy of Management Journal, 50*(5).

Cech, M. (2015). *Interventions with children and youth in Canada* (2nd ed.). Don Mills, ON: Oxford University Press.

Child and Youth Certification Board. (2018). Core competencies of child and youth care. Retrieved from https://www.cyccb.org.

Coulson, D., & Harvey, M. (2013). Scaffolding student reflection for experience-based learning: A framework. *Teaching in Higher Education, 18*(4), 401–413.

Cranton, P. (2016). *Understanding and promoting transformative learning: A guide to theory and practice* (3rd ed.). Sterling, VA: Stylus Publishing.

Crenshaw, D. (2008). *The myth of multitasking: How "doing it all" gets nothing done.* San Francisco: Jossey-Bass.

Curry, D., Lawler, M., Schneider-Munoz, A. J., & Fox, L. (2011). A child and youth care approach to professional development and training. *Relational Child and Youth Care Practice, 24*(1/2).

D'Cruz, H., Gillinham, P., & Melendez, S. (2007). Reflexivity, its meanings and relevance for social work: A critical review of the literature. *British Journal of Social Work, 37*(1), 73–90.

de la Sienra, E., Smith, T., & Mitchell, C. (2017). Worldviews, a mental construct hiding the poten-tial of human behaviour: A new learning framework to guide education for sustainable develop-ment. *Journal of Sustainability Education, 13.*

Demartinis, J. (2013). *The values factor: The secret to creating an inspired and fulfilling life.* New York: Berkeley Books.

Dewey, J. (1933). *How we think.* Buffalo, NY: Prometheus Books.

Dewey, J. (1971). *How we think: A restatement of the relation of reflective thinking to the educative process* (2nd rev. ed.). Chicago: Henry Regnery Co.

Di Fabio, A., & Bernard, J. L. (2014). The construction of the identity in 21st century: A festschrift in honour of Jean Guichard. Hauppauge, NY: Nova Science Publishers.

Didonna, F. (Ed.). (2009). *Clinical handbook of mindfulness.* New York: Springer Science.

Dominelli, L. (1998). Anti-oppressive practice in context. In R. Adams, L. Dominelli, M. Payne, & J. Campling (Eds.), *Social work.* London: Macmillan.

Drake, E. (n.d.). Similar and different: An ice-breaker activity that builds commu-nity. BYU Center for Teaching and Learning. Retrieved from https://ctl.byu.edu/tip/similar-and-different-ice-breaker-activity-builds-community.

Felder, R. M., & Soloman, B. A. (2008). Learning styles and strategies. Retrieved from http://www.ncsu.edu/felder-public/ILSdir/styles.htm.

Fereday, L. B. (2011). Counselor self-care instrument development: An exploration of cognitive-emotional, relational, physical and spiritual self care. PhD dissertation.

Fewster, G. (1990a). *Being in child care: A journey into self.* New York: Haworth Press.

Fewster, G. (1990b). Growing together: The personal relationship in child and youth care. In J. P. Anglin, C. J. Denholm, R. V. Ferguson, & A. R. Pence (Eds.), *Perspectives in professional child and youth care.* New York: Haworth Press.

Fewster, G. (2002). The road less graveled: A philosophical stroll through child and youth care. *Journal of Child and Youth Care, 15*(4), 173–175.

Fewster, G., & Beker, J. (2014). *Being in child care: A journey into self* (2nd ed.). Abingdon, UK: Routledge.

Finlay, L. (2008). Reflecting on reflective practice. *PBPL paper, 52,* 1–27.

Fox, L. (n.d.). Understanding and reducing power struggles: Transference and countertransference in treatment relationships. *Child and Youth Care Forum.* Retrieved from https://www.cyc-net.org/Documents/powercontrolhandouts.pdf.

Gannon, B. (2002). Creating moments. *E-Journal of the International Child and Youth Care Network (CYC-Net), 39*(2). Retrieved from https://www.cyc-net.org/cyc-online/cycol-0402-moments.html.

Garfat, T. (1992). Support-Education-Training (S.E.T.): A framework for supervision in child and youth care. *The Child and Youth Care Administrator, 4*(1), 2–13.

Garfat, T. (2002). But that's not what I meant: Meaning-making in foster care. *Irish Journal of Applied Social Studies, 3*(1), 113–124.

Garfat, T. (2003a). Committed to the relational. *Relational Child and Youth Care, 16*(3), 1–3.

Garfat, T. (2003b). Emerging themes in residential child and youth care practice in North America. *Irish Journal of Applied Social Studies, 4*(2), 1–18.

Garfat, T. (2003c). Four parts magic: The anatomy of a Child and Youth Care intervention. *E-Journal of the International Child and Youth Care Network (CYC-Net), 50.* Retrieved from https://www.cyc-net.org/cyc-online/cycol-0303-thom.html.

Garfat, T. (2003d). Taking our place. *Child and Youth Network, 334*(14). Retrieved from http://www.cyc-net.org/quote2/quote-334.html.

Garfat, T., & Charles, G. (2009). Child and youth care practice in North America: Historical roots and current challenges. *Relational Child and Youth Care Practice, 22*(2), 17–28.

Garfat, T., & Charles, G. (2012). *A guide to developing effective child and youth care practice with families* (2nd ed.). Cape Town, South Africa: Pretext Publishers.

Garfat, T., & Fulcher, L. (2012). Characteristics of a relational child and youth care approach. In T. Garfat (Ed.), *A child and youth care approach to working families* (pp. 7–28.). London: Haworth Press.

Garfat, T., & Newcomen, T. (1992). AS*IF: A model for thinking about child and youth care interventions. *Child & Youth Care Forum, 21*(4), 277–285.

Garfat, T., & Ricks, F. (1995). Self-driven ethical decision-making: A model for child and youth care. *Child & Youth Care Forum, 24*(6), 393–404.

Germer, C. K., Siegel, R. D., & Fulton, P. R. (Eds.). (2013). *Mindfulness and psychotherapy* (2nd ed.). New York: The Guilford Press.

Gharabaghi, K. (2008a). Boundaries and the exploration of self. *Child & Youth Services, 30*(3–4), 165–184.

Gharabaghi, K. (2008b). Values and ethics in child and youth care practice. *Child & Youth Services, 30*(3–4), 185–209.

Golding, K. S., & Hughes, D. A. (2012). *Creating loving attachments: Parenting with PACE to nurture confidence and security in the troubled child.* London: Jessica Kingsley Publishers.

Hargreaves, J., & Page, L. (2013). *Reflective practice: Key themes in health and social care.* Cambridge: Polity Press.

Härkönen, U. (2007). The Bronfenbrenner ecological systems theory of human development. Scientific Articles of V International Conference, 1–17.

Henley, M. (2008). Points, level systems and teaching responsibility. *The e-Journal of the International Journal of Child and Youth Care Network (CYC-Net), 112.* Retrieved from https://www.cyc-net.org/cyc-online/cyconline-june2008-henley.html.

Hernandez-Wolfe, P., & McDowell, T. (2010). Intersectionality, power and relational safety: Key concepts in clinical supervision. *Training and Education in Professional Psychology, 4*(1), 29–35.

Jaglowitz, J. (2015). Sheridan College Child and Youth Care Program.

Johns, C. (2009). *Becoming a reflective practitioner* (2nd ed.). Hoboken, NJ: John Wiley & Sons.

Kabat-Zinn, M., & Kabat-Zinn, J. (1997). *Everyday blessings: The inner work of mindful parenting.* New York: Hyperion.

Kakkori, L., & Huttenen, R. (2007). Aristotle and pedagogical ethics. *Paideusis, 16*(1), 17–28.

Keefer, J. M. (2009). The Critical Incident Questionnaire (CIQ): From research to practice and back again. Adult Education Research Conference. Retrieved from http://newprairiepress.org/aerc/2009/papers/31.

Kember, D., Leung, D. Y. P., Jones, A., Yuen-Loke, A., McKay, J., Sinclair, K., … & Yeung, E. (2000). Development of a questionnaire to measure the level of reflective thinking. *Assessment & Evaluation in Higher Education, 25*(4), 381–395.

Kiffiak, L. (1994). A Canadian perspective on the training of child and youth care workers. *Children and youth at risk.* Cape Town, South Africa: National Association of Child Care Workers, 147–148.

Killion, J. P., & Todnem, G. R. (1991). A process for personal theory building. *Educational Leadership, 48*(6), 14–16.

Kinsella, E. A. (2009). Professional knowledge and the epistemology of reflective practice. *Nursing Philosophy, 11*(1), 3–14.

Kokinov, B. (1999). Dynamics and automaticity of context: A cognitive modeling approach. In P. Bouquet, M. Benerecetti, L. Serafini, P. Brézillon, & F. Castellani (Eds.), Modeling and using context (pp. 200–213). *Lecture Notes in Computer Science, 1688.*

Kolb, D. A. (1984). *Experiential learning: Experience as the source of learning and development.* Englewood Cliffs, NJ: Prentice-Hall.

Koltko-Rivera, M. (2004). The psychology of worldviews. *Review of General Psychology, 8*(1), 3–58.

Kroth, M., & Cranton, P. (2014). *Stories of transformative learning.* Rotterdam, the Netherlands: Sense Publishers.

Krueger, M. (1990). *In motion.* Washington, DC: Child Welfare League of America.

Krueger, M. (1997). Using self, story, and intuition to understand child and youth care work. *Child and Youth Care Forum, 26*(3), 153–161.

Krueger, M. (Ed.). (2004). Themes and stories in youthwork practice. London: Haworth Press.

Krueger, M. (2005). Four themes in youth work practice. *Journal of Community Psychology, 33*(1), 21–29.

Krueger, M. (Ed.). (2011). *Themes and stories in youth work practice.* New York: Routledge.

Kumashiro, K. K. (2000). Toward a theory of anti-oppressive education. *Review of Educational Research, 70*(1), 25–53.

Lareau, A., & McNamara Horvat, E. (1999). Moments of social inclusion and exclusion: Race, class, and cultural capital in family-school relationships. *Sociology of Education, 72*(1), 37–53.

Lee, G. V., & Barnett, B. G. (1994). Using reflective questioning to promote collaborative dialogue. *Journal of Staff Development, 15*(1), 16–21.

Lyons, N. (Ed.). (2010). *Handbook of reflection and reflective inquiry: Mapping a way of knowing for professional reflective inquiry.* New York: Springer.

Mann, K., Gordon, J., & MacLeod, A. (2009). Reflection and reflective practice in health professions education: A systematic review. *Advances in Health Science Education, 14*(4), 595–621.

Mann-Feder, V. (1999). You/me/us: Thoughts on boundary management in child and youth care. *Journal of Child and Youth Care, 13*(2), 93–98.

Mayer, E. (2016). *The mind-gut connection: How the hidden conversation within our bodies impacts our mood, our choices, and our overall health.* New York: Harper Collins.

McCammon, L. (2012). Systems of care as asset-building communities: Implementing strengths-based planning and positive youth development. *American Journal of Community Psychology, 49*(3–4), 556–565.

McCormick Calkins, L., & Oxenhorn-Smith, A. *Small moments: Personal narrative writing.* Portsmouth, NH: Heinemann.

Mezirow, J. (1990). *Fostering critical reflection in adulthood: A guide to transformative and emancipatory learning.* San Francisco: Jossey-Bass.

Moon, J. (2004). *A handbook of reflective and experiential learning: Theory and practice.* London: Routledge Falmer.

Moon, J. (2008). *Critical thinking: An exploration of theory and practice.* London: Routledge.

Natali, C. (2013). *Aristotle: His life and school.* D. S. Hutchinson (Ed.). Princeton, NJ: Princeton University Press.

National Child Traumatic Stress Network (NCTSN). (2014). www.nctsn.org.

Ngo, V. H. (2008). A critical examination of acculturation theories. *Critical Social Work, 9*(1).

Nhat-Hanh, T. (1987). *The miracle of mindfulness: An introduction to the practice of meditation.* Boston: Beacon Press.

O'Connell, T. S., & Dyment, J. E. (2011). The case of reflective journals: Is the jury still out? *International and Multidisciplinary Perspectives, 12*(1), 47–59.

O'Connell, T. S., & Dyment, J. E. (2013). *Theory into practice: Unlocking the power and the potential of reflective journals.* Charlotte, NC: Information Age Publishing.

Orsillo, S. M., & Roemer, L. (2011). *The mindful way through anxiety: Break free from chronic worry and reclaim your life*. New York: The Guilford Press.

Pack, J. A. (2015, September 9). A collection of icebreakers and connection activities. Retrieved from https://inclusiveschools.org/wp-content/uploads/2015/09/Student_Connection_Activities_and_Icebreakers.pdf.

Pearson, M., & Smith, D. (2004). Debriefing in experience-based learning. In D. Boud, R. Keogh, C. Peterson, & M. Seligman (Eds.), *Character strengths and virtues: A handbook and classification*. Oxford: Oxford University Press.

Peterson, C., & Seligman, M. (2004). *Character strengths and virtues: A handbook and classification*. Oxford: Oxford University Press.

Phelan, J. (2005). Child and Youth Care education: The creation of articulate practitioners. *Child & Youth Care Forum, 34*(5), 347–355.

Phelan, J. (2009). A useful way to begin. *Child and Youth Care Work, 27*(6), 18–19.

Pollard, A., & Anderson, J. (2008). Part I: Becoming a reflective teacher. In *Reflective teaching: Evidence-informed professional practice*. London: Continuum International.

Ranahan, P., Blanchet-Cohen, N., & Mann-Feder, V. (2015). Moving towards an integrated approach to youth work education. *International Journal of Child, Youth and Family Studies, 6*(4), 516–538.

Richard, C. (2015). *20 quick strategies to help patients and clients manage stress*. Edmonton, AB: Brush Education.

Ricks, F. (1997). Perspectives on ethics in child and youth care. *Child and Youth Care Forum, 26*(3), 187–204.

Ricks, F., & Bellefeuille, G. (2003). Knowing: The critical error of ethics in family work. *Child & Youth Services, 25*(1–2), 117–130.

Righton, P. (1983). The child care worker and going out. In *The children's home: A place in which to grow, a place from which to go*. Papers delivered at the 1981 Biennial Conference of the National Association of Child Care Workers, Cape Town, South Africa.

Rodgers, C. (2002). Defining reflection: Another look at John Dewey and reflective thinking. *Teachers College Record, 104*(4), 842–866.

Rogers, C. (1946). Significant aspects of client centered therapy. *American Psychologist, 1*, 415–422.

Rybak, C. (2013). Nurturing positive mental health: Mindfulness for wellbeing in counseling. *International Journal for the Advancement of Counselling, 35*(2), 110–119.

Schomaker, S. A., & Ricard, R. J. (2015). Effect of a mindfulness-based intervention on counselor-client attunement. *Journal of Counseling and Development, 93*(4), 491–498.

Schon, D. A. (1983). *The reflective practitioner: How professionals think in action*. New York: Perseus Books Group.

Scott, B. (2010). Meeting the health professions council's standards of proficiency: A student's experience. *Education, 20*(4), 139–142.

Siegal, D. J. (2007). *The mindful brain: Reflection and attunement in the cultivation of well-being*. New York: W. W. Norton & Company.

Smith, M. (2006). Ethics. *E-Journal of the International Child and Youth Care Network (CYC-Net), 87*. Retrieved from https://www.cycnet.org/cyc-online/cycol-0406-smith.html.

Smith, M. (2009). Throw away the rule book. *E-Journal of the International Child and Youth Care Network (CYC-Net), 109*. Retrieved from https://www.cycnet.org/cyc-online/cycol-0308-smith.html.

Snow, K. (2006). Vulnerable citizens: The oppression of children in care. *Journal of Child and Youth Care Work, 21*, 94–113.

Steele, W., & Malchiodi, C. A. (2012). *Trauma-informed practices with children and adolescents*. New York: Routledge.

Stevens, D. D., & Cooper, J. E. (2009). *Journal keeping: How to use reflective writing for learning, teaching, professional insight and positive change*. Sterling, VA: Stylus Publishing.

Stuart, C. (2013). *Foundations of child and youth care* (2nd rev. ed.). Dubuque, IA: Kendall Hunt Publishing Company.

Sutherland, A. (2007). Writing and performing change: The use of writing journals to promote reflexivity in a Drama Studies curriculum. *South African Theatre Journal, 21*(1), 109–122.

Tsingos, C., Bosnic-Anticevich, S., & Smith, L. (2015). Learning styles and approaches: Can reflective strategies encourage deep learning? *Currents in Pharmacy Teaching and Learning, 7*(4), 492–504.

VanderVen, K. (Ed.). (1992). Developmental care through the life span. *Journal of Child and Youth Care, 7*(4).

VanderVen, K. (1999). The case against point systems and grading in behavior programs. *E-Journal of the International Child and Youth Care Network (CYC-Net), 3*. Retrieved from https://www.cyc-net.org/cyc-online/cycol-0499-karen.html.

VanderVen, K. (2016). Karen VanderVen's Point Pack: A documented analysis of the literature on the destructiveness of "Point and Level Systems" commonly employed in group and residential settings, and schools. Retrieved from https://www.cyc-net.org/Documents/VanderVen%20Point%20Pack.pdf.

VIA Institute on Character. (2004–2014). Retrieved from https://www.viacharacter.org.

Weiss, H., Johanson, G., & Monda, L. (2015). *Hakomi mindfulness-centered somatic psychotherapy: A comprehensive guide to theory and practice.* New York: W. W. Norton.

White, J. (2007). Knowing, doing and being in context: A praxis-oriented approach to child and youth care. *Child & Youth Care Forum, 36*(5–6), 225–244.

Wong, P. T. P. International Network on Personal Meaning, ppt slides. July 22–23.

Wosket, V. (1999). *The therapeutic use of self: Counselling practice, research and supervision.* New York: Routledge.